ANNE ROSS

Everyday Life of the

PAGAN CELTS

DRAWINGS BY
R. W. FEACHEM

B. T. BATSFORD LTD
LONDON
G. P. PUTNAM'S SONS
NEW YORK

for DOUGLAS GRANT

The PAGAN SYSTEM, *whether true*
Or false, its strength, like Buildings, *drew*
From many parts dispos'd to bear
In one great Whole, their proper share.
Each GOD *of* eminent *degree,*
To some vast Beam *compar'd might be;*
Each GODLING *was a* Peg, *or rather*
A Cramp, *to keep the* Beams *together;*
And Man as safely might pretend
From JOVE *the* thunder-bolt *to rend,*
As with an impious pride aspire
To rob APOLLO *of his* Lyre.

From 'The Ghost', Book II, 33–44 *The Poetical*
Works of Charles Churchill (ed. Douglas Grant), Oxford 1956

First published 1970
Text © Anne Ross, 1970
Illustrations © B. T. Batsford Ltd, 1970
7134 1685 8

Printed and bound in Great Britain by
Jarrold and Sons Ltd, Norwich and London,
for the publishers

B. T. BATSFORD LTD
4 Fitzhardinge Street, London W1

G. P. PUTNAM'S SONS
200 Madison Avenue, New York, NY 100 16

CONTENTS

5

Contents

THE ILLUSTRATIONS

ACKNOWLEDGEMENT

The debt of gratitude which is owed to one's friends and colleagues over the years, for direct help and information, and for inspiration and encouragement of an indirect nature, is immeasurable, and it is impossible even to attempt to repay it. It would not be possible to mention by name the many friends and scholars who have, in some way or another, made their contribution to the thoughts that have led to the writing of this book. And to select a few of these would be unjust to the remainder who must be nameless. But to them all, I extend my grateful thanks and most willingly acknowledge the debt.

Three scholars, however, must receive individual mention, for to them my debt is very great. Professor Kenneth Jackson, Professor of Celtic Studies in the University of Edinburgh, has been kind enough to read the manuscript of the book, and has made valuable suggestions and criticisms. It will, of course, be understood that the opinions expressed are my own responsibility. Likewise, Professor Stuart Piggott, Professor of Prehistoric Archaeology in the University of Edinburgh and Dr T. G. E. Powell, Reader and Head of the Department of Prehistoric Archaeology in the University of Liverpool, have been a constant source of encouragement and information in the researches that preceded the writing of this book; both have likewise increased my debt to them by reading the manuscript and, again, by making valuable and critical comments.

I would also like to acknowledge my gratitude to Mrs. Rachel Bromwich, University of Cambridge and Mr. J. V. S. Megaw, University of Sydney.

My grateful thanks are due to Mr Derek Allen, Secretary of the British Academy, for kindly providing me with his own drawings for figure 30 and for information about the coins; I am also indebted to him for stimulating conversation and assistance in the field of Celtic coins.

The jacket illustration is reproduced by the kind permission of the B.B.C. and I should like to extend my thanks to Miss Felicity Kinross, producer of the television programme for which they were designed, and to the model designer, Mr John Friedlander, and his assistant, Mr Laurie Warburton, for their kind help in this matter.

The debt I owe to my husband, R. W. Feachem, can never be fully acknowledged. He has worked selflessly and painstakingly by my side throughout the compilation of the book. His advice and guidance have been as invaluable as has his assistance with the more tedious tasks of typing and checking, and the general lightening of my burden has greatly facilitated the preparation of this work. He has saved me from many errors and has constantly encouraged me. All the line drawings, except figure 30, are by his hand, and place me even further in his debt.

My thanks are also due to Mr Peter Kemmis Betty for kind help throughout the preparation of the book and for his tolerant acceptance of a delay of three months in the agreed date of delivery of the manuscript. This was occasioned by the sudden and untimely death in February of this year of my brother, Douglas Grant, Professor of American Literature in the University of Leeds, while acting as external examiner in the University of Singapore. Although his scholarly interests lay in fields different from my own, his spiritual influence and his academic example, his constant encouragement, his personal integrity, and his own strong sense of the 'ideal' and the 'fitness of things' have been a powerful and enduring influence throughout my life. My debt to him is thus perhaps the greatest of all, and for this reason the book is dedicated, with humility, to his memory.

ANNE ROSS, 1969

The Author and Publishers would like to thank the following for the illustrations appearing in this book: the University Museum of Archaeology and Ethnology, Cambridge for fig. 94; the Trustees of the British Museum for figs 33, 53, 66 and 75; Corinuim Museum for fig. 49; the Dorset County Museum for fig. 59; Gloucester City Museum for fig. 89; Robert Hogg, Tullie House, Museum, Carlisle

Acknowledgement

for fig. 50; the Musée St Raymond de Toulouse for fig. 69; the Mansell Collection for fig. 27; the National Museum of Ireland for fig. 46; the Reading Museum and Art Gallery for fig. 57; the Rhein Landesmuseum, Bonn for fig. 44; the Staatliche Museum, Berlin for the frontispiece; Thames and Hudson for fig. 42; the Ministry of Public Buildings and Works (Crown Copyright) for fig. 11; the Ministry of Public Buildings and Works, Edinburgh for fig. 83; L. Flanagan, Ulster Museum, Belfast for fig. 81; Photo Yan Zodiaque (J. Dieuzaide) for fig. 71; Wurt Landesmuseum for figs 80 and 81.

Acknowledgement is also due to authors and publishers who have kindly granted permission to quote from the following books: Cross and Slover, *Ancient Irish Tales*, G. G. Harrap & Co.; M. Dillon, 'The Archaism of Irish Tradition,' *Proceedings of the British Academy*, George Weidenfeld and Nicolson Ltd; Gwyn and Thomas Jones, *The Mabinogion*, J. M. Dent & Sons; T. D. Kendrick, *The Druids*, Methuen & Co. Ltd; C. O'Rahilly, *Táin Bó Cúalnge*, Dublin Institute for Advanced Studies; J. J. Tierney, 'The Celtic Ethnography of Posidonius', *Proceedings of the Royal Irish Academy*, Royal Irish Academy; Polybius, *The Histories*, 'Loeb Classical Library', Heinemann Publishers Ltd, Harvard University Press.

Shorter quotations are acknowledged on p. 216.

PREFACE

Not long was Fer Diad's charioteer there when he saw something: a beautiful, five-edged, four-wheeled chariot approaching with strength and swiftness and skill, with a green awning, with a framework of narrow compact opening, in which feats were exhibited, a framework as tall as a sword-blade, fit for heroic deeds, behind two horses, swift, high-springing, big-eared, beautiful, bounding, with flaring nostrils, with broad chests, with lively heart, high-groined, wide-hoofed, slender-legged, mighty and violent. In one shaft of the chariot was a grey horse, broad-thighed, small stepping, long-maned. In the other shaft a black horse, flowing maned, swift-coursing, broad-backed. Like a hawk to its prey on a March day across a plain, or like a furious stag newly roused by hounds in the first chase—so were the two horses of Cú Chulainn in the chariot, as if they were on a bright, fiery flagstone, so that they shook the earth and made it tremble with the speed of their course.

(C. O'Rahilly, 218)

This passage is translated from Irish, a Celtic language. It comes from an epic tale, the _Táin Bó Cúalnge_ (_Cattle Raid of Cúailnge_), written down in Christian times, but belonging essentially to a heroic age, the age of the pagan Celtic peoples. It is utterly Celtic in tone, and fully expressive of all the sentiments and the fierce sensual delights of these restless barbarians; the keen and detailed observation of nature and living objects which was one of the great contributory factors in the development of their splendid art style: the bold, exaggerated descriptions, turning the commonplace event into a glorious achievement and the sordid, vain and childish warrior into a great, immortal hero; the lust for battle and bloodshed; the sheer joy in the use of words. All these things are present in this epic Irish tale; the whole world of the pagan Celts is evoked in its pages.

It is the purpose of this book to find out something about this pagan Celtic world; about its origins; about the people who lived in it, what they did and how they conducted their day to day affairs; and this must inevitably be limited first of all by the space available here for such an investigation, and in the second place essentially by the limitations of the evidence and our ability to interpret it.

Origins and Early History; the Sources

In considering the nature of early Celtic society one is instantly confronted with a problem which differs in two essential ways from those involved in defining and describing the society of many other ancient peoples. To begin with, the Celts had no great material civilisation to be suddenly discovered as was, for example, the civilisation of ancient Babylonia and Assyria; the sophisticated world of the ancient Egyptians or the polished cities of the Mediterranean had little in common with the simple homesteads of the mobile, 'nomadic' Celts. They did in fact leave little in the way of permanent structural remains, and their forts and burials, sanctuaries and portable goods are found scattered over wide tracts of Europe and the British Isles and cover centuries of time and of social evolution. Their society was thus essentially 'un-nucleated'. Moreover, unlike the creators of the great civilisations of the ancient world, the Celts were virtually illiterate in their own languages; much of what we know of the early forms of their speech and their learning is derived from limited and often hostile sources—the names of their tribes, place-names, and names of chieftains, for example, occur in Classical accounts of the Celts. Place-names speak for themselves: they are fixed and permanent. The names of chieftains and tribes appear on many Celtic coins and can give clues as to trade and domestic economy and politics: epigraphy provides classical forms of Celtic divine names and the names of dedicants. Over and above these linguistic fragments there are a limited number of actual

1 Celtic inscription KORISIOS in Greek script, on a sword found with other weapons, and timbers, on an old river bed at Port, nr. PETINESCA, Switzerland

sentences in Gaulish which appear on inscriptions (*1*). But there are no long king-lists for the early period of Celtic history, no mythological legends before those committed to writing by the Irish Christian scribes; no complex poems in praise of kings and chieftains which we know to have been recited in the dwellings of the aristocracy; no lists of divine names, no instructions for the performance of the priests, and the correct control of ritual. So the first aspect of the problem is that we are dealing with a scattered barbarian society, not a great nucleated ancient civilisation; and although we know the Celts to have been both educated and cultured, or at least capable of assimilating cultural influences with ease, it is a fact that their education was not of the kind we generally associate with the word. Nor is their culture readily apparent, but can only be discovered and appreciated by devious and various methods.

Secondly, the Celtic world differs from that of the ancient civilisations which are considered in this series, in that Celts have *survived*; one cannot say that, in certain limited geographical areas, Celtic society ceased to exist in a recognisable form at any given time in antiquity. Their archaic languages did not cease to be spoken in parts of the British Isles and in Brittany; and they still remain as living tongues in limited areas of Scotland, Wales, Ireland and Britanny. Much of their social structure and organisation endured, as did their oral literary tradition, their folk-tales and their superstitious beliefs. In some instances and in some areas aspects of this ancient way of life have continued down to the present day, for example amongst the crofter population of the western seaboards of Scotland and Ireland. Wales, where the language is strongest today, presents a different picture, one which is outside the scope of this book. It is this very remarkable fact of the survival of certain aspects of Celtic society which enables us to approach the formidable task of discovering something of the everyday life of the pagan Celts in Europe and in the British Isles, with greater understanding.

Because we must limit the range of our inquiry, it would seem reasonable to take the year AD 500 as the lower limit, that is, a time when Christianity was fully established in Ireland and in the wider Celtic world. But we must bear in mind the fact that much of the literary evidence from which we derive a great deal of information about the Celtic past, was written down in Ireland, at a post-pagan period, and under the aegis of the Christian

Church; and because of the impressive continuity and longevity of many aspects of Celtic society, such a temporal dividing-line, although convenient, is in fact essentially artificial.

THE CELTIC PEOPLES

Who were the Celts with whose everyday life we are here to be concerned? The word *Celt* has a very different connotation for different people. For the linguist, the Celts are the people who spoke, and still speak, languages of great antiquity and of Indo-European origin. Springing from an original common Celtic tongue, two somewhat different groups of Celtic speech came into being; when this differentiation took place is not known. One of these groups is known to philologists as *Q Celtic*, or 'Goidelic'; it is called Q Celtic because it retained the original Indo-European q^v —as q, later becoming k in sound, but written as c; this is the branch of Celtic which was spoken and written in Ireland; it was later introduced into Scotland by the Irish settlers of Dálriada in the late fifth century AD. It was also spoken in the Isle of Man, and continued there vestigially. There are some traces of it on the Continent but we know little of its distribution there. The second group is known as *P Celtic*, or 'Brythonic' or 'Brittonic'; it turned the original Indo-European q sound into p; so you have *cenn* 'head' in the Goidelic group and *penn* 'head' in the Brittonic group. This was the branch of Celtic spoken widely on the Continent and known as 'Gaulish' or 'Gallo-Brittonic'; it was introduced to Britain by the Iron Age settlers from the Continent in a form known as 'Brittonic'. It was the language of Britain during the Roman period; later it became divided up into Cornish (now extinct as a spoken language although there is a strong movement to revive it), Welsh and Breton.

For archaeologists Celts are the people who are recognisable as such on account of their distinctive material culture, and who are also known to have been Celts from written sources outside their own society. For Celtic nationalists of the present day they have yet another meaning, but this has no bearing on our present inquiry.

We start then by trying to see how it is possible to identify these people, with their widespread origins and their long, if limited survival; and since they left no pre-Christian written historical records or origin legends relating to the earliest phase of their history, we are obliged to use inferential evidence. The earliest, and perhaps the most reliable, although strictly limited source of information is the archaeological record. Later, the historical comments of the Greeks and the Romans on Celtic manners and customs, combined with what can be derived from the early Irish literary tradition give us further details and help to bring a more human element into the somewhat austere outline sketch which the archaeological evidence can depict.

Although the find-spots of some of the earliest Celtic remains— places which gave their names to the two main phases of Celtic culture—are extremely interesting in themselves, the Celts were not discovered archaeologically in high drama, nor were the personalities involved to become figures in world history on account of their finds. To begin with, the Celts were no new concept in the nineteenth century, when the first archaeological evidence for this iron-using society was brought to light. The word *Celt* began to be used for the Celtic-speaking peoples as early as the sixteenth and seventeenth centuries through the pioneer works of the linguists, George Buchanan (1506–82) and Edward Lhwyd (1660–1709). In the romantic speculations of the seventeenth and eighteenth centuries, the Celts, with their Druidic priesthood, had become a popular subject as had other 'primitive' peoples such as the Anglo-Saxons and the early Germanic folk; antiquarians such as John Aubrey, writing in the seventeenth century, and William Stukeley, in the eighteenth century, and many other literary figures liked to weave fantasies around what little real information they had about these people and their pagan past which they found engrossing and fascinating. So, in a sense, they helped to popularise them and the literate public of the British Isles and Europe had some sort of hazy, idealised and utterly romantic notion of the Celts with their Druids and their fascinating, if unfamiliar, religious habits.

THE ARCHAEOLOGY OF THE CELTIC WORLD

In order to obtain any convincing and realistic picture of the nature and origin of these earliest Celtic people—the people whom we can consider to have been Celtic as we understand the term—it is necessary to begin with a brief survey of the archaeology of the ancient Celtic world; for in the earliest phase, when written evidence is non-existent, it is our only material and

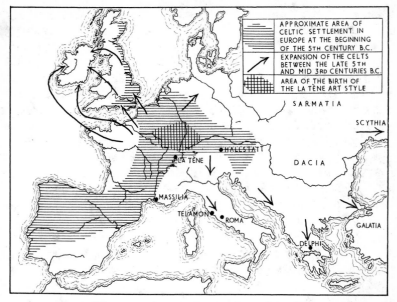

2 Culture provinces and expansions of the Celts

the information it can give is necessarily limited and sometimes ambiguous. Archaeologists have revealed two main phases in the evolution of early Celtic society; to these they have given the names Hallstatt and La Tène, both of which are derived from the place-names of significant find-spots of Celtic material (2). There is some fairly convincing evidence that their immediate ancestors in Europe, the bronze-using Urnfield people as they are called, spoke some form of Celtic language, but the Celts, as we know them, cannot be said to be earlier than this Hallstatt culture which is dated to about 700 BC. In this period, which continues until about 500 BC, a technological change of first importance has taken place in Europe; iron has replaced bronze in the manufacture of weapons and edge tools amongst these Hallstatt people. Bronze of course continued to be used, and some of the finest Celtic work-manship uses bronze as its medium. Iron, however, is the more durable and superior metal and it conveyed an inevitable techno-logical and military superiority on its users. In this period then, the first people whose material culture can be shown to have been Celtic, appear in Europe; this culture is modified and altered by about 500 BC and the La Tène material, together with other

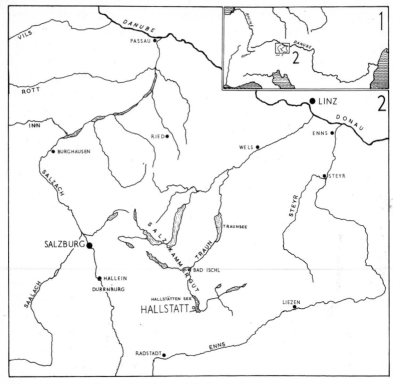

3 Location of Hallstatt, Austria

archaeological evidence, testifies to this new phase. It is this La Tène world which saw the full development of Celtic culture and expansion, and is therefore the phase with which we are primarily concerned. The Hallstatt period, however, provides the early background from which a fully developed Celtic society was to emerge and we must glance at its characteristics in order to better understand the nature and significance of the later changes in the material background of the Celtic peoples.

The site in Austria at Hallstatt, near Salzburg in the Salzkammergut (*3*), lies above the western shore of Lake Hallstatt in dramatic, mountainous country. It is not in fact the place in which the culture suddenly originated, for a long period of evolution lay behind it; but in the nineteenth century a great number of antiquities were brought to light there and for this reason the name was given to this entire phase of Celtic prehistory. At this site an ancient salt-mine and a huge prehistoric cemetery were discovered. Salt was obviously of first importance in the economy of this early Iron Age society and a major factor in the wealth of the aristocracy. Something of the everyday life of the people is revealed here, not only in the grave-goods and funerary rites, but in the more humble objects found in the mine itself. These have survived throughout the ages through the highly preservative qualities of the salt. They are of importance in that they cast light on some aspects of the life of the ordinary working people. The huge cemetery is believed to have consisted of some 2,500 graves and the fact that much of value was preserved for posterity is due to the interest and vigilance of the Director of the Hallstatt State Mine, George Ramsauer. Lubbock, writing in 1872, comments that 'M. Ramsauer, for many years Director of the salt-mines at Hallstadt . . . has discovered an extensive cemetery. . . . He has opened no less than 980 graves.' One realises what a loss to science it would have been had a less scrupulous and less interested person than Ramsauer been in charge of the mines when the great discoveries were made. In 1876, the Vienna Academy of Sciences excavated there in the place where the salt-working sites were situated. Traces of habitation and industry were found in this wild, agriculturally useless place; and numerous imported objects from all over Europe and the wealth reflected in the grave-goods points to the salt-mines as the reason for the richness of the burials. Salt was, of course, a most desirable marketable commodity which could be exchanged for riches of all kinds. Jacques Nenquin, in his study of the role of salt in the economics of prehistory, comments of this site: 'that . . . a number of objects have been discovered in the mine-galleries of Hallstatt, which have proved to be of great importance for the study of the daily life of prehistoric man. Fragments of clothing made of leather, wool or linen are known, and leather caps, shoes, and even a sort of leather gloves, probably used as a protection for their hands when the miners slid down ropes leading to the galleries. Mention must also be made of the remains of food, like barley, millet, beans, and a cultivated form of apple and cherry, fragments of pottery, wooden dishes, spoons of wood, and so on. On the surface, traces of wooden huts were found repeatedly.'

The imported material found in the Hallstatt graves shows trading connections with Etruria and Greece, and with Rome as early as the third century BC. The quantity of Italic metal imports is impressive; others come from Croatia-Slovenia. Amber points to communications with the north, and Egyptian influence may perhaps also be detected. Apart from all these imports, there was a local industry in pottery and metalwork. Both inhumation and cremation funerary rites were practised. In 1907, the Duchess of Mecklenburg, a remarkable woman who worked indefatigably, often under spartan conditions, as a field archaeologist, carried out excavations at Hallstatt. She located 26 graves, and also came upon many isolated finds. The Duchess was an Austrian noblewoman with a family tradition of archaeological interest and research. She was an avid collector, as well as an excavator; she was one of the outstanding characters concerned with Hallstatt and its cultural implications.

Hallstatt, then, consisted of a settlement with a flourishing local industry, that of salt-mining, and on this the wealth of the community depended. The huge cemetery testifies to the prosperity of the inhabitants. The people were iron-using, and on account of this extraordinarily rich and rewarding site, the early Iron Age in Europe came to be known as the 'Hallstatt phase'. There is nothing to suggest that the Hallstatt people represent a foreign intrusive element into central Europe. They were, as all the evidence indicates, basically the old indigenous Urnfield people of the late Bronze Age, with perhaps a complement of refugees and wanderers from Assyria and the Steppelands, as the horse-trappings suggest; but basically they were native people, and Celtic-speaking. It is also probable, as we have seen, that the bronze-using ancestors of these Hallstatt Celts spoke some form of Celtic language; but this can only be inferred, because we have no written evidence to prove the point. However, the distribution of early Celtic place-names in certain areas of Europe coincides with Urnfield remains in such a way as to lead us to suppose that there was a connection between the two.

The graves of these Hallstatt Celts were very singular; they seem to have derived in part from Etruscan funerary traditions. The body, burnt or unburnt, was laid under a four-wheeled wagon (*4*) in a wooden chamber under a grave mound. The wood used was frequently oak. The horse-trappings were placed in the grave, but there do not seem to be any traces of the horses themselves, so presumably these were not buried with the dead. The human skeletons found by the earlier excavators were not preserved by

4 Sketches of a 4-wheeled cart and a 2-wheeled chariot

them. Vessels, weapons of iron, personal decorations such as buckles, armlets, rings and neck ornaments were recovered, many of them bearing symbols familiar to later Celtic iconography, such as the ram-headed serpent and the cross in various forms, symbolic of the sun. Buckets and *situlae* and actual joints of meat, especially pig-meat, were excavated in these graves, and all these objects testify to the prosperity of the society, its innovating nature, and its new and exciting art style. Of Hallstatt, Mahr says: 'It was apparent that this civilisation was far superior to that of the Bronze Age, which was just then being recognised as a past stage of human culture. This superiority expressed itself in a style of art and in a perfection of craftsmanship which came as a great surprise to the learned world.' And also: 'It is difficult for us today to realise how completely the antiquarians of that time were dependent upon classical literature in their endeavours to solve the problems before them. To the majority, the scraps of evidence which they thought they could extricate from Greek and Roman sources were the final authority, and the idea never entered their heads that non-Greek and non-Roman evidence could be brought to tell its own story, or indeed that it had any value at all.' Those remarks convey very succinctly the attitude prevalent amongst antiquarians of the time, and show how undeveloped was the concept of Celtic archaeology and culture as attested by wider archaeological evidence, as recently as the late nineteenth century. So, although a Celtic civilisation cannot be said to have been dramatically *discovered*, the finding of the remains at Hallstatt, and

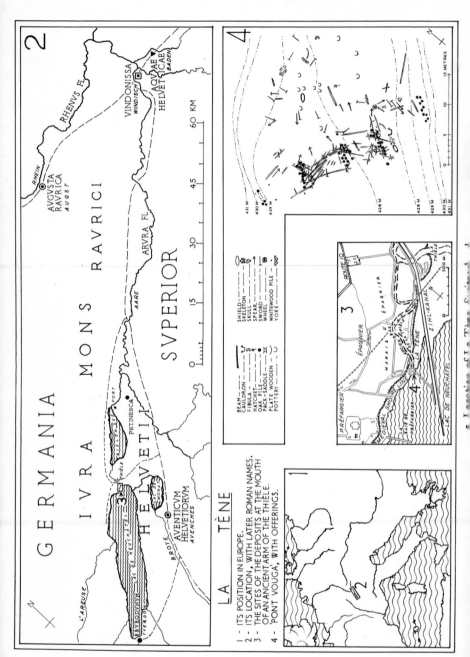

2

GERMANIA

IVRA MONS RAVRICI

RHENVS FL

AVGVSTA RAVRICA
AUGST

VINDONISSA
WINDISCH

AQVAE
HELVET ICAE
BADEN

RHEIN

ARVRA FL
AARE

HELVETIA

SVPERIOR

PETINESCA

PORT

AVENTICVM
HELVETIORVM
AVENCHES

BROYE

L'AREVSE

LAC DE NEVCHATEL

EBVRODVNVM
YVERDON

LAC DE MORAT

60 KM   45   30   15   0

3

ÉPAGNIER

PRÉFARGIER

MARAIS D'ÉPAGNIER

LA TÈNE

PONT DE PRÉFARGIER

MEDIEVAL SWORD FOUND

ROUTE 10

THIÈLE

ZIHL-KANAL

LAC DE NEUCHÂTEL

4

431 M   430 M   429 M   428 M   429 M   430 M   431 M

15 METRES   10   5   0

SHIELD
SKELETON
SKULL
SPEAR
SWORD
WHEEL
WHITEWOOD PILE
YOKE

BEAM
CAULDRON
FIBULA
OAK PILE
PACK-SADDLE
PLATE WOODEN
POTTERY

1

LA TÈNE

1 – ITS POSITION IN EUROPE.
2 – ITS LOCATION, WITH LATER ROMAN NAMES.
3 – THE SITES OF THE DEPOSITS AT THE MOUTH
     OF AN ANCIENT ARM OF THE THIÈLE.
4 – 'PONT VOUGA', WITH OFFERINGS.

the gradual appreciation of their significance for European prehistory and the origins of the European Iron Age, made an impact which was to have far-reaching implications for European archaeological thought.

Before considering the actual movements of these early Celtic peoples inside Europe and into the British Isles, we must look at the second phase of Celtic evolution in Europe. This is characterised by the finds of Celtic objects at La Tène (5), from which this phase takes its name. Less impressive in quantity, and perhaps in the nature of the site, the quality of the articles recovered, and the religious motives which must have motivated the depositors, make this second discovery in fact no less exciting and significant than that of Hallstatt. In Iron Age times the River Thièle flowed into Lake Neuchâtel through a main channel and a subsidiary arm (5). In due course the level of the lake rose, and the mouths of the river were inundated. When the water-level was reduced in about 1858 timbers were seen projecting from the mud (6), and investigations revealed that structures like bridges had been thrown across the lowest reach of the subsidiary arm (5). All round these there were found great quantities of metal and other objects which had evidently been cast into the stream after being dedicated to a deity or a group of gods, as thank-offerings or placatory gifts, in accordance with Celtic custom. Publications of the find were made in 1864 by E. Desor and in 1866 by F. Schwab; E. Vouga then explored the area and published his conclusions in 1885, and P. Vouga published a final account in 1923.

6 Timbers were revealed projecting from the mud at La Tène when the level of Lac Neuchâtel was lowered

Analysis of the objects showed that they were certainly Celtic, but that new art styles and cultural influences had come into play. Graves from the Marne district of France and from the Rhineland were discovered, fully bearing out the evidence of the material from La Tène and indicating that in this second, later, phase of Celtic culture, dating to about 500 BC, the same basic peoples were involved. It is suggested that the centre of power had shifted in a westerly direction, and that new families had usurped the older, more conservative dynasties.

The graves themselves showed innovations, one of the most striking of which was the fact that the body was laid out, not under the old four-wheeled Hallstatt cart but under a new type of light, two-wheeled war-chariot, drawn by two ponies yoked to a central pole (*4*). This chariot can be seen to have been one of the most characteristic pieces of war equipment of the early Celts, a battle-conscious people if there ever was one.

The art style had likewise developed, and revealed the influence of wider trade contacts with Etruria and the Mediterranean world and elsewhere. The founding of Massilia (Marseilles) as a Greek trading colony in 600 BC, and the consequent opening up of the Rhône Valley to Mediterranean influences, was obviously a powerful factor in this new stage of Celtic development. It is dated roughly to 500 BC, but as Mahr again so appositely remarks: 'It goes without saying that the La Tène period, like its Hallstatt predecessor, was not a clear-cut chronological unit which commenced and terminated in all its manifestations and provinces at the same time.'

An import which was clearly much in vogue with the La Tène Celts was wine, from Etruria and the Mediterranean. Decorated wine-flagons, *oinochoai*, were found in many of the graves, together with fire-dogs, drinking-vessels and joints of pork, testifying to the belief in a continuing material life in, or beyond, the grave; the stores would provide sustenance for the journey to the Other-world beyond the tomb, or material for the great Otherworld feast on arrival, the feast for which according to early Irish tradition the smith-god Goibniu brewed the inevitable ale. The Celtic conception of the Otherworld was both sensual and materialistic.

When we come to consider the early movements of the Celtic peoples, the first people whom we can confidently describe as Celts are the iron-using innovators of central Europe whom we

24

have seen to have left impressive traces at Hallstatt in Austria as elsewhere in Europe. They appear to have stemmed from the indigenous bronze-using people whose culture is known to archaeologists as the 'Northern Alpine Urnfield' culture. They spread out on conquests, and settled in areas as far apart as eastern Europe and, by 450 BC, southern and eastern parts of the British Isles. When we come to look for evidence of early Celtic settlement in the British Isles, it has to be realised that opinion is still fairly fluid about the exact dates and areas of settlement, and any outline given must be prepared for modification in the light of continuing researches in the field.

The picture at the moment is briefly as follows. There are traces of people of Hallstatt ancestry in the north-east of Scotland as early as about 600 BC. These are likely to have consisted of bands of warriors, perhaps accompanied by some of their womenfolk, and to have led to the presence of a Celtic-speaking population in this area. These people were apparently connected with late Hallstatt cultures of north Germany. Hallstatt-derived cultural influences reached southern and eastern England perhaps as early as the sixth century BC, characterised by techniques of iron-working with the resulting improved weapons and agricultural implements which gave a greater efficiency to warfare and land-use, which in turn made the settlers technologically far superior to the bronze-using native population, and ensured a rapid supremacy.

From the initial phases of settlement they moved north and west; the Scottish Lowlands, however, seem not to have been colonised by Celts until somewhat later. From about the fourth century BC the second great wave of Celtic immigrants began to arrive in parts of Yorkshire again, in Sussex, and elswhere on the south coast of England. These were composed of people of La Tène descent. It was they who introduced the light two-wheeled Celtic war-chariot, and the impressive La Tène art style, into the British Isles. They brought with them the warlike, heroic ideals which we are to meet with in later documented contexts; the intensely aristocratic nature of Hallstatt society, however, would suggest that these had a long Celtic ancestry. The tribes which settled in Yorkshire were primarily pastoralists, and cattle-raiding is likely to have been their chief sport and source of wealth. The art styles which they developed are peculiarly insular, less flamboyant, more subtle and restrained perhaps than their

25

continental counterparts. The early Irish tales are full of accounts of cattle-raiding and tribal strife, and of all the passions and the barbarities which seem to have operated throughout the Celtic world, and which we must suppose to have characterised this British La Tène phase as it did that in Ireland and on the Continent.

More than the material culture of the Yorkshire Celts, and those from south-west Scotland, is likely to have found its way into Ulster with their migrations there; some of the actual legends themselves may have been taken over into north-east Ireland by the settlers.

The latest Celts to settle in the British Isles on any scale were the Belgic peoples, from north-east Gaul. The archaeological record of their movements can now be fully borne out by the testimony of history. They came over here before 100 BC, and settled in south-east England, bringing their own brand of Celtic culture and their religious cults with them. Strabo singles the Belgae out for comment from the other Celts:

> Among them they say that the Belgae are the bravest. They are divided into 15 tribes between the Rhine and the Loire. And so they alone are said to have resisted the attack of the German tribes, the Cimbri and the Teutones. Of the size of their population the following is a proof: they say that in previous times it was shown that there were 300,000 Belgae capable of bearing arms. (*Tierney, 268*)

The warlike characteristics of these people came out very distinctly in their dealings with the Romans, who found them the most stubborn and unyielding of the Celtic population in Britain, as in Gaul. They appear to have introduced the plough into Britain, together with techniques of enamelling and their own distinctive brand of La Tène art. Belgic pottery is also very characteristic. They also introduced the system of coinage. They created urban settlements which were in fact towns, such as St Albans (Verulamium), Silchester (Calleva), Winchester (Venta) and Colchester (Camulodunum).

The coming of the Celts to Ireland is even more problematic: this is in part due to the fact that the richness of the early native texts is in no way paralleled by the archaeological evidence. However, this is most probably due to the fact that comparatively little critical archaeological investigation had been carried out in Ireland until recent years, and a lot of badly conducted excavations have confused interpretations attached to them. But work is now being done and results are being obtained which give great hope for a better understanding of the problem in the future. As we have seen, Q Celtic or Goidelic is the form of the language spoken in Ireland, Gaelic Scotland, and until recently, natively in the Isle of Man. This presents a serious problem for those concerned with the early Celtic peoples. We do not as yet know who brought Q Celtic to Ireland, and from where, nor have we any certainty that the question is in fact capable of being resolved. Also we cannot say how the Brittonic speech of the aristocratic Yorkshire and south-west Scottish colonisers of Ulster was completely swamped by the Goidelic language which we must suppose to have been spoken there. Various theories have been put forward by scholars in both the philological and archaeological spheres, but so far nothing fully convincing has been suggested. It may be possible to suppose that the Goidelic or Q Celtic form was the older of the two, perhaps even the language of the Hallstatt Celts; in which case it could have been these earlier colonisers who brought it with them to Ireland somewhere about the sixth century BC. Was it, one may ask, submerged elsewhere by Brittonic-speaking immigrants with a superior technological equipment and better battle techniques? We cannot as yet answer these questions, but it is a fact that Goidelic was dominant in Ireland in spite of the Brittonic immigrations which we know to have taken place into Ulster in the centuries immediately before the Christian era. These are all questions which archaeology and philology together may be able to resolve. Meanwhile, the phenomenon of Q Celtic is a fascinating one and at present inexplicable.

The Hallstatt colonisation of Ireland may in part have taken place from Britain, but there is evidence that it stemmed directly from the Continent and entered Ireland by way of north-eastern Scotland. As far as the introduction of the La Tène culture into Ireland can be determined, it would seem that there were two main sources, one already mentioned, through Britain, round about the first century BC with its main concentration in the north-east, and another, earlier, movement coming direct from the Continent and dating to about the late third, early second centuries BC. This movement was into western Ireland. This supposition is supported not only by the material excavated, but by the early literary tradition. This portrays a well-established rivalry between Connacht in the west and Ulster in the north-east. It is this textual tradition that does so much to augment the evidence of archaeology and to illuminate some part of the every-day lives of at least a section of the early Celtic peoples.

CLASSICAL REFERENCES TO THE CELTIC PEOPLES

Now we must consider another source of evidence for the ancient Celts, namely the commentators of the Classical world. Some of their references to Celtic movements and settlement are frag-mentary, others more detailed; all must be used with caution, but on the whole they do impart information much of which we must regard as genuine, allowing for emotive and political bias. The two earliest writers who make any comment on the Celts are the Greeks, Hecataeus, writing somewhere about the second half of the sixth century BC, and Herodotus, writing somewhat later, in the fifth century BC. Hecataeus mentions the founding of the Greek trading colony at Massilia (Marseilles), which was in Ligurian territory, near the land of the Celts. Herodotus refers to the Celts and states that the source of the River Danube was in Celtic lands. He gives evidence for widespread Celtic settlement in the Iberian peninsula, and we know of early Celtic settlement in Spain and Portugal, the amalgamated cultures of the two peoples leading to their being given the name of 'Celtiberians'; and although Herodotus confuses the geographical location of the Danube, and places it in the Iberian peninsula, he may have been basing his statement on the tradition that the Celts were associated with the source of this river. Writing in the fourth century BC, Ephorus classed the Celts as one of four great barbarian peoples; the others mentioned are the Persians, the Scythians and the Libyans. This implies that at this time, as earlier, they were a distinctive people. No matter how insubstantial their political unity may have been, they had a common language and tradi-tions, a distinctive material culture, and closely related religious ideas; all these things stand out from the inevitable regional cultural patterns caused by the fusing of Celtic traditions with those of the peoples amongst whom they settled over such wide areas of Europe (2).

Celtic social organisation was based on the tribe; the tribes each had their own individual name, while the collective term for the entire people was *Celtae*. The name *Celtici* continued in existence in south-western Spain until Roman times; but it is now thought that this was due to the Romans themselves, who recognised Celts there from their knowledge of the Gauls, and gave them the name *Celtici*. The term is not known to have been used for the Celtic inhabitants of the British Isles in ancient times, and there is no evidence to show that the Celtic inhabitants of these areas called themselves by this collective name, although they may well have done so. The Greek form of the name, *Keltoi*, originates from the oral tradition of the Celts themselves. There are two other forms of name for the Celts; *Galli*, which is what the Romans called them, and *Galatae*, which was frequently used by Greek writers. So we have the two Greek forms of the name, Keltoi and Galatae, and the equivalent Roman forms, Celtae and Galli. Caesar does in fact comment that the Galli called themselves Celtae, and it seems clear that this is the name by which they knew themselves, over and above their individual tribal names. *Gallia Cis-Alpina* was the name given to the region south of the Alps by the Romans, who also named the area beyond the Alps *Gallia Trans-Alpina*. Somewhere round about 400 BC Celtic tribes, headed by the Insubres, invaded northern Italy, coming from Switzerland and south Germany. They sacked Etruria, and penetrated down into the Italian peninsula as far as Mediolanum (Milan). Other tribes followed their example, and large-scale settlements took place. The warriors bent on conquest were followed by their families and servants and possessions, loaded into heavy, cumbersome carts. This is corroborated in an interesting statement in the *Táin Bó Cúalnge*, the Irish epic tale:

> Thereafter the hosts set out upon their march. It was difficult for them to attend to that mighty army, which set forth on that journey, with the many tribes and the many families and the many thousands whom they brought with them that they might see each other and know each other and that each might be with his familiars and his friends and his kin on the hosting. (*C. O'Rahilly, 147*)

Bands of skilled soldiers raided widely, using these newly gained territories as their base. In 390 BC Rome was successfully attacked. In 279 the Galatae attacked Delphi under their leader (or, as seems more likely, their deity) Brennos. Before this they had penetrated into Macedonia, led by Brennos and Bolgios— probably both to be regarded as gods rather than human leaders —and had attempted to settle there. The Greeks consistently opposed this move. The Celts were defeated when they attacked Delphi, but they remained in the Balkans. Three tribes entered Asia Minor, and after some conflict they settled in northern Phrygia; this then became known as Galatia. There they had a sanctuary called *Drunemeton*, 'oak grove'; they also had hill-forts, and they retained their individuality here for a long period of time. St Paul's Epistle for these Galatian settlers is famous; and once the archaeology of Galatia is recognised and explored, the results may show another interesting regional cultural development within the wider Celtic world.

Today, in the British Isles, when we think of the Celts, we incline to think of them in terms of the Celtic-speaking peoples on the periphery of the western parts of Europe—in Brittany, in Wales, Ireland and Gaelic Scotland, and vestigially, in the Isle of Man. But we must be aware that for archaeologists they are people whose culture covers huge areas of territory and time. For eastern European archaeologists moreover, the more easterly dwelling Celts have an importance and an interest equal to that of the—to us—better-known Celts of the West. And much more archaeological research throughout the entire ancient Celtic regions, as well as linguistic studies, especially perhaps in the important sphere of onomastics (place-names studies) must be carried out before we can feel the picture is anything like as complete as it can be.

To return to the early history of the Celts as seen through Classical eyes, the lands of Gallia Cis-Alpina began to be lost to the Celts as early as 225 BC; this process began with the crushing defeat of a huge Gaulish army at Telamon. It included amongst its troops the famous Gaesatae 'spear-bearers', the impressive Gaulish mercenary soldiers who used to hire themselves out for service with any tribe or group of tribes who required their assistance. These troops would seem to bear some resemblance to the Irish *Fiana*, bands of warriors who lived outwith the tribal system and roamed the countryside fighting and hunting, under their legendary leader, Finn mac Cumaill. The Gaesatae are vividly described by the Roman writer Polybius in his account of the Battle of Telamon. His remarks on the appearance of the Celts in general are discussed in Chapter 2. He tells us that the Celtic tribes taking part in the battle, the Insubres and the Boii, wore trousers and cloaks, but the Gaesatae were naked. Gaius, the Roman Consul was killed in the first action, and decapitated according to Celtic custom. The Celts were then effectively trapped between two Roman forces, and in spite of their almost suicidal courage and stamina, were heavily defeated. This was the beginning of the retreat of the Celts from Gallia Cis-Alpina; in 192 BC the Romans, by defeating the Boii at their stronghold, now Bologna, gained final supremacy over the whole of Cis-Alpine Gaul. From then on, the story is the same everywhere; a gradual shrinking of independent Celtic territory as the Roman Empire advanced and expanded. By the first century BC Gaul, which alone then remained as independent Celtic territory on the Continent, was to become incorporated into the Roman Empire with its final defeat by Julius Caesar which began in 58 BC; it took some seven years to complete the subjugation of the country, and after that Romanisation was rapid.

The native speech and religious traditions continued to be perpetuated, but now under the aegis of Rome, and modified to fit in with Roman ideas; and the Latin tongue was widely in use amongst the privileged classes. The Celtic priests, the Druids, were discredited but this was probably due as much to their threat to Roman political supremacy as to their crude religious practices which allegedly so offended Roman taste—human sacrifice had long been abandoned in the Roman world. Much of our knowledge of Celtic life and religion has to be sifted out from under this Roman veneer, both in Gaul and in Britain. The native religious cults have likewise to be divorced from their Classical overlay and this is by no means an easy task, and in some cases seemingly impossible. However, we have enough information and comparative material to allow us to draw a fairly convincing sketch of native life in Roman Gaul and Britain. The coming of Christianity brought about great changes, as did the final conquest of the barbarian hordes from northern Europe. After this, apart from Ireland, we are dealing with a dying Celtic world, and the areas that remained Celtic-speaking after this mark a Celtic survival, which is outside the scope of this book.

To return to the British Isles. We know little from the written sources of the history of the Celts, less in fact than we do of that of the Celts in Europe. Caesar's report of Belgic migrations to south-east Britain is the first true historical account of a Celtic movement into the British Isles; but there are one or two other fragments of evidence, apart from the archaeological record. In the poem *Ora Maritima*, written in the fourth century AD by Rufus

Festus Avienus, fragments of a lost Massiliot sailing-manual, known as the *Massiliote Periplus*, are preserved. This dates to about 600 BC and consisted of an account of a voyage, starting from Massilia (Marseilles), and proceeding down the eastern Spanish coast as far as the city of Tartessos which was probably located near the mouth of the Guadalquivir. This account included a reference to the inhabitants of two large islands, Ierne and Albion, namely Ireland and Britain, who were reputed to trade with the Oestrymnians, the inhabitants of what is now Brittany. The words are Greek forms of names which survived amongst the Goidelic-speaking Celts, namely Old Irish Ériu and Albu. They are Indo-European words and most probably of Celtic origin. Next we have the voyage of Pytheas of Massilia, about 325 BC, in which Britain and Ireland are referred to as *pretannikaē*, the 'Pretanic Isles', a presumptively Celtic word again. The natives would be *Pritani* or *Priteni*. The name Pritani appears in Welsh as *Prydain*, seemingly used to connote Britain; this was misunderstood and came through as the *Britannia* and *Britanni* of Caesar. Later geographers use these names and it is clear that the Pretanic Islands were indeed *Ierne* and *Albion*.

ROME AND THE COMING OF CHRISTIANITY

After the various waves of Celtic migrations into the British Isles which we have already discussed, the next major event in the history of early Britain was, of course, its incorporation into the Roman Empire. Julius Caesar came to Britain in 55 and again in 54 BC. The Emperor Claudius finally began the subjugation of the south in AD 43 and from then on the story is one of Roman expansion, military conquest, Roman civil rule and the Romanisation of the foremost native chieftains. But the pattern here must be seen in the same light as in Gaul, less sophisticated and on a smaller scale; the native languages persisted, although Latin was used by the aristocracy as in Gaul. Roman manners were learnt, cities built in Mediterranean fashion, and stone temples based on Classical models were erected in which the gods of the two traditions were worshipped alike. The native element seems gradually to have reasserted itself, and by the fourth century AD we find evidence of a renewed interest in native religious cults; this included the construction of one or two impressive temples to Celtic deities, such as that to Nodons at Lydney Park on the

Severn Estuary, and that to an unknown deity, characterised by a bronze representation of a bull with three goddesses on its back, at Maiden Castle, Dorset. Each of these sites originated as an Iron Age hill-fort. Christianity too was becoming established, bringing with it its own modifications and influence upon the native society.

This is the wide background we have to envisage, against which the Celts lived their everyday lives; it varies greatly both in time and in geographical range as we have seen, beginning about 700 BC and ending, for us, somewhere about AD 500. We have seen how between the times of Herodotus and Julius Caesar, the fortunes of this restless people had risen to great heights and fallen with equal drama. Their language, with its two main branches, was common in one form or the other, to the whole Celtic world; their religious attitudes were likewise universal. Their individuality or 'nationhood' if we may use such a term for a people with no strong central political control, made them distinctive and recognisable to their more sophisticated and literate neighbours. And it is partly the observations of these neighbours that enable us to learn what it was about the Celtic way of life that made them noteworthy as a people; and the other sources of evidence for the early Celts take us a step further in this quest. We now want to know something about the more intimate and personal lives of these pagan Celtic peoples; we want to see something of their literary expression and their religious ideas, of the laws which governed their everyday lives. We must learn something of the actual structure of their society, of their appearance and dress which singled them out for comment by the Classical writers. The Classics tell us that the Celts were one of the four barbarian peoples of the known world—what did they mean by this, how can we verify it, and how reliable are our sources? In the rest of the book we will attempt to answer at least some of these questions.

The Structure of Society; Appearance and Dress

Because of the scattered nature of the Celts in Europe and in the British Isles, the long periods of time involved in their evolution and decline, and the fragmentary and varying nature of the evidence for their habits and customs, it is necessary to generalise to some extent in considering the pattern of their everyday lives. The Celts in some areas must, of course, have been more backward (conserving) than the Celts in other areas, who would be progressive (innovating) according to their contact with other peoples and their cultural and technological ideas. Those living on busy trade routes would have had access to influences which were denied to the Celts living in geographically and culturally isolated regions, or having fierce barbarians as neighbours; these would inevitably be conservative rather than innovating, warlike rather than pacific. The insular Celts must always have had distinctive cultural peculiarities which made them differ from their continental cousins. Celtic art, for example, once it reached the British Isles, immediately developed its own distinctive style and quality, yet remained essentially Celtic art and its affinity with the continental styles was never obscured; likewise the people themselves on settling in Britain must have developed their own peculiar insular character and modified cultural pattern while remaining completely and positively Celtic. Geographical and economic factors play a vital part in social evolution and the Celt living on the shores of the Mediterranean must be, to some extent, a very different person from his racial fellow living in the boglands of Ireland or on the exposed Yorkshire moors, and require very different food and clothing and housing conditions. But although geographical distribution and foreign manners may have affected the outward Celt, so strong and individual is the Celtic personality

—the Celtic character is so distinct and positive—that all these people in all these various areas can be seen from the evidence at our disposal to have been fundamentally Celtic.

The picture we shall draw, of the everyday life of the early Celts is the one most probable in the light of the evidence of the Classical writers, of archaeology and of the vernacular literatures of Ireland and, to a lesser extent, of Wales. These last are concerned with the insular Celts, but the picture they present coheres remarkably with that outlined by the remaining source material. Although the Irish texts describe a world which was already archaic (in their earliest form they cannot be dated to earlier than the eighth century AD) such was the longevity and strength of the oral tradition in Celtic society, where information was handed on by a professional class of tradition-bearers trained in the art, that when the native tradition was finally committed to writing under the aegis of the Christian Church, it contained memories of a more archaic world which can be seen to be valid and reliable. Allowing for regional and temporal variations, then, and details based on individual tribal choice or preference (tight or loose trousers; ringlets or tightly tied back hair and so on), the following chapter presents some picture of the fundamental nature of Celtic society during its most powerful and influential period.

THE STRUCTURE OF SOCIETY

Basically, the structure of Celtic society must have been the same throughout the pagan Celtic world. The Classical writers commented on it; the Irish law tracts in particular deal with a society whose structure is recognisably that known to the Classical writers. Archaeological evidence testifies to this same organisation of the social orders in so far as it can; that is to say, it can testify to its essentially aristocratic nature. From these various sources we learn that at the top of the social structure came the king—by the time Caesar conquered Gaul, the system of kingship had been to a large extent replaced in the leading tribes by chief magistrates (*vergobretos*) who ruled together with the aristocracy. Below the king came his chief nobles who were highly aristocratic and powerful. This class included the priests, who were always recruited from the aristocracy in Gaul, and this is likely to have been the case in Ireland also. Below them again were the non-noble freemen, like gentlemen farmers, owning land and property and including the finest craftsmen, especially the blacksmith who had a high position in early Celtic society; his craft was believed to have been of a semi-supernatural character and the smith-god held an equally elevated position in the divine society of the Celtic deities. These were the three main divisions of Celtic society that counted; the rest of the population consisted of the unfree members of society, people without franchise, men who were not allowed to bear arms, who had neither land nor property. This section was little higher in status than were the slaves and consisted of families which had fallen on hard times, conquered peoples, and the slaves themselves and so on. That this element in the society of the early Celts resembled slaves is actually stated by Caesar who, in his comments on Celtic society in general, says:

> Throughout Gaul there are two classes of men of some dignity and importance. The common people are nearly regarded as slaves; they possess no initiative and their views are never invited on any question. Most of them being weighed down by debt or heavy taxes, or by the injustice of the more powerful, hand themselves over into slavery to the upper classes, who have all the same legal rights against these men that a master has towards his slave. One of the two classes is that of the Druids, the other that of the Knights. The Druids are concerned with the worship of the gods . . . they have the right to decide nearly all public and private disputes and they also pass judgment and decide rewards and penalties in criminal and murder cases and in disputes concerning legacies and boundaries. When a private person or a tribe disobeys their ruling they ban them from attending at sacrifices. This is the harshest penalty. Men placed under this ban are treated as impious wretches; all avoid them, fleeing their company and conversation, lest their contact bring misfortune upon them; they are denied legal rights and can hold no official dignity. The Druids have at their head one who holds the chief authority among them. When he dies either the highest in honour among the others succeeds, or if some are on an equal footing they contend for leadership by a vote of the Druids, but sometimes even in arms. At a fixed time of the year they meet in assembly in a holy place in the lands of the Carnutes, which is regarded as the centre of the whole of Gaul. All who have disputes come here from all sides and accept their decisions and judgments. . . . The Druids are wont to be absent from war, nor do they pay taxes like the others; they are dispensed from military service and free of all other obligations. . . . The second class is that of the Knights. They all take part in war whenever there is need and war is declared. Before the arrival of Caesar it used to happen nearly every year that they either

attacked another tribe or warded off the attacks of another tribe. The greater their rank and resources, the more dependents and clients do they possess. This is their only source of influence and power. (*Tierney, 271–2*)

Strabo further testifies to the high rank of the Druids and the Bards or Vates:

> Among all the tribes generally speaking, there are three classes of men held in special honour: the Bards, the Vates and the Druids. The Bards are singers and poets; the Vates interpreters of sacrifice and natural philosophers while the Druids in addition to the science of nature, study also moral philosophy. (*Tierney, 269*)

This Classical portrayal of the structure of Celtic society is strikingly similar to that described in the early Irish tales and in the law tracts, even down to small details. It is also strongly reminiscent of Scottish Gaelic society down to the eighteenth century, the clan representing the tribe, and the chieftain at the head of it, having his cadet nobles and kinsmen almost on a level with himself, with the remainder of the clan owing allegiance to him, depending on him, and fighting for him in skirmishes and larger issues. Each tribe, then, in pagan Celtic areas, had its king, his power indicated by the extent of the lands over which he ruled, the size of his tribe, and the number of his clients; below him were the noble freemen, and the priests and seers. Caesar mentions this custom of clientship as we have seen, and it is a basic feature of Celtic society. It is a commonplace in early Irish law and is seen in the tales and is known in Ireland as *céilsine*. One freeman would become the client or vassal of another more influential freeman. The arrangement could be terminated by agreement between the two parties. In this way nobles became rich and powerful according to the number of their clients because the client borrowed capital from the lord and paid it back with interest. As in the case of the clan in Scotland, the client fought in the service of his lord and attended him on public occasions. The lord, in return, protected his client from danger and concerned himself with his affairs. In this way a freeman could become a powerful noble, not necessarily on account of his aristocratic birth, but because of the number of clients he possessed. The Celtic custom of clientship is commented on by Athenaeus who says: 'The Celts have in their company even in war (as well as in peace) companions whom they call parasites.'

The other very typical feature of Celtic society is that of fosterage; this again persisted in Gaelic Scotland until the eighteenth century as recognised practice. The sons of lesser nobles used to be sent to live with and be reared in the household of more powerful nobles; there they were taught the rudiments of warfare and all the other accomplishments proper to a nobleman. This, of course, also gave additional power to the lord over his client as he had his sons in his control. In the early Irish tradition, the bond between foster-child and foster-parent was extremely close and real; that between foster-brothers was almost sacred in nature. This custom of fosterage is suggested by Caesar:

> In the rest of their way of life, nearly their sole difference from other peoples is that they do not allow their sons to approach them in public unless they have grown up to the age of military service, and they think it a disgrace for a boy under this age to sit in public within sight of his father. (*Tierney, 273*)

The foster-child was only returned to his father when his training was completed and thus could not accompany him in public until this time. Girls were also sent to foster-parents with whom they learnt to sew and embroider; boys were taught to swim, to ride, to use the sling and to play games like *fidchell* and *brandub*. The fee payable to the foster-parent varied according to the rank of the foster-child. In Ireland boys were apparently returned to their parents at the age of 17 while girls went home at 14 years of age. The foster-children were obliged to support their foster-parents in old age. The bond between children fostered in the same home was a very close one and it is well illustrated in the *Táin Bó Cúalnge*, as elsewhere. Fer Diad, one of the great heroes of this epic tale, is obliged to engage in single combat against his foster-brother, Cú Chulainn; this is a deeply tragic moment in the story and demonstrates very clearly the strength of the bond between foster-brothers in the ancient world. Fer Diad is forced against his will to fight his foster-brother, by the wiles of the great queen, Medb.

> Then messengers and envoys were sent for Fer Diad. Fer Diad refused and denied and again refused those messengers and he did not come with them for he knew what they wanted of him which was to fight with his friend and companion and foster-brother Cú Chulainn mac Sualtaim and so he came not with them. Then Medb

sent the Druids and satirists and harsh bards for Fer Diad that they
might make against him three satires to stay him and three lampoons,
and that they might raise on his face three blisters, shame, blemish
and disgrace, so that he might die before the end of nine days if he
did not succumb at once, unless he came with the messengers. For
the sake of his honour Fer Diad came with them, for he deemed it
better to fall by shafts of valour and prowess and bravery than by
shafts of satire and reviling and reproach. (*C. O'Rahilly, 211f.*)

The bonds of foster-brotherhood were powerful, but the fear of
satire was even more compelling to the Celt.

In pagan Ireland too the Druid occupied an exalted place; no
one, including the king, could speak before the Druid had spoken.
Conchobar mac Nessa, King of Ulster, had the powerful Cathbad
as his Chief Druid; he was also the King's father. In the early
texts the Druids do not appear so much as priests as prophets, but
this is because the Christian scribes did not include direct references to actual pagan religious practices in the stories they committed to writing, although traces of these can in fact be detected.
Even the charioteer was a freeman, and his relationship with the
chariot warrior whom he served was a very close one. Lóeg had
much influence over Cú Chulainn and indeed his clever inter-
vention saved the day on many occasions.

This, then, is the structure of pagan Celtic society, and the sort
of background we must envisage all the ensuing details of everyday
life to have operated against—the religion, the learning, the
domestic arrangements, the laws, the warfare. Everything refers
to a society constituted in this way, and in the main to the free
classes—the rest of the people are hardly mentioned; they were of
no interest to Classical commentators, or to early story-tellers, or
later to archaeologists as they had little in the way of material
possessions to endure the test of time. Caesar is commenting
correctly when he says they were little better than slaves. Diodorus
Siculus is probably not exaggerating when he says of the Celts:
'They transport the wine by boat on the navigable rivers and by
wagon through the plains, and receive in return for it an in-
credibly large price; for one jar of wine they receive in return a
slave, a servant in exchange for a drink.' Slavery, and the extent
of the slave trade suggested by this comment, is further confirmed
by the finds of slave chains and slave-gang chains amongst Celtic
deposits such as those at La Tène and Llyn Cerrig Bach in
Anglesey (7).

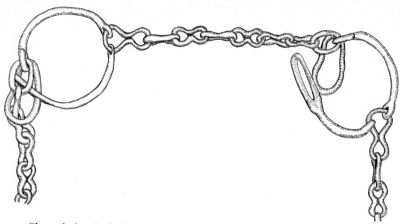

7 Slave chains, included in the votive material recovered when Llyn Cerrig Bach, Anglesey, was drained

PHYSICAL APPEARANCE

In the eyes of the Mediterranean commentators, the Celts were essentially a distinctive people. This shows that their personal appearance and their sartorial habits were different from those of the Classical world, and therefore noteworthy. We can in fact obtain a fair idea of what the Celts looked like, and learn something of their own standards of beauty, from various sources of evidence. Taking their physical appearance first, and their dress next, the Classical writers give a certain amount of space to details about Celtic looks. The early Irish texts again support these remarks to an impressive degree. It is clear that even to the alien world of the Mediterranean, with its own different standards of looks, the Celts were a fine-looking people, the women vying with the men in size and comeliness. Diodorus Siculus tells us that short beards were worn by some of the Celtic men; others of them shaved off the beard: 'The nobles shave the cheeks, but let the moustache grow freely, so that it covers the mouth.' These remarks are well borne out by Classical portrayals of the Celts, and by

8 Coarse hairdressing as exemplified on a Celtic coin

40

native religious iconography. Strabo mentions their hair, and the Irish sources again support his comments.

> Their hair is not only naturally blond, but they also use artificial means to increase this natural quality of colour. For they continually wash their hair with lime-wash and draw it back from the forehead to the crown and to the nape of the neck, with the result that their appearance resembles that of Satyrs or of Pans, for the hair is so thickened by this treatment that it differs in no way from a horse's mane (*8*). (*Tierney, 249*)

In the Irish tales the aristocracy is continually described as having fair hair, oval faces and light skin. Strabo speaks of the 'very moist and white' flesh of the Gauls—presumably in contrast to the dark skins of the Mediterranean peoples—and their tall stature. Men, alike with women, wore their hair long, and there are vivid descriptions in the early tales of the hair of the various heroes. The importance to the Celts of fine hair is everywhere stressed. In the epic tale, the *Táin Bó Cúalnge*, for example, we are told that one of the bands of warriors which came to support the queen, Medb, against the Ulaidh (Ulstermen) 'had flowing hair, fair-yellow golden streaming manes', supporting the Classical writers' statements that the hair of the Celts was long and yellow.

This could be further verified by dozens of examples from the vernacular literatures. The hero of the *Táin*, Cú Chulainn, is described as having dark hair, in contra-distinction to the ideal blond Celtic type, but it was in three shades—dark at the roots, brown near the middle and fair at the ends; clearly dyed hair. It is described as being so stiff that an apple could be impaled on the tip of each lock.

> His hair curled about his head like branches of red hawthorn used to refence the gap in a hedge. Though a noble apple tree weighed down with fruit had been shaken about his hair, scarcely one apple would have reached the ground through it, but an apple would have stayed impaled on each single hair, because of the fierce bristling of his hair above him. (*C. O'Rahilly, 202*)

This, of course, refers to his hero's battle distortion, which came upon him when great feats of strength and skill were required of him; and not to his everyday appearance. It is reminiscent of the Celtic coins on which the chariot is manned by a frantic warrior, his hair streaming and stiff behind him, his whole being

9 Battle ardour depicted
on a Celtic coin

epitomising frenzy and inhuman battle ardour (9). Elsewhere, when Cú Chulainn's more pacific beauty is restored to him, and his heroic boyhood deeds have been accomplished, he is calmed, bathed and dressed and thoroughly groomed, and brought in to sit beside his uncle Conchobar the King. The description runs: 'Fifty tresses of hair he had between one ear and the other, bright yellow like the top of a birch tree or like brooches of pale gold shining in the sun. He had a high crest of hair, bright, fair, as if a cow had licked it.' Again in the *Táin*, the three colours of his hair are described as follows: 'Three kinds of hair he had, dark next to the skin, blood-red in the middle, and hair like a crown of red-gold covering them. Fair was the arrangement of that hair with three coils in the hollow at the back of his head, and like gold thread was every fine hair, loose-flowing, golden and excellent, long-dressed, distinguished and of beautiful colour, as it fell back over his shoulders.'

In spite of the fact that many of these descriptions are conflicting, and therefore clearly formulaic, as in Scottish Gaelic traditional love-songs where the girl is described as having rich brown hair but the refrain constantly refers to 'my golden yellow-haired maiden' (*nighean bhuidhe bhán*)—they serve to emphasise the importance of hair to the early Celts, and its role in the 'ideal' of beauty, with which they were greatly preoccupied. And the constant references to the elaborate styling and dressing of the hair, exaggerated though they undoubtedly were, serve to bear out the Classical writers' observations and comment on the vanity of the Celts and their preoccupation with their coiffeur. Men as well as women plaited their hair, and some pieces of Celtic religious iconography illustrate this. Helmets tended not to be worn, presumably because they would both hide and spoil an elaborate hair-do. Women wore their hair long, and their ultimate beauty was always dependent on their tresses, and the colour-quality of the hair. It could be elaborately curled or plaited, and was often caught within combs, or the ends of two pigtails were secured with gold and silver ornaments. There is an impressive description in the *Táin* of the hair of the prophetess Fedelm, when she comes to encounter Medb, the Queen of Connacht. 'She had long, fair-yellow, golden hair; three tresses of her hair wound round her head, another tress falling behind, which touched the calves of her legs.' Perhaps some of the closest parallels in iconography to the verbal descriptions of the long and elaborately curling hair of the Irish warriors are to be found in the religious sculptures of south-west England. The group of reliefs of native deities, clad in short kilted tunics, bearing weapons, their long curled hair usually devoid of any protective head-gear, found in Gloucestershire and Wiltshire, are an example of this.

As an ideal of Celtic beauty, then, hair was usually, but not always, fair, rich, thick and elaborately styled. There must certainly have been a dark element among the Celtic aristocracy, and Cú Chulainn is not the only hero who is described as being dark-haired. But some passages appear to imply that he was regarded as a stranger, an incomer to Ulster society; and his beauty was accepted even though it differed from the normal standards. But other heroes are dark-haired, and are not scorned on account of it. In the description of the various hosts in the *Táin* we hear of 'A thick-necked corpulent warrior in the van of that company. He had black, cropped hair and a scarred, crimson countenance. A grey bright eye in his head.' 'Who was that?' asked Ailill of Fergus. 'We know him indeed,' said Fergus. 'He that came there is the starting of strife; he is the stormy wave which drowns; he is a man of three shouts; he is the sea pouring over ramparts. That was Munremur mac Gerrcind from Modorn in the north.' No tall, slender, long-haired, pale-skinned ideal type here, but a mighty and revered warrior just the same. So although the Celtic ideal of beauty was of the tall, blond kind, there must have been a strong admixture of racial types in such a complex and widespread society. The small dark Celt of popular tradition is in fact epitomised by the semi-divine Cú Chulainn, as we have seen. The blond ideal can only have been applicable to a section of the aristocracy. The lower classes must have been very mixed in type, but no one bothers to comment on these.

Celtic men were very figure-conscious. It was considered a disgrace to grow corpulent. Strabo writes: 'The following is a further peculiar trait: they try not to become stout and fat-bellied, and any young man who exceeds the standard length of the girdle is fined.' The size and power of their bodies is described by the Classical observers of the Belgae. Strabo also writes: 'Their arms correspond in size with their physique.' Their violent and frightening manners are also described. Diodorus Siculus says: 'Physically the Gauls are terrifying in appearance, with deep-sounding and very harsh voices.' Of the Celtic women he says: 'The Gallic women are not only equal to their husbands in stature, but they rival with them in strength as well.' Ammianus Marcellinus, a Roman writer, tells us more about Celtic stature and general appearance, and again comments on the tall, fair nature of the Gauls:

Almost all the Gauls are of tall stature, fair and ruddy, terrible for the fierceness of their eyes, fond of quarrelling, and of overbearing insolence. In fact a whole band of foreigners will be unable to cope with one of them in a fight, if he calls in his wife, stronger than he by far and with flashing eyes; least of all when she swells her neck and gnashes her teeth, and poising her huge white arms, begins to rain blows mingled with kicks like shots discharged by the twisted cords of a catapult. (*Loeb, 195: M.A., XV.12.1*)

The Icenian Queen, Boudicca, is also described in some detail, in this instance by the Roman writer Dio Cassius, who says: 'She was huge of frame and terrifying of aspect and with a harsh voice. A great mass of bright red hair fell to her knees.' The descriptions of these people, both Classical and native, all support the evidence that the Celts in Gaul, as in the British Isles, were basically a tall, fair-skinned, fair- or red-haired people, having blue eyes, powerful bodies, faces 'broad above and narrow below'—(Classical sculptures provide further evidence for this feature)—and also demonstrate that they were indeed very much concerned with their personal appearance. They took great pains to decorate themselves with ornaments, and to enhance by artificial means their already long and abundant hair. It is also clear that they emphasised other features by artifice. In the Irish tale concerning the fate of the sons of Uisliu (the famous *Deirdre* story) Deirdre, in the earliest version (probably eighth century AD) laments 'I do not redden my finger-nails', implying that her sorrow is so great that she cannot be bothered to heighten her attractions any more. Irish women also dyed their brows black with berry juice, and heightened the colour of their cheeks with a herb called *ruam*. The use of cosmetics by Celtic women on the Continent is also attested; in Rome the poet Propertius reviles his mistress for making up like the Celts. The Celts seem also to have paid attention to personal hygiene, and there are many references in the early tales to their washing and bathing habits. Unlike the inhabitants of the Mediterranean world, they used soap and water. Also, according to the Irish tales, they used oil and sweet herbs for anointing their bodies. Archaeologists have discovered many fine mirrors and razors which were used to aid the toilet of the aristocracy, and these are mentioned in the textual material as well. Their fastidious attitude to things in general is reflected also in what Athenaeus says of their meat-eating habits: 'they partake of this in a cleanly but leonine fashion, raising up whole limbs in both hands and biting off the meat'. Anyone who has watched the incredible skill and delicacy with which a present day Scottish Gael will eat a salt herring with his fingers will appreciate Athenaeus' comment more fully.

The general impression we gain from all the sources of evidence at present at our disposal of early Celtic aristocratic society is that of tall, physically powerful men and women, having fair or reddish hair, grey-blue eyes, light skins, oval faces and fresh complexions. The women's fecundity is mentioned by the Classical writers. Talking of Celtic tribes Strabo says: 'I have already described the numbers of the Helvetii and of the Arverni and their allies, and all this shows the great size of the population, and moreover, a point which I have already mentioned, the excellence of their women in bearing and rearing children.' Diodorus Siculus makes an odd remark when he says of the Gallic women: 'Their children are born, for the most part, with grey hair, but as they advance in age they are assimilated to the hair colour of their parents.'

The abundance of the hair of these peoples is everywhere emphasised, and it was worn flowing or braided, according to preference, and caught with combs and other ornaments. The men could be clean-shaven or moustached, or bearded and moustached; and the forked or otherwise elaborately dressed beard described in the tales is paralleled in native iconography.

DRESS

The information we have about their clothing, combined with references to their fastidiousness, both in the Classics and in the Irish tales, shows that the Celts had, in fact, a most distinctive appearance and mode of dress which made them immediately distinguishable and different from their neighbours in the eyes of the Classical world—and this in spite of inevitable variations in fashion both regionally and temporally.

Trousers were favoured by the men, and this particularly impressed the toga-wearing Mediterranean world. They were foreign to Classical dress, and the tight version was borrowed by the Romans for cavalry wear, some of the finest cavalry in the Roman Empire being recruited from amongst the Celts. Strabo says: 'Although they are all [i.e. Gauls and Germans] naturally fine fighting-men, yet they are better as cavalry than as infantry, and the best of the Roman cavalry is recruited from among them.' The custom of wearing trousers came from contact with horse-riding peoples, such as the Scythians and the Iranian horsemen. The Hallstatt chieftains wore trousers (*bracae*) (*16*). Very close trousers which seem to reach only to the knee are worn by the warriors on the Gundestrup cauldron (*26*); tight trousers are also seen on the fine bronze portraying a musician, from Neuvy-en-Sullias (*10*). Trousers seem to have been virtually unknown amongst the Irish aristocracy, although they were worn by the servants.

10 The instrument is now missing from this bronze figure of a musician from Neuvy-en-Sullias, Loiret, France

The earliest sources describe the clothing in some detail; this would seem to have consisted of a knee-length tunic of linen, caught in at the waist with a girdle. The tunics were often elaborately fringed and embroidered. Amongst the continental Celts belts and girdles were decorated with ornaments of bronze and gold; no doubt this was also the case with the Irish girdles. Over the tunic a cloak was worn, and this was a most important garment both in Europe and in the British Isles, having both a functional and social aspect (*11*). The length and copiousness of the cloak would seem to have indicated its wearer's social status. Women, alike with men, wore this garment. The prophetess Fedelm is wearing a cloak when she is described in the *Táin* on her encounter with

11 Cloaks, as worn by figures on a relief at Housesteads, Northumberland

Medb, Queen of Connacht. It is a many-spotted green cloak and is reminiscent of the Classical descriptions of the cloaks of the Gauls, striped and checked and many-coloured. The cloak was fastened with a brooch of gold or silver, and it was made of wool, light in summer and heavy in winter. Of the British queen Boudicca's appearance Dio Cassius says: 'She wore a great twisted golden necklace, and a tunic of many colours, over which was a thick mantle, fastened by a brooch.'

This would seem to have been one of the heavy-weight garments mentioned by the Classics. Celtic cloaks were famous: in Roman times these garments, made in Gaul and in Britain, were heavily taxed and continued to be praised until well into the medieval period. Their excellence and fame indicates the skill and prosperity of the sheep-rearing industry in the Celtic countries; *sagi* (woollen cloaks) were exported to Italy from Gaul and this trade is mentioned by Strabo, who also comments on the export of salt pig-meat from Gaul to Rome and Italy. The cloaks would seem to have been rectangular in shape, without sleeves or hoods, as far as we can gather. The cloaks of the Irish kings are referred to in the early texts as having been five-folded. They were clearly as gaudy and decorative in appearance as those of the Gauls. The *Táin* contains many important descriptions of the dress and

47

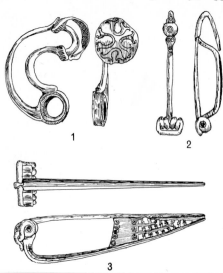

appearance of the early Irish nobility, both men and women, and the ancient laws provide interesting information on cloth-dyeing and the art of weaving. Fedelm, when she meets Medb, is described as follows: 'The girl was weaving a fringe, holding a weaver's beam of white bronze in her right hand with seven strips of red-gold on its points.'

The common dress of the free Irish, then, about the turn of the Christian era seems to have consisted of a short, linen tunic, and an elaborate long woollen cloak, brooch-fastened, its size and the elaborate nature of its decoration indicating social status and rank.

12   Brooches: 1, Beckley, Oxfordshire; 2, Cold Kitchen Hill, Wiltshire; 3, Deal, Kent

Bells were used for purposes of adornment, and many personal ornaments were worn by the aristocracy. Strabo comments:

> To the frankness and high-spiritedness of their temperament must be added the traits of childish boastfulness and love of decoration. They wear ornaments of gold, torques on their necks, and bracelets on their arms and wrists, while people of high rank wear dyed garments besprinkled with gold. It is this vanity which makes them unbearable in victory and so completely downcast in defeat. (*Tierney, 269*)

Archaeological evidence fully attests to the Celtic passion for personal decoration, and many brooches (*12*), finger-rings, ankle-rings, necklets and elaborate metal belts have been found.

Amongst the other garments mentioned in the Irish textual sources is a short, fitted, leather coat which was apparently worn by charioteers. A splendid description of Lóeg, Cú Chulainn's charioteer, before an encounter, is given in the *Táin*:

> Then the charioteer arose and put on his hero's outfit for chariot-driving. Of the outfit for chariot-driving which he put on was his

smooth tunic of skins, which was light and airy, supple and of fine texture, stitched and of deerskin which did not hinder the movement of his arms outside. Over that he put on his outer mantle black as raven's feathers. . . . The same charioteer now put on his helmet, crested, flat-surfaced, four-cornered, with variety of every colour and form, and *reaching past the middle of his shoulders*. This was an adornment to him and was not an encumbrance. (*C. O'Rahilly, 200*)

This description of the charioteer's elaborate helmet, reaching down at the back to between the shoulder-blades may well be taken to be the pure invention of the *literati*; on the other hand we cannot quite overlook the fantastic helmets worn, for example, by the warriors depicted in stone from sites in Gaul; one in particular, from Sainte-Anastasie (Gard) represents the bust of a warrior wearing a great helmet which comes right down to his shoulders, and is decorated with various signs (*13*). Another bust of a warrior comes from Grezan (Gard) (*14*); the helmet is similar to that from Sainte-Anastasie. Again, a seated warrior from Entremont wears a closely fitted jerkin seemingly of pigskin, having short sleeves which 'would not hinder the movement of his arms outside'. These sculptural details, provided by archaeology, suggest that such a description as that above may not have been merely due to the inventiveness of the scribes, but could rest upon an oral memory of a genuine tradition of the dress of the pagan Celtic peoples.

13 Helmeted bust from Sainte-Anastasie, Gard, France

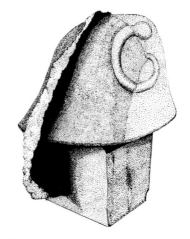

14 Bust of warrior from Grezan, Gard, France

Leather shoes and sandals were worn, and sometimes linen shoes with soles made of leather were used; sandals made of wood are also known to have been worn by the Celts. Hooded shirts and tunics are mentioned, but head-gear of any kind does not seem to have been popular, the elaborate hair-styling making it superfluous for most occasions. When the young Cú Chulainn has had his famous battle ardour quenched by drastic measures, and his normal, everyday appearance has returned to him, he is groomed and dressed and becomes once more the calm, beautiful hero: 'He had a high crest of hair, bright, fair, as if a cow had licked it. He wore a green mantle in which was a silver pin and a tunic of thread of gold.' Diodorus Siculus might have been describing Cú Chulainn's tunic here when he says:

> In this way they accumulate large quantities of gold and make use of it for personal adornment, not only the women but also the men. For they wear bracelets on wrists and arms, and round their neck thick rings of solid gold and they wear also fine finger-rings and *even golden tunics*. (*Tierney, 249*)

The Gauls are similarly described in the Classical sources and their close affinity to the Irish (trouser-wearing excepted) is clear. Trousers were worn with tunics over them; Strabo describes some of these as being slit and having sleeves. The wheel-players on a La Tène sword-scabbard wear peculiar tunics like modern dress jackets (*15*). The figures on the silver cauldron from Gundestrup seem to be wearing one-piece garments made of a ribbed, knitted fabric with V-necks, long tight sleeves, and trousers which end at the knee-cap; they wear decorated belts round their waists. The tunics in the main seem to have been short, ending below the thighs, but it is clear that there must have been many regional preferences and changes in fashion over the years. The bronze of a god of the Cernunnos-type from Besançon wears a tunic over loose trousers. Polybius in his description of the Battle of Telamon in 225 BC mentions the Celtic breeches and cloaks, necklets and bracelets. Diodorus Siculus describes the Gaulish garments in pleasing detail:

> They wear a striking kind of clothing—tunics dyed and stained in various colours, and trousers, which they call by the name of *bracae*; and they wear striped cloaks, fastened with buckles, thick in winter and light in summer, picked out with a variegated small check pattern . . . some wear gold-plated or silver-plated belts round their tunics. (*Tierney, 250*)

Strabo speaks of 'linen works amongst the Cadurci'; he also says of the Belgae, the tribes living in the region between the Rhine and the Loire:

> They wear the *sagus*, let their hair grow long and wear baggy trousers. Instead of ordinary tunics they wear divided tunics with sleeves, reaching down as far as the private parts and the buttocks. Their wool is rough and thin at the ends, and from it they weave the thick *sagi* which they call *laenae*. (*Tierney, 268*)

The Irish word for shirt was *léine* and the modern Irish and Scottish Gaelic word for shirt is still *léine*.

The Irish texts tell us that women wore tunics which reached to the ground, cloaks, brooches and other ornaments, and wore their hair in two or three plaits, the ends being fastened with some form of decorative ball or bead. Their great physique is commented on by the Classics, as also was their beauty. In the *Táin*, the Queen is described as wearing a golden diadem; there is also a fine description of her in the *Táin*: 'There came to me there a woman,

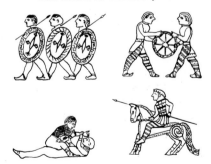

15 Figures engraved on a bronze scabbard found with an inhumation burial at Hallstatt, Austria

tall, beautiful, pale and long-faced. She had flowing, golden-yellow hair. She wore a crimson, hooded cloak with a golden brooch over her breast. A straight ridged spear blazing in her hand.' Another detailed description of an early Irish woman comes in the story of the wooing of Étaín. Eochaid the King is seeking for a suitable wife, and his messengers have seen Étaín; he goes to seek her and finds her at a well:

> He saw a woman at the edge of the spring, with a bright silver comb ornamented with gold, washing her hair in a silver bowl with four golden birds on it, and little flashing jewels of purple carbuncle on the rims of the bowl. She had a shaggy purple cloak made of fine fleece, and silver brooches of filigree work decorated with handsome gold, in the cloak; a long-hooded tunic on her, stiff and smooth, of green silk with embroidery of red gold.
>
> Wonderful ornaments of gold and silver with twining animal designs, in the tunic on her breast and her shoulders and her shoulder-blades on both sides. The sun was shining on her, so that the men could plainly see the glistening of the gold in the sunlight amid the green silk. There were two golden-yellow tresses on her head; each one was braided of four plaits, with a bead at the end of each plait. The colour of her hair seemed to them like the flower of the water-flag in summer, or like red gold that has been polished.
>
> (*Jackson, A Celtic Miscellany, 196*)

This description is borne out by the other sources of evidence; that she was an ideal Celtic female type is stressed by a remark following after the description of her physical beauties: 'This is the maiden concerning whom is spoken the proverb: 'Every lovely form must be tested by Étaín, every beauty by the standard of Étaín.'

It would not be proper to leave the difficult question of the clothing worn by the Celtic peoples without glancing at the remarkable decorated pots from Sopron in Hungary. These date to the seventh century BC and illustrate some aspects of Hallstatt everyday activity and clothing; the men are wearing trousers which indicate that these were adopted at the beginning of the Iron Age culture. The women wear tight-waisted bell-shaped or 'A-Line' skirts and these are elaborately decorated and perhaps hung with bells or little balls. They are engaged in tasks such as spinning and weaving and add a little fascinating detail to this period of Celtic prehistory (*16*).

Throughout the Celtic world we can see how the emphasis was on personal ornament, the loading of the body, both male and female, with every kind of eye-catching and valuable trinket; and the gay and flamboyant decoration of both dress material and personal equipment. As in all heroic societies the giving of rings and personal ornaments had a high status value. The lavish nature of early Celtic clothing, together with their passion for personal display in the form of fine ornaments and weapons, contrasts strikingly with the stark simplicity of their domestic arrangements and living habits.

This, then, is the picture we can build up from the Classical comments on Celtic dress and appearance, from iconographic and archaeological portrayals

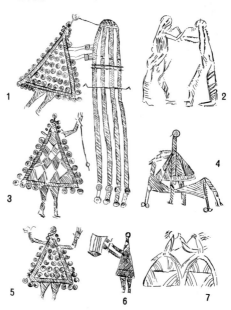

16 Figures incised on pottery from Sopron in NW Hungary: 1, Woman weaving on upright loom; 2, men fighting; 3, woman spinning; 4, riding a horse; 5, dancing; 6, playing the lyre; 7, women fighting

and discoveries, and from the descriptions in the Irish tales which contain much that is archaic. Although we cannot suppose any description to have been typical of *all* the Celts at any one given period of time, the overall picture of the general attitude to dress and adornment which those various sources present is a convincing one. It demonstrates clearly how widespread the general mode of clothing, and the passion for adornment must have been, if such heterogeneous sources of evidence could produce such closely similar and convincing observations. The earliest Irish evidence supports the Classical and iconographic information to a remarkable degree. All this allows us to conclude that these differing documents do present a reasonably valid picture of the appearance and personal attire of the Celtic aristocrats, in pre-Roman times for Europe and Britain, and in Ireland at least until the advent of Christianity in the fifth century AD.

3

Warfare, Communications, Forts and Houses

In pagan Celtic societies (and down into comparatively modern times in the surviving Celtic areas) war was regarded as the norm, and highly desirable; and fighting and success in single combat were right and proper for the young warrior and hero-elect. The Celts were not much concerned about who fought whom or for what particular reason, or when or where the battle took place, provided some excuse could be concocted for a set-to. This could consist of a mass skirmish, with flamboyant and aggressive 'mustering of the hosts', as the old Irish tales put it, or the single combat between two warriors, a typically heroic feature and one especially enjoyed by the Celts. Any alarm, any fancied insult resulted in an instant seizing of weapons. Anyone who happened to be near by could be fallen upon and viciously attacked in the frenzied moment—and as this sort of situation was usually brought about by over-indulgence, any sense of responsibility there might have been in sober moments was completely obliterated.

A nice parallel is provided by the Classical comments to a situation which is commonplace in the Irish tales. In the Irish story, *Bricriu's Feast* (*Fled Bricrend*), the narrative, paraphrased here, runs:

> When Bricriu had displayed his feast to the Ulstermen, they asked him to leave the hall as he had promised; and, as he went out he bade them give the Hero's Portion to the greatest warrior among them. The carvers arose to divide the food, and at once Loegaire's charioteer claimed the prize for his master. The charioteers of Conall and Cú Chulainn claimed it too. The three warriors sprang up, seized their weapons and began to fight, Loegaire and Conall against Cú Chulainn, so that one side of the house was like a blaze of fire from the clash of swords and spears, and the other was like a flock of

white birds from the dust of the shields. The house was in a tumult, and Conchobar was angry at the unfairness and untruth of two men attacking one. But none dared to hinder them until Sencha, the Druid, told Conchobar to separate the men. For Conchobar was the earthly god of the Ulstermen at that time. (*Dillon, 20*)

Athenaeus' statement takes on a new veracity and interest in the light of such a typical pagan Irish situation. Quoting Posidonius, he says:

'The Celts sometimes engage in single combat at dinner. Assembling in arms they engage in a mock battle—drill and mutual thrust and parry. But sometimes wounds are inflicted, and the irritation caused by this may lead even to the slaying of the opponent unless the by-standers hold them back.' 'And in former times', he says, 'when the hindquarters were served up, the bravest hero took the thigh piece, and if another man claimed it they stood up and fought in single combat to the death.' (*Tierney, 247*)

The warlike attitude of the early Celts is thus well attested, as is their predilection for carrying on the quarrel, indeed provoking it, even at table. The aspirations and priorities of a hero-elect are nicely described in the boyhood deeds of Cú Chulainn, and we may accept them as being typical of the pagan Celtic world.

Cathbad the Druid was teaching his pupils to the north-east of Emain,* and eight pupils of the class of druidic learning were with him. One of them asked his teacher what omen and presage was for that day, whether it was good or whether it was ill. Then said Cathbad, that a boy who should take up arms on that day would be splendid and famous, but would be short-lived and transient. Cú Chulainn heard that. . . .

The aspirant hero goes to the King, his uncle Conchobar mac Nessa, to demand a set of weapons from him. The Druid comes upon them and says:

'Is that boy then taking arms?' 'He is indeed,' said Conchobar. 'Not by your mother's son would I wish arms to be taken today,' said Cathbad. 'Why is that? Is it not you who advised him?' said Con-chobar. 'Not I indeed,' said Cathbad. 'What do you mean, you distorted sprite? Have you deceived me?' said Conchobar. 'Do not be angry, father Conchobar,' said the little boy, 'for it is he who advised

* 'Emain Macha', Navan Fort, one and a half miles west of Armagh.

me; for his pupil asked him what omen was for the day, and he said that a boy who took arms on this day would be splendid and renowned, but short-lived and transient.' 'I spoke the truth,' said Cathbad. 'you will be splendid and renowned, but short-lived and transient.' 'It is a wonderful thing, if I am but one day and one night in the world, provided that my fame and my deeds live after me.'

(C. O'Rahilly, 164)

Strabo, like others, makes comments which support this warlike attitude and disregard of personal safety and longevity:

The whole race, which is now called Celtic or Galatic, is madly fond of war, high-spirited and quick to battle, but otherwise straightforward and not of evil character. And so when they are stirred up they assemble in their bands for battle, quite openly and without forethought; so that they are easily handled by those who desire to outwit them. For at any time or place, and on whatever pretext you stir them up, you will have them ready to face danger, even if they have nothing on their side but their own strength and courage.

(Tierney, 267)

War and the technique of warfare had clearly a high priority in the everyday life of the Celtic peoples everywhere. As a result we may expect strong emphasis on weapons, battle tactics and elaborate codes of honour. This predilection for battle and single combat is reflected not only in all the evidence for their daily life, but is very much emphasised in their religious traditions and cult legends. The tribal god is first and foremost a superb warrior. The semi-divine hero may stand in for the god in single combat; the god could come and aid the semi-divine hero in a similar situation. The weapons of the great heroes were alleged to be inhabited or motivated by gods.

WARFARE, WEAPONS AND CHARIOTS

We must now consider the evidence for Celtic weapons and battle-gear. What did these battle-thirsty barbarians actually use as equipment in the fight? The earliest evidence for Celtic weapons and the prototypes for later examples comes, of course, from burials. The sword has always been of vital importance in battle; in the Hallstatt graves (dating from about 700 BC) the bronze cut-and-thrust sword popular in the late Bronze Age has been replaced by the long sword of iron which was also used in the cut-and-thrust technique of fighting. This use of a new metal—iron—

did, of course, make a vital difference to the
quality and durability of weapons, and their
efficiency in battle. Polybius comments on
the Gaulish swords in his description of the
famous Battle of Telamon:

> The Gaulish sword being only good for a cut
> and not a thrust. [He also says:] From the
> way their swords are made, only the first cut
> takes effect; after this they at once assume the
> shape of a strigil, being so much bent length-
> wise and sideways that unless the men are
> given leisure and rest them on the ground and
> set them straight with a foot, the second blow
> is quite ineffectual. (*311f.*)

There are references in the early Irish tales
to the straightening of a sword with the foot;
the teeth were also used on such an occasion!
Perhaps the Celts were wise to place emphasis on the spear as the vital piece of battle
equipment. The swords were often described
as having hilts of gold. In the *Táin*, Cú Chulainn and Fer Diad are described as fighting
with ivory-hilted swords.* Later in the same
single combat Fer Diad chooses 'heavy hard-
smiting swords' as the weapons for the day.
A pair of broad-bladed spears, used for
thrusting, were also carried by Celtic warriors
(*17*). The early Irish tales frequently refer to
these. At one stage in his single combat with his foster brother Cú
Chulainn choses spears as the weapons for use:

17 Iron spear-head
with bronze decora-
tion found in the
river Thames near
Datchet, Berkshire

> 'Let us then,' said Cú Chulainn, 'take to our great long spears today.
> For we think that thrusting with the spears today will bring us nearer
> to a decisive victory than the casting of missiles did yesterday. Let
> our horses be harnessed for us, and our chariots yoked, that we may
> fight from our horses and chariots today.' (*C. O'Rahilly, 223*)

In Hallstatt times a broad-bladed dagger was used; when the
light iron sword, used for thrusting, became popular, the dagger

* Professor Jackson points out that the Fer Diad episode is an interpolation
of the eleventh century, but it is probable that it derives from early material.

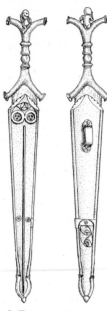

18 Dagger with sheath, dredged from the river Witham, Lincolnshire

was used for close fighting. In La Tène weapons we can see the influence of archaic Greek examples as well as discerning the indigenous Hallstatt elements.

Celtic swords were carried in scabbards covered with decorated bronze sheets as well as iron ones, and these are further discussed in Chapter 7. The dagger was similarly sheathed (*18*). Bows and arrows seem not to have been in vogue, although there is a reference to them in Strabo. He says of human sacrifice: 'There are also other accounts of their human sacrifices; for they used to shoot men down with arrows and impale them in their temples.' That their use was not entirely ritual is suggested by his further comment, in reference to the weapons of the Celts, 'Some also use bows and slings', suggesting that the bow may have actually been used in warfare by certain of the Celts at some period. The bow and arrow are certainly unknown in the early Irish texts and words for them do not come into the Irish language before the ninth century AD. Helmets, although fine examples are known, were not common items of battle equipment. The Celts preferred to go bare-headed into battle, their hair elaborately coiffed. Helmets worn by chieftains were conical (*19*), or shaped like a cap and elaborately ornamented (*20*); or exaggerated and sweeping like those from Grezan and Entremont (*14*) and that described as being worn by Lóeg, Chulainn's charioteer. Round wooden shields were used according to the Irish tales, and shields of leather. From the mid third century BC the long oval shield is used (*21*), and this shape is also described in the Irish tales, although the round shield is more common. In Irish contexts, the shield is made of alder wood and has a rim of metal, elaborately decorated. The oval shield was some three feet long, fashioned from wood or made of wickerwork. At Hjørtspring, in Denmark, long oval wooden shields were found preserved in peat; they appear to have been placed in a bog as a votive offering. The wooden shield had sometimes an umbo of iron.

Two features of Celtic methods of fighting must now be considered. These are typical of the entire Celtic race; they are the habit of fighting from chariots, and the heroic custom of single combat, the fight between two warriors, for which as we have seen the Celts had a particular liking. The light, two-wheeled war-chariot to which a pair of smallish, specially bred ponies was harnessed, was used regularly in Celtic campaigns. There are many references to the chariot in the early Irish texts, and representations are known from the Continent. Parts of chariots have been found. One assemblage, from Llyn Cerrig Bach in Anglesey, found amongst a great many other objects forming a votive hoard, has served as the model for the well-known reconstruction (4). The body of the chariot would seem to have been of light wickerwork, although wooden-sided chariots may well also have been in use. The fittings were of bronze, the tyres of iron. One elaborate description by the Roman historian Florus refers to a chariot entirely plated with silver. Knowing the Celtic predilection for pomp and display and their ready supplies of precious metals, this need not be taken to be a literary exaggeration any more than we may suppose the elaborate description of material goods and personal ornament in the early texts to be entirely verbal fancies of the *literati*. The highly decorative horse-trappings and richly adorned horse-harness likewise support this overall picture.

19 Wrought bronze helmet decorated with corals from La Gorge-Meillet, Marne, France

20 Bronze and iron helmet, its decoration enhanced with gold, found in an old channel of the river Seine near Amfreville-sous-les-Monts, Eure, France

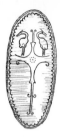

21 Oval shields carved, amongst other trophies, on the gateway arch at Orange, Vaucluse, France

The early texts mention chariots having sharp protruding points or edges, but there is as yet no archaeological evidence for this feature. Later Irish texts speak of chariots as having sickles on the hubs. The chariot carried two men, the charioteer and the warrior. The charioteer was a freeman, the close friend and confidant of the warrior if we can judge from the evidence of the Irish texts. Certainly the warrior depended upon the skill, courage and loyalty of his charioteer. A goad was used to spur on the ponies, and the vehicle was driven wildly against the enemy. The warrior then leaped down from the chariot and prepared to engage in single combat. The warrior hurled spears from the chariot before he left it, and the chariot would then wait in the background ready to pick up the hero again when required to do so. Great feats of skill and daring were apparently performed by the warriors and the Classical sources, alike with the Irish texts, contain references to such a mastery of the art of chariot warfare. Several splendid descriptions of Celtic heroes and their command of chariotry occur in the *Táin*. One of these comments on Cú Chulainn's general appearance and weapons as he prepares to display himself to the hosts:

> Then he puts on his dress for assembly that day. Of that raiment was a fair mantle, well-fitting, purple, fringed, five-folded. A white brooch of white silver inset with gold over his white breast, as it were a bright lantern that men's eyes could not look at for its brilliance and splendour. A tunic of silk next to his skin, bordered with edges and braidings and fringes of gold and of silver and of white bronze, reaching to the top of his dark apron, dark red, soldierly, of royal satin. A splendid dark purple shield he bore with a rim of pure white silver round it. He wore a golden-hilted ornamented sword at his left side. In the chariot beside him was a long grey-edged spear together with a sharp attacking dagger, with splendid thongs and rivets of white bronze. He held nine heads in one hand and ten in the other. (*C. O'Rahilly, 204*)

Compare this description with that of Strabo, who also had clearly envisaged Celtic warriors on their way to a fight:

Their arms correspond in size with their physique; a long sword fastened on the right side and a long shield, and spears of like dimension, and the *madaris*, which is a kind of javelin. There is also a wooden weapon resembling the 'grosphus' which is thrown by hand and not by means of a strap, with a range greater than that of an arrow, and which they mostly use for bird-hunting as well as in battle. (*Tierney, 268*)

Again, in the *Táin*, as we have seen in the Preface, the arrival of Cú Chulainn's chariot is described as he goes to meet his mighty rival Fer Diad and engage in single combat at the ford, a typical Celtic situation. One of the tales in the Ulster Cycle* of Irish stories, *The Wooing of Emer*, gives an interesting account of the pastimes of the pagan Irish and their mastery of the chariot; and although it is a late tale, it seems to contain some genuine early traditions.

Now once when the men of Ulster were in Emain Macha with Conchobor, drinking from the beer-vat known as the 'Iron-Chasm'; a hundred fillings of beverage went into it every evening. Such was the drinking of the 'Iron-Chasm', which at one sitting would satisfy all the men of Ulster. The chariot chiefs of Ulster were performing on ropes stretched across from door to door in the house at Emain Macha. Fifteen feet and nine score was the size of that house. The chariot chiefs were performing three feats—the spear-feat, the apple-feat and the sword-edge-feat. (*Cross and Slover, 154*)

Again, in the same tale, Emer asks one of her companions to look out and tell her what is the commotion she hears approaching; the girl reports:

I see a chariot of fine wood with wickerwork, moving on wheels of white bronze. A pole of white silver with a mounting of white bronze. Its frame very high, of creaking copper, rounded and firm. A strong curved yoke of gold; two firm-plaited yellow reins; the shafts hard and straight as sword-blades. (*Cross and Slover, 156*)

Descriptions such as these give detail to the Classical comments and add veracity to them. Allowing for the personal inventiveness

* This group of stories, written down in medieval Ireland, but having its origins in the oral tradition of the pagan Celtic world, is so called because it is concerned with the deeds of the warriors of Ulster; their king is Conchobar mac Nessa, their chief hero is Cú Chulainn. The royal seat is at Emain Macha, which excavations in the summer of 1969 strongly suggest was in fact a pagan sanctuary. The *Táin* is the longest story in the Ulster Cycle.

22 Enamelled harness mounts, Santon Downham, Suffolk

of the story-tellers, Cú Chulainn's chariot in the combat with Fer
Diad differs from what we believe the Celtic chariots to have been
like, but it may represent a different type of vehicle. In spite of the
Irish passion for wordy and grand descriptions which could
elevate the commonplace and make it remarkable, there is an
underlying nucleus of truth here in these Ulster tales, and a reality
which makes a valuable addition to the stark facts of archaeology
and the Classics. The story suggested by the archeological record
of swords and spears, chariots and shields, comes to life in the
early texts, and one gets a glimpse of these things in action against
a human background of pathos and hope. The chariots used in
Celtic warfare, and the ponies bred for them, were, as the archaeological evidence demonstrates, elaborately adorned with decorated
metalwork—chariot-fittings, bronze strips, probably with inlays,
harness-mounts (*22*), snaffle-bits, and so on. The Celtic warrior on
his way to battle or on parade with his plumed, adorned horses,
gaudy personal attire and bedecked vehicle must indeed have
presented a striking picture to the Classical world. Chariots were
used in Britain also and were presumptively introduced into Ulster
from Yorkshire; but as yet, no remains of chariots have been
recognised by archaeologists in Ireland, although they are a
commonplace in the early texts, and continued in use into probably
Christian times. They were used in Scotland until the second
century AD. Chariot-wheels have been found in wells in Scotland,
for example at Newstead in Roxburgh and at Bar Hill in
Dunbarton. The practice of chariot warfare had died out in Gaul
by the time of Julius Caesar's campaigns there in the first century
BC. Much is always made of the impact of the chariots and their

frantic drivers on the invading Romans in the British campaigns. Over and above the light two-wheeled chariot, which may or may not have been used primarily for parade purposes, four-wheeled wagons were in use in the Celtic world. The description of Cú Chulainn's 'four-wheeled' chariot may in part have originated as a result of confusion between the two vehicles by the scribes concerned with committing the tale to writing. Finally, there is a splendid description in the *Táin* of the mode in which Medb, the Queen of Connacht, used to travel:

> For this is how Medb was wont to travel; with nine chariots for herself alone, two chariots before her, two behind, two on each side and her chariot between them in the very middle. And the reason she used to do that was so that the clods of earth cast up by the horses' hooves or the foam dripping from the bridle-bits or the dust raised by the mighty army might not reach her and that no darkening might come to the golden diadem of the Queen. (*C. O'Rahilly, 153*)

SINGLE COMBAT

Another important feature of Celtic warfare was the custom of fighting in single combat. There were strict Irish rules about this, and one of these was known as the *fír fer*, lit: 'fair play', whereby a man offering single combat should only be opposed by a single opponent. Once the campaigns against the Romans began, this must have been modified on the Continent, but it is very much to the fore in the insular literatures, especially those of Ireland. In the *Táin*, the Connachtman Ferchú Loingseach with his 12 men go to attack Cú Chulainn: 'And they came forward to the place where Cú Chulainn was, and they did not grant him fair play or single combat but all 12 of them attacked him straight away.'

The custom of single combat is also remembered in the *Mabinogion*, the collection of medieval Welsh stories which contains a remarkably rich repository of mythology, thinly masked by the later conventions of the Christian *literati*. In the magnificent story of *Culhwch and Olwen*, probably the earliest of the group, two heroes, who are deities in origin, are described as engaging in single combat until the Day of Doom. Gwyn, son of Nudd, and Gwythyr, son of Greidawl, are contesting for the hand of Creiddylad, daughter of Lludd Silver-Hand. Arthur makes peace between them:

This is the peace that was made: the maiden should remain in her father's house, unmolested by either side, and there should be battle between Gwyn and Gwythyr each May-calends for ever and ever, from that day till Doomsday; and the one of them that should be victor on Doomsday, let him have the maiden. (*Jones, 129*)

Again, in another story from the *Mabinogion, Pwyll, Prince of Dyfed*, Arawn, King of Annwn—the Otherworld—comes to Pwyll and asks his assistance in single combat against his rival, Hafgan. The motif of the god seeking the aid of a mortal occurs elsewhere in the Celtic literary tradition. In accordance with Celtic custom, the fight takes place at a ford. Arawn says to Pwyll: 'A year from tonight,' said he, 'there is a tryst between him and me at the ford. And be thou there in my likeness,' said he, 'and one blow only thou art to give him; that he will not survive.' The year passes and Pwyll meets Hafgan:

And the moment he came to the ford, a horseman arose and spoke thus. 'Gentles,' said he, 'give good heed. It is between two kings that this meeting is, and that between their two bodies. And each of them is a claimant against the other, and that for land and territory; and each of you may stand aside and let the fight be between them.' And thereupon the two kings approached each other towards the middle of the ford for the encounter. (*Jones, 6*)

Two Celtic heroes, spoiling for a fight, would begin by reviling each other, and at the same time praising their ancestors and family, and their own prowess in feats of arms. This stirred them up to battle fury and lust for blood and glory; it caused any human compassion to sink back and yield to the sheer brute strength and viciousness which now took over and made these combats violent and bloodthirsty. The charioteer played his own part in these slanging matches; and if, as seems likely, the *Táin* provides a true account of single combat as waged in the ancient Celtic world we get a vivid picture of his role as illustrated by Cú Chulainn and Lóeg before a fight. When Cú Chulainn, in the eleventh-century version of the *Táin*, is about to encounter his foster-brother and sees him performing boastful and provocative feats of arms, he gives instructions to his charioteer:

Cú Chulainn too came to the ford and he saw the many brilliant wonderful feats of arms performed by Fer Diad. 'You see yonder, my friend Láeg, the many brilliant wonderful feats performed by

Fer Diad, and in due course now all those feats will be directed against me. Therefore, if it be I who am defeated this day, you must incite me and revile me and speak evil of me, so that my ire and anger shall rise the higher thereby. But if it be I who inflict defeat, you must exhort me and praise me and speak well of me that thereby my courage rise higher.' (*C. O'Rahilly, 226–7*)

Fer Diad reviles Cú Chulainn in no uncertain manner before battle is engaged:

'I have come, a wild boar of the herd, before warriors, before troops, before hundreds, to thrust you beneath the waters of the pool. In anger against you and to prove you in a many-sided encounter so that harm may come to you as you defend your life. Here is one who will crush you. It is I who will slay you, for it is I who can. The defeat of their hero in the presence of the Ulstermen, may it be long remembered, may it be to them loss.' (*C. O'Rahilly, 219*)

This evidence from the early texts is strikingly supported by the Classical comments on Celtic warfare. Diodorus Siculus, for example, remarks on the custom of reviling the enemy: 'And when some one accepts their challenge to battle they proudly recite the deeds of valour of their ancestors and proclaim their own valorous quality at the same time abusing and making little of their opponent and generally attempting to rob him beforehand of his fighting spirit.' Again, in the *Táin*, the warrior, Etarcumal, approaches Cú Chulainn and incites him to combat. Cú Chulainn says:

'But if only you knew it, the little creature you are looking at, namely myself, is wrathful. And how do you find me as you look at me?' 'I think you are fine indeed. You are a comely splendid handsome youth with brilliant, numerous, various feats of arms. But as for reckoning you among goodly heroes or warriors or champions or sledge-hammers of fighting, we do not do so or fight you at all.'
(*C. O'Rahilly, 183*)

The outcome of that jibe was as follows:

Cú Chulainn dealt him a blow on the crown of his head which split him to the navel. He gave him a second blow crosswise so that the three sections into which his body was cut fell at one and the same time to the ground. Thus perished Etarcumal, son of Fid and Leithrinn. (*C. O'Rahilly, 184*)

Cú Chulainn was alleged to have been in the possession of a mysterious weapon called the *gae bulga* which people have tried to envisage in a number of different ways. It does, however, seem to have been an actual weapon, and was used only in the last resort, in a ford. Its particular and fatal peculiarity was that it entered the body as a single spearhead, but when it was withdrawn, barbs opened out along its sides to that the victim was virtually disembowelled. Fer Diad was finally overthrown by this weapon, as was many another hero who engaged in single combat with Cú Chulainn. The account of its use against Fer Diad is as follows:

> Cú Chulainn . . . asked Láeg for the *ga bulga*. Such was the nature of the *ga bulga*: it used to be set downstream and cast from between the toes; it made one wound as it entered a man's body but it had 30 barbs when one tried to remove it and it was not taken from a man's body until the flesh was cut away about it. (*C. O'Rahilly, 228*)

This has been interpreted as a magical weapon bestowed on Cú Chulainn by his divine progenitors—for he was the son of the great Celtic god Lugh mac Eithlenn—but there is Classical evidence to suggest that this was no artefact of the gods, but had its origin in a memory of a type of spear used also by the Celts on the Continent. Diodorus Siculus in his description of Celtic weapons

23 Iron helmet with bronze crest, from Ciumeşti, Maramures, Romania

24 Bronze helmet with iron crest from Filottrano, Ancona, Italy

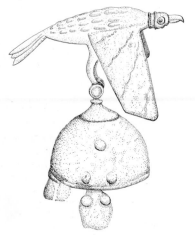

says: 'Some of their javelins are forged with a straight head, while some are spiral with breaks throughout their entire length so that the blow not only cuts but also tears the flesh, and the recovery of the spear tears open the wound.' This is a remarkable parallel to the description of the *gae bulga* and its effects in the *Táin*.

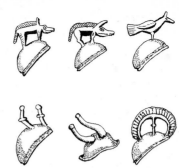

25 The decorated helmets shown on the silver cauldron found in a bog at Gundestrup, Jutland, Denmark, include examples with horns

The Irish heroes, then, like their continental counterparts, went into battle, the chief warriors in their chariots, carrying a thrusting spear, one or two casting javelins, a long iron cutting sword, a shield of wood decorated with a metal rim, no doubt with regional variations according to tradition and straightforward preference. The sling was also used, and there are many references to this weapon in the Irish tales. Diodorus Siculus again provides details of Celtic battle-gear in the following statement:

Their armour includes man-sized shields* (*21*) decorated in individual fashion. Some of these have projecting bronze animals of fine workmanship which serve for defence as well as decoration. On their heads they wear bronze helmets which possess large projecting figures (*23–4*) lending the appearance of enormous stature to the wearer. In some cases horns form one piece with the helmet (*25*), while in other cases it is relief figures of the foreparts of birds or quadrupeds. Their trumpets again are of a peculiar barbaric kind; they blow into them and produce a harsh sound which suits the tumult of war. Some have iron breastplates of chain-mail, while others fight naked, and for them the breastplate given by Nature suffices. Instead of the short sword they carry long swords held by iron or bronze chains and hanging along their right flank. Some wear gold-plated or silver-plated belts round their tunics. The spears which they brandish in battle, and which they call *lanciae*, have iron heads a cubit or more in length and a little less than two palms in breadth; for their swords are as long as the javelins of other peoples, and their javelins have points longer than swords. (*Tierney, 251*)

* Huge shields are suggested in the *Táin*: in the description of the hosts towards the end of the tale, the hero Celtchair Mór mac Uthechair appears with 'a brown mound, namely, his shield'.

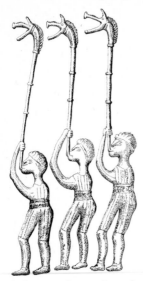

Even the small details of this descriptive passage are paralleled in the earliest Irish sources. The shields decorated in individual fashion, for example, find an echo in the *Táin* and elsewhere. Reochaid mac Faithemain has 'a white shield with emblems of animals in red gold upon it'. Again, a band of warriors is led by a hero, Erc son of Fedilmid Nóchruthach, who bears 'a white shield with animal designs in red gold'. In the description of Cú Chulainn as he goes in his finest array to woo Emer, we learn that he had 'over his shoulders a crimson shield with a rim of silver, chased with figures of golden animals'. Likewise, of Maine Máithremail and Maine Aithremail, Medb's sons, 'two bright shields they carried, ornamented with animal designs in silver'.

26 Carnyx players, from the Gundestrup cauldron

The horned helmets mentioned by Diodorus Siculus are also found in the early literatures: Furbaide Ferbend, for example, was alleged to have a three-horned helmet, two horns being of silver and one of gold. Three-horned sacred animals are a commonplace in Celtic mythology. The other descriptions of weapons are also neatly paralleled in the Irish texts. The war-trumpets Diodorus Siculus mentioned were much used; they were called *carnyxes*. They figure, for example, on the Celtic coinage, and are in evidence on the Gundestrup cauldron (*26*). Noise was very much a feature of Celtic warfare; its intention was to cause confusion, panic and sheer terror in the enemy camp. Tacitus refers to the noise made by the Britons when Paulinus was about to attack them at their sanctuary on Anglesey:

On the shore stood the opposing army with its dense array of armed warriors, while between the ranks dashed women in black attire like the Furies, with hair dishevelled, waving brands. All around the Druids, lifting up their hands to heaven and pouring forth dreadful imprecations, scared our soldiers. (*Kendrick, 93*)

The sheer noise of shouting and reviling, and supplication to

the gods for strength and aid, would be intensified by the braying
of the trumpets; these had animal heads of bronze and wooden
tongues which served as clappers, and the overall noise must have
been appalling. The remains of one carnyx, a bronze boar-head
terminal or mouth, were found near Deskford, in Banffshire. This
object dates to about the second century A D. Trumpets are also
mentioned in the Irish texts as forming parts of the battle equipment, as is the use of noise. In the *Táin* we hear of:

> The noise and the tumult, the din and the thunder, the clamour and
> the outcry which he heard there was the shock of shields and the
> smiting of spears and the loud striking of swords, the clashing of
> helmets, the clangour of breastplates, the friction of the weapons and
> the vehemence of the feats of arms, the straining of ropes, the rattle
> of wheels, the trampling of the horses' hooves, and the creaking of
> the chariots, and the loud voices of heroes and warriors.
>
> (*C. O'Rahilly, 252*)

The finest Classical account of the equipment and behaviour of
Celts in battle is given by Polybius in his famous description of the
Battle of Telamon in 225 B C. It is important enough to quote in
full, and illustrates many of the points mentioned already:

> The Insubres and the Boii wore their trousers and light cloaks, but
> the Gaesatae had discarded their garments owing to their proud
> confidence in themselves, and stood naked with nothing but their
> arms, in front of the whole array, thinking that thus they would be
> more efficient as some of the ground was overgrown with brambles
> which would catch in their clothes and impede the use of their
> weapons. At first the battle was confined to the hill, all the armies
> gazing on it so great were the numbers of cavalry from each host
> combating there pell-mell. In this action Gaius the Consul fell in the
> mêlée fighting with desperate courage, and his head was brought to
> the Celtic kings. . . . The Romans, however, were on the one hand
> encouraged by having caught the enemy between their two armies,
> but on the other they were terrified by the fine order of the Celtic
> host, and the dreadful din, for there were innumerable horn-
> blowers and trumpeters and, as the whole army were shouting their
> war-cries at the same time, there was such a tumult of sound that it
> seemed that not only the trumpets and the soldiers but all the country
> round had got a voice and caught up the cry. Very terrifying too
> were the appearance and the gestures of the naked warriors in front,
> all in the prime of life and finely built men, and all in the leading
> companies richly adorned with gold torques and armlets. The sight

of them indeed dismayed the Romans, but at the same time the prospect of winning such spoils made them twice as keen for the fight . . . reduced to the utmost distress and complexity some of them (the Gaesatae) in their impotent rage, rushed wildly on the enemy and sacrificed their lives, while others, retreating step by step on the ranks of their comrades, threw them into disorder by their display of faint-heartedness. (*Loeb edition, 311f.*) (27).

Polybius mentions the Gaesatae, the mercenary bands from outside the tribal system, and in this respect as we have seen they

27 A Roman copy in marble of a bronze representing a dying Gaul set up at Pergamon, in modern western Turkey, about 200 B C

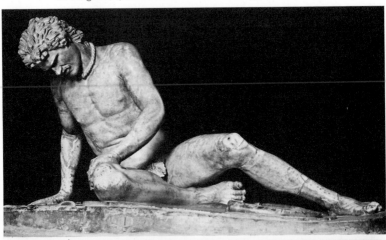

may be paralleled by the Fenian bands in Ireland, round whom a colourful literature grew up. These Gallic warriors hired themselves out to fight for different factions, and we must now see what can be discovered about such powerful, ruthless men. The name simply means 'spearman'—and the word *gae*, for a spear or dart, occurs in Old Irish and comes through as Scottish Gaelic and Irish *gath*.

These tough troops fought naked and this custom was clearly misunderstood by the Romans who knew nothing of its ritual implications. Others over and above the Gaesatae appear to have fought without clothing, or body protection of any kind. Diodorus Siculus says, without mentioning the Gaesatae in particular: 'Some of them so far despise death that they descend to do battle unclothed except for a girdle.'

The legendary Fenian bands which roamed Ireland in the early centuries of the Christian era, hunting and fighting and taking their living from the various tribes there, resembled the Gaesatae in that they would hire themselves out to various factions, and lived outwith the jurisdiction of the tribe (they were *écland*, 'without a tribe'). They tend to be portrayed as mercenary soldiers, and there is much reason to believe they had a strong mythological basis in the native tradition.

HORSEMANSHIP AND HEAD-HUNTING

As chariot warfare, in which the Celts so delighted, gave way gradually to cavalry warfare the Gauls became famous for their prowess in horsemanship. These horsemen are the *equites*, 'knights', mentioned by Caesar—the aristocracy. After the Roman occupation of Gaul, Gaulish cavalry troops became a distinguished feature of the Roman Army and served widely in the Empire. With their tight trousers, fine physique, flowing cloaks and legendary acrobatic skill, the Gauls deeply impressed by their parade drill and polished cavalry exercises. Arrian, writing in 136 AD, describes cavalry exercises borrowed by the Romans from the Celtic horsemen who formed so important an element in their mounted force:

> Then those of them who are conspicuous for rank or for skill in horsemanship ride into the lists armed with helmets made of iron or brass and covered with gilding to attract the particular attention of

the spectators. . . . They have yellow plumes attached to them, not to serve any useful purpose but rather for display. . . . And the horsemen carry oblong shields, not like shields for real battle but lighter in weight—the object of the exercises being smartness and display— and gaily decorated. Instead of breastplates they wear tunics, made just like real breastplates, sometimes scarlet, sometimes purple, sometimes parti-coloured. And they have hose, not loose like those in fashion among the Parthians and Armenians, but fitting closely to the limbs. (*J. Curle, 173*)

The Romans had indeed much to learn from the Celtic horsemen. Pausanius mentions *trimarcisia*, literally a set of 'three riders', i.e. a chieftain or nobleman with two attendants, as a feat of Celtic riding custom. This again perhaps can be paralleled by passages in the early texts. A nice example, with a strong mythological flavour, occurs in the weird tale *Togail Bruidne Da Derga, The Destruction of Da Derga's Hostel*. Conaire the King, at a significant moment in the drama, sees 'the three Reds' (*na trì Deirg*). These are three men having red hair, dressed entirely in red, and riding red horses. The non-mortal nature of these three riders is fully revealed when Conaire's son, having found it impossible to overtake them, is told: 'We ride the steeds of Donn Détscorach; though we are alive we are dead.' Red was the colour associated with battle and with the Celtic gods of war. Strabo says: 'Although they are all [i.e. Gauls and Germans] naturally fine fighting-men, yet they are better as cavalry than as infantry, and the best of the Roman cavalry is recruited from among them.'

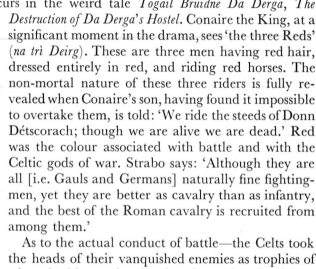

As to the actual conduct of battle—the Celts took the heads of their vanquished enemies as trophies of triumph; this practice also played a profound religious and superstitious role in Celtic everyday life. One or two illustrations of this practice are as follows: the heads were often set up in the sanctuaries of the Celts and offered up to the gods. The great stone shrine at Roquepertuse (Bouches-du-Rhône) had, like other sanctuaries, skull-niches in the walls for the display of human heads; many of the sanctuaries contained

28 Pillar with 12 incised faces, all without mouths, from the sanctuary at Entremont, Bouches-du-Rhône, France

representations of severed heads as well as real skulls. At Entremont, a splendid stone slab is covered with schematic heads, oddly arranged (*28*). Diodorus Siculus says of the practice of decapitating the enemy:

> They cut off the heads of enemies slain in battle and attach them to the necks of their horses. The blood-stained spoils they hand over to their attendants and carry off as booty, while striking up a paean and singing a song of victory; and they nail up these first fruits upon their houses, just as do those who lay low wild animals in certain kinds of hunting. They embalm in cedar oil the heads of the most distinguished enemies, and preserve them carefully in a chest, and display them with pride to strangers, saying that for this head one of their ancestors, or his father, or the man himself, refused the offer of a large sum of money. They say that some of them boast that they refused the weight of the head in gold; thus displaying what is only a barbarous kind of magnanimity, for it is not a sign of nobility to refrain from selling the proofs of one's valour. It is rather true that it is bestial to continue one's hostility against a slain fellow man.
>
> (*Tierney, 250*)

This battle custom is a regular feature in the early texts, as is the religious veneration of the head. A typical scene is described in the *Táin*, where head-hunting is much to the fore; Cú Chulainn has slain the two sons of Nera and their charioteers, and decapitated them. Cormac Conn Longes is sent by Medb to see what has been going on at the ford:

> And when he got there he saw only the forked pole in the middle of the ford with four heads on it dripping blood down the stem of the pole into the current of the stream, and the hoof-marks of the two horses, and the track of a single charioteer and of a single warrior leading eastwards out of the ford. (*C. O'Rahilly, 154*)

On the very first expedition as a warrior-elect the youthful Cú Chulainn makes in the *Táin*, he takes heads. He decapitates the three sons of Nechta Scéne. When he returns in wild triumph to the fortress at Emain Macha a woman looking out sees his approach and reports: 'A single chariot-warrior is here . . . and terribly he comes. He has in the chariot the bloody heads of his enemies.' In his encounter in the same tale with Ferchú Loingseach and his followers we learn:

> And they came forward to the place where Cú Chulainn was, and when they came they did not grant him fair play or single combat,

but all 12 of them attacked him straightway. However, Cú Chulainn fell upon them, and forthwith struck off their 12 heads. And he planted 12 stones for them in the ground, and put a head of each one of them on its stone, and also put Ferchú Loingseach's head on its stone. So that the spot where Ferchú Loingseach left his head is called Cinnit Ferchon, that is, Cennait Ferchon (the Head-place of Ferchú). (*C. O'Rahilly, 209*)

This passage not only demonstrates the elaborate ritual of decapitation and the display of heads, but it incorporates the concept of *fír fer* which is mentioned on page 115, the code of battle behaviour which it was considered outrageous to violate. The Romans were clearly not in sympathy with this universal Celtic custom of decapitation, and regarded it, together with human sacrifice and other customs, as an inherently barbaric and renegade practice.

CONDUCT IN BATTLE, TRADITIONS AND TALES

There are various Classical references to conduct in battle. The Celts were clearly brave to the point of foolhardiness, reckless and savage; their lack of efficient organisation and staying power as a group were constant hindrances to permanent victory and the consolidation of gains. The textual sources very much bear out what the Classics have to say about Celtic battle behaviour and organisation. Polybius, for example, remarks:

Such was the end of the war against the Celts, a war which, if we look to the desperation and daring of the combatants, and the numbers who took part and perished in the battles, is second to no war in history, but is quite contemptible as regards the plan of campaigns, and the judgement shown in executing it, not most steps but every single step the Celts took being commended to them rather by the heat of passion than by cool calculation. (*Tierney, 327*)

This is the story throughout the early history of the Celts. Inflamed as they must have been by habitual drinking, quarrels were bound to break out in the course of festivity and revelry, resulting in hero fighting against hero in single combat, in tribe fighting against tribe; or in members of the same tribe turning against each other. The *Táin* itself, the great legendary cattle-raid, was alleged to have begun first of all with a heated quarrel between Ailill and Medb, King and Queen of Connacht; this led finally to bitter war between the provinces of Connacht and Ulster. The war came about as a result of drunken indiscretion, leading to insult and threats on the part of the emissaries sent out by Medb to borrow a bull from Cúailnge in the province of Ulster, owned by Dáire.

The episode is graphically described in the story: Mac Roth, the chief emissary, has extracted a promise that the bull shall go on loan to Connacht. The entertainment then begins: 'Then they were attended to, and straw and fresh rushes were strewn underfoot for them. The choicest food was served to them, and a drinking feast provided until they were merry.' A conversation breaks out amongst the emissaries, which is very indiscreet, and ends with one of them saying: 'I should like to see a gush of blood and gore from the mouth from which that talk comes, for were the bull not given willingly, he would be given perforce.' Dáire's servant overhears this remark, and goes to his master in a rage. Dáire at once revokes his promise, and says: 'I swear by the gods whom I worship, unless they take him thus by force they shall not take him by fair means.' Mac Roth is amazed when he is refused the bull the next day, and says to Dáire: 'Whatever messengers might say as a result of indulging in your meat and drink, it should not be heeded or noticed.' But Dáire will have none of it, and war ensues. This must have been a typical Celtic situation, with inevitable results. Many tales in the early literature are based on the same motif, i.e. feasting, over-indulgence in drink and the ensuing squabble, followed by bloodshed and ultimately involving the whole tribe. Diodorus Siculus bears this out when he remarks: 'At dinner they are wont to be moved by chance remarks to wordy disputes and, after a challenge, to fight in single combat, regarding their lives as naught.' In the story *Bricriu's Feast*, again, the quarrels and fighting began at dinner.

The continual internecine warfare indulged in by the Celts is commented on by Caesar as a custom pertaining to the past. He says: 'Before the arrival of Caesar it used to happen every year that they either attacked another tribe, or warded off the attacks of another tribe.' Prisoners of war were sometimes sacrificed to the gods. Caesar again says: 'After deciding on battle they frequently vow to Mars whatever they may take in the war; whatever captured animals remain over they sacrifice, and everything else they bring together in one place.'

75

Religion thus played a major role in the conduct of battle as in every other sphere of Celtic life. There were lucky days and unlucky days for engaging in conflict; the omens often caused a warrior seeking battle to avoid it. To see a crane, for example, was thought to portend ill to a battle-bound warrior. In one Irish text it was said that to see the three cranes of the god Midir was sufficient to drain away a warrior's entire battle ardour and ability.

Encampment was a feature of tribal war. In the *Táin*, Ailill says to the hosts:

> 'Let us pitch our tents and pavilions and let us prepare food and drink and let us make music and melody and let us eat and take food, for it is unlikely that the men of Ireland ever at any time experienced a night of encampment that held more hardship and distress for them than last night.' Their encampments were set up and their tents pitched. Food and drink was prepared by them, music and melody played, and they ate a meal. (*C. O'Rahilly, 156*)

Military exploits, as we have seen, appear to have involved movement of virtually the whole tribe while a 'hosting' was in progress. Strabo says of the Celts: 'They are wont to change their abode on slight provocation, migrating in bands with all their battle array, or rather setting out with all their households when displaced by a stronger enemy.'

War, weapons, and heroic exploits, these are so much a feature of the everyday life of the pagan Celts that one could well say that they are the most typical feature round which a great body of tradition of every kind has gathered. They have given rise to the main theme of many of the tales. The early Welsh *Triads** which contain so much of the ancient pagan tradition and morality abound in references to warfare and heroic exploits. One of these is entitled *Three Pillars of the Islands of Britain*, for example, and another *Three Red-Speared Bards of the Island of Britain*; and in another, Arthur states:

> *These are my three battle-horsemen:*
> *Menedd and Lludel of the breastplate*
> *And the pillar of Cymry, Caradawg.*

Yet another triad is concerned with *Three Battle-Diademed Men*

* A form of composition characterised by arranging statements in groups of three.

of the Island of Britain, and another refers to *Three Slaughter-Blocks of the Island of Britain*, and so on. The tradition, then, is everywhere concerned with battle. Cult legends recount the strivings of the gods as they pursue their immortal objectives and engage in battle to achieve their goal; the aid of mortal heroes is often enlisted in these tales. Laws were passed controlling the conduct of war, feasts prepared to honour the triumphant hero, often ending in further fighting and bloodshed. The Celts who counted were the warrior aristocrats—powerful, savage, brave, unstable, obsessed with individual glory, and bent on the success of their own tribe or faction.

We have seen some of the barbaric accounts of Celtic heroes decked provocatively in splendid arms and equipment, in search of adventure. It will provide a contrast if we end this section with a passage from medieval Welsh literature, no less barbaric in its undertones than the Irish tales, but the primitive element is tactfully subdued and partially concealed by the grace and elegance of the language; even in translation it makes its impact. It is the account of the young hero-elect, Culhwch, journeying to the Court of Arthur in search of initiation and adventure:

Off went the boy on a steed with light-grey head four winters old, with well-knit fork, shell-hoofed, and a gold tubular bridle-bit in its mouth. And under him a precious gold saddle, and in his hand two whetted spears of silver. A battle-axe in his hand, the forearms length of a full-grown man from ridge to edge. It would draw blood from the wind; it would be swifter than the swiftest dew-drop from the stalk to the ground, when the dew would be heaviest in the month of June. A gold-hilted sword on his thigh, and the blade of it gold, and a gold-chased buckler upon him, with the hue of heaven's lightning therein, and an ivory boss therein. And two grey-hounds, white-breasted, brindled, in front of him, with a collar of red gold about the neck of either, from shoulder swell to ear. The one that was on the left side would be on the right, and the one that was on the right side would be on the left, like two sea-swallows sporting around him. Four clods the four hoofs of his steed would cut, like four swallows in the air over his head, now before him, now behind him. A four-cornered mantle of purple upon him, and an apple of red-gold in each of its corners: 100 kine was the worth of each apple. The worth of 300 kine in precious gold was there in his footgear and his stirrups, from the top of his thigh to the tip of his toe. Never a hair-tip stirred upon him, so exceedingly light his steed's canter under him on its way to the gate of Arthur's Court. (*Jones, 97*)

ROADS AND WHEELED VEHICLES

Soldiers went to battle with wheeled vehicles in Celtic times, goods were bartered, coins and slaves were offered to foreign traders, by the Celts, in return for exotic goods. People moved about the countryside with all their households and possessions and settled in new areas; the dead were carried along ancient routes to their final resting-place which would be a place of sanctuary and ritual practice. That some provision for all this activity and coming and going must have been made in the way of roads is clear; and it is an aspect of Celtic life which cannot simply be ignored. But it is an extremely difficult subject because the evidence for roads is scant and unsatisfactory in the Celtic countries as elsewhere in the barbarian world in pre-Roman times. It was not until the first and second centuries A D, under the Roman Emperors, that the great network of roads in Europe took shape. It has been claimed that this was possible because there was already an existing and efficient system of native roads which the Romans proceeded to improve upon, but this is a debatable point. Evidence for water transport is fuller than that for roads and land travel in general. As far as the actual roads are concerned, and in so far as they existed at all, we must suppose them to have been crude in construction, and very infrequent. The use of wheeled transport does, however, suggest that there were some tracks of a fairly permanent and maintained nature. The custom of chariot-fighting and travel by chariot, would also imply reasonably functional routes and tracks. Anyone who has ever driven along mud roads in the west of Scotland and elsewhere, after a long drought and during a gale, is able to appreciate more fully the passages in the *Táin* which describe such conditions. Mac Roth, the emissary sees extraordinary sights on the plain before him. He cannot interpret them and goes to Ailill and Medb to ask what they are. The great hero Fergus knows:

> The grey mist he saw which filled the void between earth and sky was the expiration of the breath of horses and heroes, and the cloud of dust from the ground and the roads which rises above them driven by the wind so that it becomes a heavy, deep-grey mist in the clouds and the air. Later Fergus says: The flock of varied, wonderful, numerous birds which he saw there was the dust of the ground and the surface of the earth which the horses flung up from their feet and their hooves and which rose above them with the driving of the wind. (*C. O'Rahilly, 251*)

That roadways of some kind existed in Celtic Europe is suggested by Diodorus Siculus, for example: 'They are exceedingly fond of wine . . . and therefore many Italian merchants with their usual love of lucre look on the Gallic love of wine as their treasure trove. They transport the wine by boat on the navigable rivers and by wagon through the plains. . . .'

Such active trade as this, involving the transport of bulky goods over large tracts of land, must imply that everything possible would have been done to speed up and facilitate the supplies. The driest, hardest land would naturally be chosen. Any unavoidable bogland would be made as penetrable as possible by artificial means. Accustomed as we are to the Roman system of roads throughout Europe and Britain, one tends to forget what a marvel and what an extraordinary phenomenon the brilliantly engineered Roman roads and bridges were in the ancient Western world; and it is useful to bear in mind the fact that, after the collapse of the Roman Empire, right down to comparatively recent times, when the military roads were constructed, there was nothing at all to compare with them. The Romans must in fact have utilised old trackways and existent routes and systematised them. In many isolated districts of the British Isles, right down to the eighteenth century and later, wheeled transport simply did not exist. Dr Johnson, during his famous tour of the Scottish Highlands in 1773 was not merely talking from English prejudice when he commented, on leaving Inverness for the west coast: 'We were now to bid farewell to the luxury of travelling and to enter a country upon which perhaps no wheel has ever rolled.'

Spoke-wheeled vehicles appear in Europe as early as between 1500 and 1250 BC, in the Middle Danube basin. Model wagons and wheels were made, and in some instances at least these are probably to be regarded as having a votive significance. The Celtic equivalent of Jupiter, Taranis, 'Thunderer', is symbolised in the ancient Celtic world by a wheel (*29*). The presence of many metal models of wheels and wheel-shaped brooches as well as wheels drawn on pottery vessels in votive deposits and on sacred sites may have a double significance. It may emphasise the veneration with which the Celts regarded the wheel as symbolising the sun; this rather vague and general significance may also link up with a specific relationship with the wheel-god himself, and indicate a very widespread worship of this deity in Celtic countries which other evidence would support. In one early Irish text

29 Wheel represented on pottery, Housesteads, Northumberland

Elatha, the divine suitor, comes to woo Ériu, the eponymous goddess of Ireland; he is described as having five wheels of gold on his back. Again in the earliest Irish tales, certain of the warriors are described as wearing wheel-shaped brooches which would seem to provide a verbal parallel for those known from archaeological sources. This reverence for the wheel and its mythological associations would imply that it was not altogether a commonplace everyday object. Its function as a vital part of a vehicle would cause wonder and awe. Chariot-wheels have been found in wells, and knowing the Celtic predilection for making offerings to the gods in wells, it may be that this is a further example of the reverence which was accorded to the symbol of the wheel, and its importance in functional but essentially aristocratic life.

The earliest wagons—those, that is, that were not built for ceremonial purposes—may have been used as farm transport rather than for long-distance travel. These were apparently drawn by two oxen yoked to a pole. The fact that both the wagon and the chariot were in use among the Celts would seem to imply that their territories were in fact served by roads of some kind, no matter how crude. According to the Irish sources, in so far as they can be used as reliable records of the period in question, these were laid with wood and stone, and there is no reason why this should not have been the case. Some must always have been little better than simple but well-demarcated trackways, of the kind still to be seen in the Scottish Highlands and other regions today. The Irish texts describe five main roads which converged on Tara in Meath, an ancient sanctuary of the Celts and seat of the High Kings. There are references to other named roads, but it is difficult to determine how far back into antiquity they go; or whether, in fact, they reflect a situation pertaining to Ireland in Christian times alone. Knowing, however, the conservative nature of Celtic tradition, and the reverence with which the old legends, place-names and customs were regarded, it is probable that there is a hard core of truth underneath the verbal elaborations of the Christian *literati*.

ROAD REPAIRS, BRIDGES AND FERRIES

The evidence suggests that it was regarded as of prime importance that the roads should be efficiently maintained; the Brehon Laws stipulate the regulations governing the making and repair of roads in Ireland. Roads must be kept clean. Cormac, in his ninth-century Irish glossary, states: 'A road of whatever class must be cleaned on at least three occasions, that is, the time of horse-racing, winter and war.' He also classifies the roads of ancient Ireland. These roads had to be kept clear of brambles, weeds and so on. Certain people were compelled to make a road through a wood in times of war. Thus, although there is strong evidence for a system of roads in early Ireland, it is not easy to determine from the texts alone whether they were in fact of such a quality as the laws and stories would suggest, or if they were really of a con-siderably more crude nature. Strabo, though, does mention roads in Narbonnensis, and one would expect these to have been superior to any insular roads.

Causeways were certainly constructed across bogs where necessary. They consisted of layers of trees, brushwood, earth and stones trampled down to make a foundation of considerable efficiency. Sometimes they were covered over with planks to make a corduroy road.

The early bridges were of wood: there is no Irish evidence for the building of stone bridges before Anglo-Norman times. Ferries were much in use on rivers and straits, and these were subject to strict regulations, according to the early accounts. They must have been of considerable importance in facilitating movement and transport; and the withdrawal of any particular established ferry would be extremely inconvenient. Strabo, in his account of the Celtic tribes, comments: 'You cross the river by ferry to the city of Cavaillon.' In the tale of *Branwen*, one of the Four Branches of the *Mabinogion*, Matholwch, the Irish ruler, who is married to Branwen, sister of the euhemerised Bran the Blessed, wishes to cut off communication with Britain. His advisers council him in the following terms: 'Aye, Lord,' said his men to Matholwch, 'set now a ban on the ships and the ferry-boats and the coracles, so that none may go to Wales, imprison them and let them not go

30 Some examples of boats on Gaulish coins (after D. F. Allen)

back. . . .' Ancient Irish boats were apparently of three kinds: canoes, which were made from hollowed-out trees; wicker boats; ships with sails or oars or both. *Curraghs* were covered with hide and propelled with oars or sails. Caesar used British models for curraghs, which he had built. The Latin *Voyage of St Brendan* describes in some detail the building of a curragh.

Celtic tribes were famed for their skill as boatmen. Strabo mentions that the Massiliotes 'have a natural ability in seafaring'; and the Veneti of Armorica (*30*) were distinguished amongst these. Strabo comments:

> After the tribes already described the rest belong to the Belgae, who live along the ocean. Among these are the Veneti, who fought the naval battle against Caesar. For they used the trading station there, and were ready to hinder his voyage to Britain. He defeated them easily by sea, not using rams for the timber of their boats was thick, but when they bore down upon him with the wind the Romans tore down their sails with long-handled hooks; for their sails were made of leather, owing to the force of the winds, and chains pulled them up instead of ropes. They make their boats with broad bottoms and high sterns and prows, on account of the ebb-tides. The material is oak, of which they have a large supply, and therefore they do not joint their planks closely, but leave openings which they stop with seaweed, so that when the boats are in dock the wood may not dry up for lack of moisture, the seaweed being naturally rather moist, while the oak is dry and without fat. (*Tierney, 267*)

This provides an interesting picture of the methods of boat-building of one Celtic tribe, at least. There is other very good evidence for Celtic nautical skill and regular use of transport by water. The Pictish navy was famous in the early centuries of the Christian era, and there is no reason to believe that this was a late development. Wainwright says: 'It is quite clear that the Picts were not a negligible factor in the northern political scene. They possessed a fleet of considerable strength, which implies navigational skill, familiarity with difficult waters, and a knowledge of shipbuilding.'

The real evidence for Celtic roads is slight, then; but the

presence of active markets and centres of trade and commerce all over Europe and in the British Isles in pre-Roman times must imply the existence of certain efficient and well-maintained routes, if nothing else. The widespread Celtic use of the chariot also suggests the presence of functional roads of some kind. The Irish laws which contain the most archaic written record of the Celtic way of life as organised from *within*, give a strong, even if exaggerated, impression that road-making and maintenance were activities of vital public concern. In his discussion of the siting of Celtic workshops and regional schools of Celtic art in Britain, Fox demonstrates how the old routes like the Jurassic route and the Icknield Way must have been used by the Celtic artists and traders. The extent of trade and movement of goods must certainly imply reliable routes, but, as Fox goes on to say: 'The "ifs" in this problem, as in others, are sadly frequent. For example, the inter-tribal commerce of the time must have been extensive, but its fundamental bases are unknown.'

Archaeological evidence can as yet determine little of the nature of Celtic roads before the development of the superbly engineered and systematised network of Roman roads throughout Europe. But, just as Roman temples and eventually Christian shrines tended to be constructed over the foundations of pagan sanctuaries, so one may suppose the Romans to have built some, at least, of their sophisticated roads over the ancient tracks which had been proved by their predecessors to have been the most efficient and practical cross-country routes for trading and transport in general. Traces of actual roads do remain, and can be determined, when, for example, they run through cemeteries. Coffin tracks have always been vital and known and marked by such things as barrows or, even at the present day, mounds of stones, at which the coffin containing the remains of the dead was rested.

Locomotion and transportation were by chariot, by four-wheeled wagon, on horseback, with pack-horse, or on foot; boats of various kinds were in use, ferries were plentiful and frequent and of great importance. Bridges were apparently of the simplest wooden kind.

As we see throughout this inquiry into the everyday life of the early Celtic peoples, religion permeates its every sphere and nothing is entirely and truly secular. Magic, superstition, and the great host of gods and goddesses with their requirements from Man and the benefits they bestowed in return for gifts and proper propitiation, are everywhere present. Fox, again, in considering the nature of trade, and the routes taken in the exchange of goods, and the factors determining the siting of the Celtic *ateliers* in Britain—and the reasons for the richness of the Iceni in East Anglia and so forth—brings this out most appositely, when he says: 'There is another possibility. It is that the Druidic hierarchy may have organised the gold traffic along the route mentioned above, primarily for their own ritual purposes; if so, it would partly explain why remote Mona became the centre of this British cult, and suggest that the port for the gold trade to the Continent was in Norfolk. The fanatic antagonism to Rome illustrated by the dreadful scenes in Anglesey in AD 59, when the legionaries under Suetonius destroyed groves and priests and worshippers, will then have been fed by economic as well as religious and political motifs.'

FORTIFICATIONS

The economics of trade and domestic economy, and the necessities of warfare led, as we have seen, to the demand for some sort of functional, traversible trade routes and roads, no matter how rudimentary and crude. Domestic life necessitates dwelling-houses of some kind, and warfare implies fortifications and defences. The fact that the Celts were prodigious fort-builders and that forts constitute one of the most typical and important features of their material culture, serves to demonstrate once again how important a feature of their everyday life warfare in fact was. There is as yet very much more material evidence for Celtic fortresses at all stages of their history than there is for their houses and their domestic equipage in general. The Celts, unlike their Mediterranean neighbours, were never concerned with permanent settlement and the domestic sophistication this implies. Architectural elaboration and urban development were features which they adopted at a very late period in their early history, under the example of, and for the most part under the aegis of, Rome. But the earlier restless, ranging Celt with his mobile tribal organisation and his aggressive, touchy temperament, thought primarily in terms of fortified sites rather than stately homes. Such sites were imperative, while sophisticated houses were supererogatory.

The Celts constructed both places of comparatively temporary refuge, defended by stockades or banks and ditches, for use particularly in times of population movement, and forts designed for more permanent use. At first the forts occupied hill-tops that themselves added to the strength of the defences; but shortly before and during the period of the earliest contacts with the Romans they also built large 'towns', or *oppida*, down on the plains or in the valleys.

The defences of forts of all kinds include several different principles; the simple stockade, the bank and ditch—single or multiple—the wall and ditch, the wall alone. Walls were either simple drystone constructions or were reinforced, made more resistant to attack, by being tied internally with timber, in one method or another, with or without iron clamps. Caesar encountered a form of this during his campaigns in Gaul, and named it *murus gallicus*. In some cases at least timber houses were attached to the inner face of the wall; and either when these were set on fire by accident or design, or when attackers piled brushwood up against the wall and lit it, it often happened that the whole wall began to burn, and the heat generated in the airless interior caused some of the stones to melt, and to fuse into a vitrified mass.

The size of Celtic fortified enclosures varies greatly, from the mere family stronghold to towns hundreds of acres in extent. The largest were the latest. At Bibracte, for example, on Mont-Beuvray near Autun, France, the *murus gallicus* wall was some five kilometres in length, enclosing an area of some 335 acres. It is of some interest to compare this with Homeric Troy, less than five acres in extent. In the area enclosed by the wall at Bibracte there were buildings, mainly rectangular, and streets, suggesting the influence of the Mediterranean world. Some of the buildings that were excavated, typical Celtic post-framed structures, had been enamellers' workshops; others were stalls and booths of different kinds. The great *oppidum* at Manching, in Bavaria, is another such example, testifying to the size and power these late Celtic plain-forts could attain.

Forts both large and small, early and late in date, are found scattered widely throughout Europe. They are recorded by the Classics from Galatia (modern western Turkey) but as yet have not been recognised there by archaeologists. In the eastern Celtic world, for example, at Zavist in Czechoslovakia, there is a fort some 80 acres in extent. In Britain, Belgic *oppida* occur at several places, such as Colchester (Camulodunum), St Albans

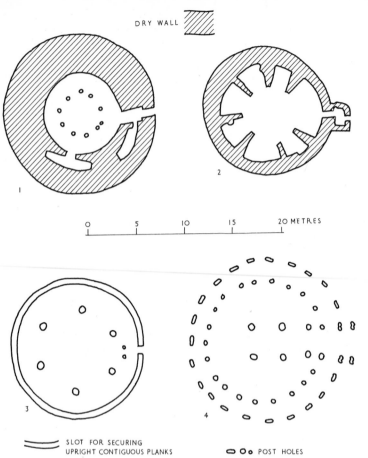

DRY WALL

0   5   10   15   20 METRES

SLOT FOR SECURING
UPRIGHT CONTIGUOUS PLANKS   ⬭ ⬭ₒ POST HOLES

31 Ground plans of four kinds of circular house: 1, broch, Dun Troddan, Inverness-shire; 2, wheelhouse, Jarlshof, Shetland; 3, Harehope, Peebles-shire; 4, Little Woodbury, Wiltshire

(Verulamium) or Silchester (Calleva). Earlier than these are such famous forts as Maiden Castle, Dorset, which contains 45 acres, Traprain Law, East Lothian with 40 acres, and Stanwick, York-shire which, in its latest phase, reached the acreage if not the standard of the *oppidum*—850 acres. The ramparts and ditches here extend for more than six miles, and, as Piggott says, it serves the needs of a pastoral people with large flocks and herds to be protected.

In regions outside the Roman sphere of influence the construction of forts went on unchecked. The timber-laced fort at
Burghead, Morayshire, has recently been dated to the fifth
century AD.

Forts were as much a feature of the everyday life of the Irish
Celts as they were throughout the rest of the Celtic world. There
seems to have been a professional class or guild of fort-builders, a
supposition that is substantiated by Irish textual sources. Graham
demonstrates that this is also borne out by the workmanship of the
brochs, thick but hollow-walled, circular dwellings of a unique
character of which some 600 have been recorded all in modern
Scotland (*31*). Graham says: 'The technical standard of broch
masonry being so high as to enforce the conclusion that the work
was done by professionals.' Literary sources support the archeological evidence for the vast quantities of wood which were used
in the construction of forts. King Brude's fort in Inverness, for
example, is alleged to have had folding doors with bolts. At Tara,
the great fortified stronghold of the Irish kings, a door and door-
keepers are mentioned. Forts were the appurtenances of kings and
high-ranking nobles; many of these must have been small. The
Irish chief's hall was surrounded by a defensive rampart, having
a parapet walk and a stockade. This is attested again by the
material evidence.

There was a gateway, a door-keeper's lodge and a *faithche* or
parade ground where military practice, training exercises and ball
games, such as hurley, would take place. In the early Irish story
of *The Exile of the Sons of Uisliu* we are told that: 'On one occasion,
then, the aforementioned Noisiu was alone on the rampart of the
earthwork.' Fortification, then, was an essential feature of the
Celtic way of life, the simpler structures of the early phase
developing and becoming more elaborate and complex during the
La Tène period, according to the degree of Mediterranean
influence and the borrowing of its architectural tradition; and as
a result of the pressure and siege tactics of Rome, which presented
a more formidable situation than that caused by mere inter-tribal
strife.

HOUSES

Celtic houses were circular or rectangular on plan; in the pre-
Celtic or Urnfield period of European prehistory rectangular

houses were favoured and these predominate in the Hallstatt and La Tène phases. Round houses were the choice of the western European world; they were common in Spain and Portugal and continued to be built right up to the period of the Roman Conquest. The round house also is found in Britain and Ireland with an ancestry reaching back to at least the Bronze Age, and the evidence suggests that this was an essentially Atlantic building tradition. There are references to rectangular structures in the Irish texts, but there is some evidence to suggest that these may refer to ritual structures, while the circular house was the domestic norm; the great hall, however, appears to have been rectangular. Archaeology has not recognised circular houses in Europe east of the Rhine. Strabo says of the Belgae: 'Their houses are large and circular, built of planks and wickerwork, the roof being a dome of heavy thatch.' This seems to be an exact parallel to the circular insular houses as evidenced by such examples as the well-known Little Woodbury house (*31*), and others. In central Europe, then, the rectangular house has an ancestry which goes back ultimately to the Neolithic Age, while along the Atlantic coasts, the circular shape has its antecedents in the Bronze Age at least. The round house was a permanent dwelling, made of wood, and supported by poles. No examples of this type have been excavated in central Europe to date.

32 Cauldron suspended over the fire by iron chains

The interior arrangement of these Celtic houses must have been extremely crude, and all the evidence suggests that the Celts were much given to personal decoration and display whereas they were unabashed by crude living-quarters. The fire in these circular houses would be central in the room with a hole in the thatch for the escape of smoke. The great cauldron in which the huge quantities of meat consumed by the Celts would be boiled—when it was not roasted on a spit—was suspended above the fire from a

88

cross-beam (*32*). Bread was used in small quantities by the nobles; fish would be boiled, or baked. Athenaeus, quoting Posidonius, mentions some of the gastronomic preferences of the Celts and these are well attested in the early Irish texts.

> Their food consists of a small number of loaves of bread, together with a large amount of meat, either boiled or roasted on charcoal or on spits . . . those who live beside the river or near the Mediterranean or Atlantic eat fish in addition, baked fish, that is, with the addition of salt, vinegar, and cummin. (*Tierney, 247*)

All round the walls of these houses, as far as we can tell from the early accounts of Irish houses, were compartments, known as *imdae*; these must have been like cubicles and in them the various activities of the aristocratic household took place. Presumably these could be closed off from the rest of the hall by screens or material or leather or wickerwork, when privacy was required. If the Classical comments on Gaulish sleeping habits are to be taken for fact, people must have slept together in these cubicles no doubt often on the floor. Diodorus Siculus comments: 'Their custom is to sleep on the ground upon the skins of wild animals and to wallow among bed-fellows on either side.'

The typical diameter of a circular Iron Age house was round about 50 feet. The actual cubicles must have been demarcated by wooden or wickerwork partitions.* In the so-called 'wheel-houses' of the Western Islands of Scotland (*31*) stone replaced wood in these divisions, wood being a rare commodity in the treeless west: the cubicles are thus made of radiating stone piers. The earliest Irish tales do correspond to a striking degree with the information provided by the Classical record and the ground-plans and so on of Celtic houses as known to archaeologists. The hall of the Celtic nobleman must have been quite a substantial building, consisting of a fortified enclosure, a parade ground, or *faithche* in Irish, outside the enclosure, which was probably a home pasture as well as the sports and military training ground. Inside the enclosure would be the king or noble's residence and various other essential buildings of wood—the servant's quarters, agricultural sheds and so on. The framework of the Irish houses, as elsewhere in the Celtic world, was of wood; weather-boarding was used and also

* At Glenmoriston, Inverness-shire, Boswell, on his tour of the Highlands with Dr Johnson, comments: 'The house was built of thick turfs and thatched with thinner turfs and heath. It had three rooms and a little room which projected . . . the side-walls were wainscotted with wicker very neatly plaited.'

wicker work; the roof was of shingles, or thatched. It was supported by pillars which seem often to have been elaborately
carved, and these must have been another great medium for the
skilful convolutions of the Celtic artists employed to decorate them.
There would be a great gate outside and a porter's lodge where
watch was kept for visitors and trouble-makers. The role of
watchman is always stressed in the tales; nothing of vital
importance ever occurs without its being observed by the watchman. The closing of the gate at dusk was of first importance; even
in the houses of non-noble freemen, that is superior craftsmen,
etc., this is done. ⟍

When the King, Conchobar, Cú Chulainn's uncle, goes to the
house of Culann the smith, to receive the hospitality that was his
right, Cú Chulainn, who is a little boy at that time, says he will
stay behind until he has finished playing with the boys at Emain
Macha and then come to Culann's fort: 'I shall follow the trail of
the company and the horses and the chariots.' Conchobar arrives
before the boy, attended by the number of his followers that the
law allows him on such an occasion: 'The King was served, and
they were honoured according to rank and profession and rights
and nobility and accomplishments. Reeds and fresh rushes were
strewn beneath them. They began to drink and make merry.'
When Culann finds out that no one else is to follow—for the King
has forgotten his young nephew—he releases his mighty watch-
dog which he uses to guard the settlement; the dog goes swiftly
round the enclosure: 'His dog-chain was loosed from the blood-
hound and he made a swift circuit of the canton* and he came to
the mound where he was wont to be while guarding the dwelling
and he lay there with his head on his paws.' The little boy comes,
is attacked by the hound and kills it with his bare hands; this is
one of his greatest feats because as a result of it he gets his name,
without which no hero could have a positive identity. This
happens as follows: the King hears the baying of the dog, remem-
bers the boy and says:

'Alas my warriors, would that we had not come to enjoy this feast.'
'Why so?' asked they all. 'The little boy who arranged to come after
me, my sister's son, Sétanta mac Sualtaim, has been killed by the
hound.' All the famous Ulstermen rose with one accord. Though the
gateway of the dwelling was wide open, they all went to meet him
over the palisades of the stronghold.

* 'Canton', a subdivision of country.

The smith, when he sees what has happened, is devastated by the loss of his dog: 'Would that you had not come to consume my drink and eat my food for my substance now is substance wasted, my livelihood a lost livelihood. Good was the servant you have taken from me. He used to guard my herds and flocks and cattle for me.' The boy volunteers to act as watch-dog for the smith until such time as he can rear a puppy sired by the blood-hound until it is old enough to guard the fortress. Cathbad the Druid on hearing this says: 'Why shall you not be called Cú Chulainn—Culand's Hound—because of this?' The boy agrees to this and his name changes to his real, heroic name, Cú Chulainn.

This is one of many realistic descriptions of the life and manners and the domestic background of early Irish life which coheres well with the other sources of evidence. The social unit, then, in Ireland as in Britain, seems to have been predominantly the isolated, single, circular farmstead with its defences and its related buildings, not the village with its rectangular houses, as found in much of Celtic Europe. The British and Irish type of single domestic unit was almost unknown in Europe in the Hallstatt and La Tène periods.

To return to the interior of a Celtic house; the nobles sat each in his own cubicle to dine, surrounded by his attendants and chosen companions. He could see into the rest of the hall and listen to the communal entertainment—music, recitals of poetry and tales, the feats of jugglers and so on—he was protected by his own servants and spearsmen. Athenaeus, quoting Posidonius, would seem to describe just some such arrangement when he comments:

> The Celts sit on dried grass and have their meals served up on wooden tables raised slightly above the earth . . . when a large number dine together they sit around in a circle with the most influential man in the centre, like the leader of the chorus, whether he surpass the others in warlike skill, or nobility of family or wealth. Beside him sits the host and next, on either side, the others in order of distinction. Their shieldsmen stand behind them while their spearmen are seated in a circle on the opposite side and feast in common like their lords. (*Tierney*, *247*)

This description is strikingly paralleled by the Irish passage we have just considered, where reeds and grasses are strewn in Culann's house for the entertainment of the royal party, and people are seated as Athenaeus says, according to pre-eminence for whatever reason it may be. Variations in arrangement would, of course, be expected, especially in the case of a rectangular as opposed to a circular house. Furniture must have been scarce, and chairs seem not to have been used, for eating at any rate, in pre-Roman times. Chests are mentioned by the Classics. There is some evidence that the Irish houses were two-storeyed. On the level of the upper floor there was some kind of room or protected balcony which projected outwards, known as the *grianán*, literally 'sun-room'. This was occupied by the women and was probably situated in the front over the common living-room. Here the women must have sat and sewed and embroidered and gossiped, away from their raucous, touchy menfolk. In the enigmatic story *Bricriu's Feast*, which may date to an eighth-century text, Bricriu builds a house in sumptuous style in which to entertain Conchobar and the heroes of Ulster; he is a sinister trouble-maker and has undertaken not to be present at his own feast. He builds a sun-room, with windows of 'glass' so that he can see into the hall and observe what is going on. One of the amusing episodes in this remarkable tale, the longest in the Ulster Cycle after the *Táin*, concerns the eagerness of the women, who are drunk, to be considered the first in beauty, wisdom and eloquence of the women of Ulster. When three of the women have made a speech in praise of their husbands, the three men tear down the pillars of the house in their drunken excitement in order to let the women, who have left the house, get back in. Cú Chulainn merely lifts up his side of the house and his wife and other women are then able to enter. When it falls back to the ground, the entire fort is shaken and the sun-room falls down. In spite of the humour and the ludicrous nature of the situation, the descriptions of the house and its light-weight nature, and the positioning of the sun-room would seem to reflect genuine traditions of such Iron Age structures as we have been considering.

4

Games and Hunting; Music and Entertainment; Food and Drink

These, then, are the things which formed the background to Celtic everyday life; their physical appearance, and distinctive style of dress and personal ornament; their modes of warfare and the weapons they used; the roads and the water routes which were vital for the conduct of war, for expansion and conquest, for trade and for travel; and the forts with which they defended themselves, the houses in which they passed their domestic days. How did the Celtic nobles pass their time when they were *not* fighting? In the *Táin* again we learn of Conchobar, the King:

> For this is how Conchobor spends his time of kingship since he assumed sovereignty: as soon as he arises, settling the cares and business of the province, thereafter dividing the day into three, the first third of the day spent watching the youths playing games and hurling, the second third spent in playing *brandub* and *fidchell* and the last third spent in consuming food and drink until sleep comes on them all, while minstrels and musicians are meanwhile lulling him to sleep. (*C. O'Rahilly, 158*)

BOARD GAMES AND FIELD GAMES

Although it is the King who is described here, this can probably be regarded as a fairly typical day in the life of a high-ranking Iron Age nobleman, when he was not engaged in warfare. Games played an important part in the social life of the pagan Celts. The nobles regularly played a kind of board game called *fidchell*, 'wooden wisdom'; it occurs in the Welsh tales as *gwyddbwyll*, having the same meaning. It was not chess as we know it, but it does seem to have consisted of two sets of men which were pegged into position on the board. Sometimes it was played for mere amusement; sometimes the stakes were high and vital, as in the case of *The Wooing of Étaín*; in this mythological tale the goddess Étaín, wife of the god Midir, undergoes a variety of metamorphoses until she is finally reborn as Étaín, daughter of a noble Ulsterwoman. She is wooed by Eochaid Airem, King of Ireland, and becomes his wife; her rebirth is one thousand and twelve years after her original birth as daughter of the god Ailill. Midir still desires his wife, and comes to her in the form of Ailill, Eochaid's brother, who is sick with love for her. On the third night of these meetings Midir tells Étaín who he is, and who she is, and of their original relationship which he still desires. She refuses to go with him without her husband's consent. One day Eochaid climbs on to the ramparts of Tara, his seat, and sees a splendid man approaching him. It is the god Midir. 'I know you not,' said the King. 'But I know you,' said the stranger. Midir then takes out a superb 'chess'-board of silver with 'men' of gold. He invites the King to play with him, and loses to him. He gives the King 50 grey horses with enamelled reins as a prize. Next morning at sunrise Midir is there again; they play another game, Eochaid is again the winner, and another huge prize is given to him by Midir. This happens three times, and each time the King is triumphant. But on the fourth occasion, the stakes are to be named by the winner when the game is over. Midir of course wins, and demands to take Étaín in his arms and kiss her. Eochaid agrees to this, and tells Midir to return 'one month from today'. On that day he has gathered all his warriors together, and the doors are locked. Even so, Midir appears in the banqueting hall in all his radiant beauty. He goes to Étaín and takes her in his arms:

> He took his weapons in his left hand and the woman beneath his right shoulder; and he carried her off through the smoke-hole of the house. And the hosts rose up around the King, for they felt that they had been disgraced; and they saw two swans circling around Tara.
>
> (*Cross and Slover*, 92)

In *The Dream of Rhonabwy*, one of the stories in the *Mabinogion*, this game is again played for high stakes, and the supernatural element is once more predominant. Arthur says to Owein: 'Owein, will you play *gwyddbwyll*?' 'I will, Lord,' said Owein. And the redheaded servitor brought the *gwyddbwyll* to Arthur and Owein.

Once again it consists of 'gold pieces and a board of silver.' They begin to play, and a series of strange events ensues; Owein wishes to cease from playing and go and attend to things, but Arthur repeatedly says with grim oblivion to what is going on around him: 'Play thy game.'

Another board game, known as *brandub*, 'black raven', was also played. Gaming pieces and dice were actually found in a recently excavated Belgic grave at Welwyn Garden City

Some sorts of board games were very popular, and no doubt helped to pass the long evenings. Field games were also encouraged; like rugby football in public schools today, the sons and foster-sons of the nobility were taught to play at an early age. The hero Cú Chulainn excelled at such games. A nice description of his sports equipment is given in the *Táin*. Just as Culhwch, in the *Mabinogion* sets out to find his Cousin Arthur's Court and establish himself there, so in the *Táin*, Cú Chulainn sets out, against his mother's will, to find Emain Macha and become a member of the King's household; for the King, Conchobar, is his mother's brother:

> The boy went forth and took his playthings. He took his hurly stick of bronze and his silver ball; he took his little javelin for casting and his toy spear with its end sharpened by fire; and he began to shorten the journey by playing with them. He would strike his ball with the stick, and drive it a long way from him. Then with a second stroke he would throw his stick so that he might drive it a distance no less than the first. He would throw his javelin and would cast his spear, and would make a playful rush after them. Then he would catch his hurly stick and his ball and his javelin; and before the end of his spear had reached the ground he would catch its tip aloft in the air.
>
> (C. O'Rahilly, *159*)

So, juggling in this carefree fashion, the hero-to-be makes his way to his uncle's Court to seek his fortune and cement his fate. When he comes to Emain Macha the little boys of the Court are playing hurley; he outrages them by not observing the pro-hibition that it is taboo for anyone to come on to their playing-field without first securing their protection. They all attack him, but he makes short work of them—150 boys, in fact. Fergus is playing chess with the King while the game is in progress. The chess-board is named *Cendchaem*, 'smooth head', as are the weapons of the great heroes and gods given individual names. This suggests that the board, like those weapons, was accredited with supernatural powers and qualities.

95

33 Part of a ritual crown from Hock-wold - cum - Wilton, Norfolk

Pottery mould from Kettering, Northamptonshire

A game like hurley—probably closely similar to the modern *caman* played in the Scottish Highlands, for example, and somewhat akin to hockey—was very popular in the earliest tales. Cú Chulainn will not follow his uncle to Culann's fort until he has finished playing this game:

> Conchobor went to the playing-field and saw something that astonished him: thrice 50 boys at one end of the field and a single boy at the other end, and the single boy winning victory in taking the goal and in hurling from the thrice 50 youths. When they played a hole-game—a game that was played on the green at Emain—and when it was their turn to cast the ball and his to defend, he would catch the thrice 50 balls outside the hole, and none would get past him into the hole. When it was their turn to keep goal and his to hurl, he would put the thrice 50 balls unerringly into the hole.
>
> (*C. O'Rahilly, 160*)

This team game was known as *báire*; the goal was a hole dug in the ground. Two figures from Romano-British contexts seem to be playing, or equipped to play, a game like hurley or hockey. One, from Kettering, and now in the British Museum, occurs on a clay mould from a Roman kiln. The figure is naked, and carries a stick like a hockey-stick and a ball and probably a head; he is addressing a second ball (*33*). The other figure, also in the British Museum, appears on a plaque from a ritual crown or diadem found at Hockwold-cum-Wilton, Norfolk. He holds a stick like a hockey-stick in front of him in his right hand, and raises a ball in his left hand. Four balls decorate the corners of the plaque. He too is naked (*33*).

HUNTING

Apart from playing *fidchell*, 'chess', and another game called *brandub*, and the playing of field games by the young, hunting was much indulged in for pleasure as well as for necessity. Bird-hunting was a popular pastime, and for this a sling was used. There are many fantastic descriptions of bird-hunts, some of which, as in the case of Conaire's bird-hunt in the story of *The Destruction of Da Derga's Hostel*, have a clear mythological significance. Conaire has been borne by Étaín the daughter of Étaín daughter of Etar, after her union with a great mysterious bird that becomes a man at will. This creature has his retinue of followers who likewise shape-shift and become birds or men as required. One day Conaire, who is playing with his foster-brothers, becomes bored and looks for other amusements:

> He turns his chariot with his charioteer so that he was at Ath Cliamh. He saw great white speckled birds there of unusual size and colour. He turns after them until the horses grow tired. They went the length of a cast before him, and they did not go further. He alights, and he takes his sling from the chariot. He turns so that he pursues them by the sea. The birds settle upon the waves. He approaches them and raises his hand to strike them. The birds put aside their bird cloaks, and turn upon him with spears and swords.
>
> (*Knott*, 5 *f.*)

The widespread popularity among the Celts of hunting birds is also attested by the Classical writers. Strabo says: 'There is also a wooden weapon resembling the "grosphus" which is thrown by hand and not by means of a strap, with a range greater than that of an arrow, and which they use mostly for bird-hunting as well as in battle.' Bird-hunting is the sport in which Cú Chulainn's only son indulges on his way to meet his father and his fate—death by his father's hand—in the tragic tale of *The Death of Aife's Only Son*. The men of Ulster are standing on the shore at Tracht Eisi when they see a boat of bronze coming towards them. In it is a boy; he is bringing down birds alive with his sling, and then letting them go free again. His own father performed a similar feat on the day he first took arms and proved himself in combat. He is returning to Emain Macha loaded with heads, live stags and booty, and he sees a flock of white swans fly past.

> 'What kind of birds are those, Ibar?' said the boy, 'are they tame, or just birds?' 'Just birds,' said Ibar, 'they are a flock of swans which come in from the crags and rocks and islands of the ocean to feed on the plains and level spots of Ireland.' 'Which would be more wonderful, to bring them alive to Emain, or to bring them dead, Ibar?' said the boy. 'More wonderful indeed to bring them alive,' said Ibar, 'for not everyone can catch the living birds.' Then the boy cast a small stone at them. He brought down eight of the birds. Then he cast a big stone and brought down 16 of the birds . . . then Ibar tied the birds to the shafts and cords and thongs and strips and ropes of the chariot. (*C. O'Rahilly*, *170*)

Once, in the *Táin*, Cú Chulainn's predilection for the bird-hunt almost earns him disgrace. Nath Crantail, a powerful warrior in the service of Medb, Queen of Connacht, goes to attack Cú Chulainn; he scorns the youth and declines to take any weapons other than 27 spits of holly, which have been sharpened, charred and pointed in the fire.*

> And Cú Chulainn was on the pond before him. And as for the pond, it was not safe but there were nine spits fixed in it, and Cú Chulainn used not to miss a single spit of them. Then Nath Crantail cast a spit at Cú Chulainn. Cú Chulainn stepped on to the upper point of the spit which Nath Crantail had cast. Nath Crantail cast a second spit. He cast a third spit, and Cú Chulainn stepped from the tip of the second spit to the tip of the last spit. Then the flock of birds flew out of the plain. Cú Chulainn pursued them as swift as any bird.
>
> (C. O'Rahilly, *185*)

These passages epitomise the Celtic attitude to life and pastimes —the bombastic, fantastic, grand feats, the achievement of the impossible by the legendary semi-divine heroes, the unsophisticated joy which they felt in describing such feats and in attempting to emulate them in real life. They did not hunt only birds. They regarded the boar as the supreme beast of the chase as well as the finest food at the feast. They hunted the pig, they ate it, and they revered and venerated it as an essentially Otherworld, magical animal.

Many of the tales are concerned with a boar-hunt, and this persists right through the Celtic tradition. The Classical writers testify to the Celtic preference for pig-meat, as do the joints found in graves. Strabo notes of the Belgae: 'They have large quantities of food together with milk and all kinds of meat, especially fresh and salt pork. Their pigs are allowed to run wild, and are noted for their height, and pugnacity and swiftness. It is dangerous for a stranger to approach them.' The hunting of a great supernatural boar is the theme of several tales in the early Irish and Welsh traditions. The hunting of the great mysterious

---

* One is reminded here of the small wooden spears mentioned by Arrian as being used in cavalry exercises; something similar may perhaps also be envisaged in the following passage from the *Táin*: 'And the royal hero [Cú Chulainn] took his ivory-hilted, bright-faced sword with his eight little swords; he took his five-pronged spear with his eight little spears; he took his javelin with his eight little javelins; he took his *deil chliss* with his eight little darts.' (C. O'Rahilly, *201*)

Twrch Trwyth of the *Mabinogion*,* a metamorphosed prince with his retinue, provides the main theme in the story of Culhwch and Olwen; he is paralleled in Irish tradition by Orc Tréith. The young Culhwch, Arthur's cousin, seeks the hand of Olwen, daughter of the giant Ysbaddaden, 'Chief Giant'. Before he can win her, he must accomplish many superhuman tasks, one of which is to catch the magical boar. The giant tells him: 'There is no comb and shears in the world with which my hair may be dressed, so exceeding stiff it is, save the comb and shears that are between the two ears of Twrch Trwyth, son of Taredd Wledig. He will not give them of his own free will, nor can you compel him.' Culhwch performs the many near-impossible deeds he has been forced to do, and the Welsh warriors have gone across to Ireland where the great boar is:

> Dogs were let loose at him from all sides. That day until evening the Irish fought with him; nevertheless he laid waste one of the five provinces of Ireland. And on the morrow Arthur's war-band fought with him; save for what evil they got from him they got nothing good. The third day Arthur himself fought with him; nine nights and nine days he slew of his pigs but one pigling. His men asked Arthur what was the history of that swine, and he told them 'he was a king and for his wickedness God transformed him into a swine'.
>
> (*Jones, 131*)

Magical boars as well as straightforward mundane pigs are also hunted in Ireland. One, the legendary boar of Formael, is the subject of a vast hunt; it is described in one tale in graphic terms:

> The description of that huge boar were enough to cause mortal terror, for he was blue-black with rough bristles . . . grey, horrible, without ears, without a tail . . . and his teeth standing out long and horrid outside his big head . . . and it raised the mane on its back on high, so that a plump wild apple would have stuck on each of its rough bristles. (*Ross 1967, 317*)

The boar, then, was a favourite animal for hunting purposes, and the vernacular traditions contain many references to the hunting of pigs, natural and supernatural. Deer were also animals

---

*The *Mabinogion* cannot, of course, be considered to be a first source of evidence for pagan Celtic customs; but there are traces of what appear to be pagan elements in these sophisticated tales which make them worth considering in the light of the wider evidence.

of the chase. Cú Chulainn shows his magical power over animals again in the episode in the *Táin* immediately prior to that in which he brought down the swans alive with his sling and returned to the fort at Emain Macha with them fluttering from his chariot:

> They saw in front of them a herd of wild deer. 'What are these numerous fierce cattle, Ibar?' said the boy, 'are they tame or are they deer?' 'They are deer indeed,' said Ibar, 'that is a herd of wild deer which frequent the recesses of Sliab Fuait.' 'Ply the goad on the horses for us, that we may catch some of them.' (*C. O'Rahilly, 170*)

The charioteer plied the goad on the horses. The King's fat horses could not keep up with the deer. The boy dismounted and caught two swift, strong stags. He tied them to the shafts and thongs and ropes of the chariot.

Hunting is a regular pastime in the Welsh tales also. In the *Mabinogi of Math*:

> Pwyll prince of Dyfed was lord over the seven cantrefs of Dyfed. And once upon a time he was at Arberth, a chief court of his, and it came into his head and heart to go hunting. . . . And on the morrow in the young of the day he arose and came to Glyn Cuch to loose his dogs into the wood. And he sounded his horn and began to muster the hunt, and followed after the dogs, and lost his companions. And whilst he was listening to the cry of the pack he could hear the cry of another pack, but they had not the same cry, and were coming to meet his own pack. And he could see a clearing in the wood as of a level field, and as his pack reached the edge of the clearing he could see a stag in front of the other pack. And towards the middle of the clearing, lo, the pack that was pursuing it overtaking it and bringing it to the ground. And he looked at the colours of the pack, without troubling to look at the stag, and of all the hounds he had seen in the world he had seen no dogs the same colour as those. The colour that was on them was a brilliant shining white, and their ears red; and as the exceeding whiteness of the dogs glittered, so glittered the exceeding redness of their ears. And with that he came to the dogs and drove away the pack that had killed the stag, and baited his own pack upon the stag. (*Jones, 3*)

Red-eared white animals are the colours of the supernatural beasts in Celtic tradition, and these are in fact the dogs of Arawn, King of Annwn, the Otherworld. Later in the same tale, when Pwyll is spending a year in Annwn in place of Arawn, we learn: 'The year he spent in hunting and song and carousel', and this would seem largely to epitomise the life of a Celtic nobleman when he wasn't fighting or engaging in military exercises.

INSTRUMENTAL AND VOCAL MUSIC

The Celts delighted in music, instrumental and vocal, and at their festive gatherings were entertained by harpists and by players on the *timpan*, and by bards who chanted their repertoire to the company. An illustration of a lyre dating to Hallstatt times appears on a decorated pot from Sopron, Hungary (*16*). The Otherworld, which was as much a part of Celtic everyday life as a foreign country which could be reached after travel, excelled in the sweetness and beauty of its music. The harpist of the Dagda, the great pagan Irish god, could play such magical music that it caused people to laugh, weep, or fall into a blissful sleep. Descriptions of the Otherworld are full of musical references. For example, Bran, when he is tempted into the Otherworld by the goddess, is told by her: 'There is nothing rough or harsh, but sweet music striking on the ear.' In the Irish *Adventure of Cormac*, Cormac is on the rampart of Tara (a regular setting for the beginning of a supernatural encounter), when he sees a warrior draw near with one branch on his shoulder, bearing three golden apples. When it was shaken the branch made such a sweet music that the wounded would fall asleep peacefully, as would the sick when they heard it. Music is a regular feature of the delights of the Otherworld, and music and feasting much enjoyed by the Celts in life. In the story of *The Wasting Sickness of Cú Chulainn*, the Otherworld is described in these terms:

> Before the entrance to the east three trees of purple crystal in which birds sing softly without ceasing to the children from the royal fort . . . there is a tree at the entrance of the enclosure—it were well to match its music—a silver tree on which the sun shines, brilliant as gold. (*Dillon, 121*)

In another Otherworld setting Áne, daughter of Eogabul, comes out of the *síd* (fairy) mound with a bronze lyre in her hand which she is playing. Again, in the same tale (*The Battle of Mag Mucrama*), the two heroes Lugaid mac Con and Eogan go to visit Lugaid's uncle, Art mac Con; and on their way they hear music in a yew tree over a waterfall. They capture the musician. He turns out to be Fer Fí, son of Eogabul; Oilill made him play. He played a sad strain so that everyone wept; he then played a gay tune which reduced his audience to near-hysterical mirth. Next he played a lullaby and his audience fell asleep and did not wake up for 24 hours; by then, of course, he had disappeared. Celtic divinities and dwellers in the Otherworld must excel mortal efforts in all the most desired and desirable accomplishments. As the telling of tales was a deeply cultivated art in the Celtic world, so must the gods be superlative story-tellers; music likewise was (and has remained) one of the basic passions of the Celts, and the Otherworld people must be able to sing and play instrumental music better than any mortal. Another instance of the use of music to bring oblivion to those who heard it occurs in the tale known as *The Destruction of Dind Ríg*. Craiphtine, the Dagda's harper, goes with Labraid, the Prince, to the west where Labraid seeks the hand of the King of Fir Morca's daughter. The harpist plays sleep music so that the girl's mother, who keeps perpetual guard over her daughter, falls asleep in a trance. The lovers are then enabled to sleep together. Next day the mother says to her husband: ' "Get up Scoriath," said she. "Yours is an unlucky sleep. Your daughter breathes like a wife. Listen to her sigh after her lover has left her." '

34 Bronze figure of girl dancing, Neuvy-en-Sullias, Loiret, France

In the *Táin* an interesting reference occurs in which the harpers are supernatural:

Then came the harpers of Caín-bile from Ess Ruaid to entertain them. The men of Ireland thought that they had come from the Ulstermen to spy on them, so the hosts hunted them vigorously for a long distance until they escaped from them, transformed into wild deer, at the standing-stones at Lia Mór. *For though they were called the harpers of Caínbile,* they were men

35 Bronze figure of man dancing, Neuvy-en-Sullias, Loiret, France

of great knowledge and prophecy and magic. (*C. O'Rahilly, 173*)

The Classics also refer to these sung entertainments and musical instruments. Athenaeus, quoting Posidonius, says: 'Their entertainments are called Bards. These are poets who deliver eulogies in song.' Diodorus Siculus, moreover, tells us, of the Celts: 'They have also lyric poets whom they call Bards. They sing to the accompaniment of instruments resembling lyres, sometimes a eulogy and sometimes a satire.' Other musical instruments, such as the pipes are mentioned in the early texts, and trumpets are also known from archaeological sources.

Music, then, instrumental and vocal, was ever important at Celtic social gatherings; at certain of the calendar festivals—at the Festival of Carman, in Wexford, for example, held every three years on 1 August—there were contests in music and poetry.

Horse-racing was also very popular at these open-air celebrations, which often lasted for several days. They were under the auspices of some eponymous deity, usually an earth-goddess, closely bound up with the geographical locality. The goddess Macha, for example, gave her name to the royal fortress where she died in giving birth to twins after racing against the King's horses and winning; the name 'Emain Macha' was probably interpreted as meaning 'Macha's Twins'. Any breach of the divine peace at these great calendar festivals was instantly punishable by death. There are also references to fools and buffoons in the early texts, and it is clear that entertainers of this kind were kept in the noble households to amuse the company, when the less serious pleasures, those that did not involve intellectual effort, were in demand. Strangely enough, there are no references to dancing in the early Irish texts, but this must surely have taken place as in other societies. There are three small representative pieces from the continent which seem to strengthen this supposition. One dates back to the Hallstatt phase, and is the portrait of a woman dancing on a piece of decorated pottery from Sopron (*16*). The other two are bronzes from Neuvy-en-Sullias (Loiret) dating to the Gallo-Roman period. One depicts a naked girl dancing (*34*) and the other a naked man, also dancing (*35*). Another bronze from Saint-Laurent-des-Bois, portrays another naked woman who is in a position that suggests dancing.

FOOD AND DRINK

The Classical writers were very intrigued by these aspects of Celtic life and make many comments on them; their drinking habits made a particularly marked impression on the Mediterranean world. The Celtic capacity for strong liquor in great quantities is one which has persisted throughout their history, often with sorry results (*36*). For example, Athenaeus, quoting Posidonius, says:

> They also use cummin in their drinks . . . the drink of the wealthy classes is wine imported from Italy or from the territory of Marseilles. This is unadulterated, but sometimes a little water is added. The lower classes drink wheaten beer prepared with honey, but most people drink it plain. It is called *corma*. They use a common cup, drinking a little at a time, not more than a mouthful, but they do it rather frequently. The slave serves the cup towards the right not towards the left. (*Tierney, 247*)

A huge feast was prepared by the King, Louernius, in Gaul. This is a convincing echo of what we learn of the preparation of feasts in the early Celtic texts:

> . . . he made a square enclosure one and half miles each way, within which he filled vats with expensive liquor and prepared so great a quantity of food that for many days all who wished could enter and enjoy the feast prepared, being served without a break by the attendants. (*Tierney, 248*)

Such Classical descriptions of the elaborate preparations for a feast, and its long duration, would apply equally to such fateful Irish festivities as that of *Bricriu's Feast*, where we learn that Bricriu made a feast for Conchobar mac Nessa and all the Ulstermen. He gathered food for a whole year, and he built a house at

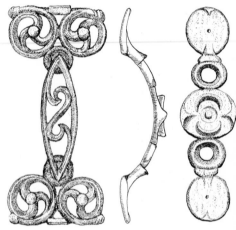

36 Tankard (and bottom of tankard) from Shapwick Heath, Somerset; tankard handle from Trawsfynydd, Merioneth; tankard handle from Waddon Hill, Stoke Abbott, Dorset

Dún Rudraige from which to serve it, even as Louernius constructed a vast square enclosure for his feast. 'Bricriu then prepared a Hero's Portion he had made ready; a milk-fed hog; an ox that had been fed only on milk, grass and corn; and 100 wheaten loaves baked in honey.' Athenaeus also mentions this tradition of the Hero's Portion which is such a feature of the Irish feasts: 'And in former times, when the hindquarters were served up, the bravest hero took the thigh piece, and if another man claimed it they stood up and fought in single combat to the death.' Diodorus Siculus says: 'Beside them are hearths blazing with fire, with cauldrons and spits containing large pieces of meat. Brave warriors they honour with the finest portions of the meat.' A similar type of elaborately prepared feast is mentioned in the story of Lludd and Llefelys in the *Mabinogion* and although it is a late source it is of interest here: 'The third plague was that however much might be the provision and food prepared in the King's courts, *even though it were a year's provision* of meat and drink, never a thing of it would be enjoyed save what was consumed the very first night.' The man who destroys the feast is a supernatural being: the King, keeping watch, sees 'a man of huge stature, clad in strong heavy armour, coming in with a hamper . . . and putting all the provisions and store of meat and drink into the hamper, and making off with it'. This is the man who also, as we have seen in Irish contexts, 'through his magic and enchantment causes everyone to sleep'. He does this 'by much rare pastime and variety of song'.

Diodorus Siculus, like other Mediterranean writers, comments on the quantity drunk at meals by the Celts, and the inevitable ensuing violence. The women took their share too, and there is a very amusing episode in the story *Bricriu's Feast* again. The wives of the heroes are described as leaving the feasting hall with their women 'after drinking much wine'. A great quarrel then ensues amongst them as to who is the most distinguished for every virtue and charm amongst them; and there follows *The Word Battle of the Women of Ulster*.

Wine was frequently drunk at the insular feasts, but the most common intoxicating drink was in fact ale (*cuirm*, Gaulish *corma*). Barley was the grain most often used in its manufacture, but rye, oats and wheat were also utilised. The grain was first converted into malt (*brac* or *braich*); next it was dried in a kiln until it was hard. The ground malt was then made into a mash with water, and this was fermented, boiled and strained until the process was complete. Ale was often made in private houses for family use. There were also professional brewers, *cerbsire* (from Latin *cervisia*, *cervisiarius*, which is itself a borrowing from the Gaulish). Other kinds of ale were drunk, and mead; the name of the goddess Medb means 'she who intoxicates', or 'drunk woman'; mead was perhaps the most characteristic Celtic intoxicating drink. A god invoked on an altar found in Derbyshire and now at Haddon Hall is called Mars Braciaca, 'Mars of the Malt or Ale'. Various other alcoholic drinks were made of berries, etc.; but although whisky has come to be regarded as the typical drink of

37 Cups—Keshcarrigan,Co. Leitrim, Ireland; Rose Ash, Devon. Such cups could be used for domestic or ritual purposes

the Gaels, the first notice of whisky in the Irish Annals would seem to be in AD 1405. Its manufacture was, of course, dependent upon the use of a still, which was not invented before the twelfth century AD. (*37*)

Food and drink seem to have been in good supply among the Celts, at least in the upper classes. Their ready access to salt, of course, enabled stock killed in the autumn to be salted and preserved. Athenaeus refers to the small amount of bread that was eaten, together with large quantities of meat; and the Irish texts bear this out. Fish was also a valued food; the Irish liked to bake salmon with honey and herbs, and Athenaeus, as we have seen, refers to fish baked with salt, vinegar and cummin. In the *Táin*, Cú Chulainn mentions the eating of wild game and herbs. He says to Fergus:

'If a flock of birds pass over the plain, you shall have one wild goose and the half of another. If fish swim into the estuaries, you shall have a salmon with the half of another. You shall have a handful of watercress and a handful of seaweed, and a handful of water-parsnip.'

(*C. O'Rahilly, 182*)

Perhaps the seaweed here mentioned is the edible *carrigeen* still used in Ireland and the Gaelic-speaking islands of Scotland today, as elsewhere, boiled with milk and then strained to form a kind of blancmange. The laver bread eaten in South Wales may also be comparable.

Porridge, as well as bread, was an important secondary item of diet; also dairy produce—milk, butter, cheese, curds. In the *Táin* we learn of Flidais (a goddess of the wilds like the Greek Diana) that 'it was she who every seventh night in that hosting quenched with milk the thirst of all the men of Ireland, King and Queen and prince, poet and learner'. Beef and pork were the favourite foods at feasts. Strabo mentions these foods when he says of the Belgae:

'They have large quantities of food together with milk and all kinds of meat, especially fresh and salt pork.' Diodorus Siculus mentions the great quantities of wine imported into Gaul from the Mediterranean; he actually mentions the transporting of it 'by wagon through the plains'. This is echoed by the description of Medb's catering in the *Táin*. 'Not for all and sundry does Medb intend the liquor which is served to Fer Baeth, for only 50 wagon-loads of it were brought into the camp'—no mean measure, one would feel.

But in spite of the plenty which the Classical writers and the Irish texts make clear the Celts enjoyed, they were very conscious of their figures. A pot-belly was regarded with scorn, and Strabo is so struck by this attitude that he remarks: 'they try not to become stout and fat-bellied, and any young man who exceeds the standard length of a girdle is fined'. Who, one wonders, was responsible for imposing such a fine?

5

The Laws; the 'Fitness of Things';
Learning and Literature

This brings us to the ways in which Celtic society was controlled, and to the laws. The Irish laws are the repository of much ancient and genuine tradition; the Welsh laws are important likewise, but do not reflect quite such an archaic attitude as do those of Ireland. There, the law tracts, in written form, go back to the seventh century AD, with centuries of oral tradition behind them, which takes us to the turn of the Christian era, and probably far back into the Iron Age. The Classical writers also provide certain comments which give us an idea of how Celtic society on the Continent was controlled, and the moral codes which defined its actions.

The Celtic 'ideal' and the Celtic way of life have always been at odds. Ideally, their passion has been for classification, for the elaborate working out and setting down of everything. If their theories had been put into practice in everyday life their subsequent career and history would have been very different from what has, in fact, been the case. They would have formed strong political centres, they would have developed efficient governments both local and central; and the disintegration which is always apparent in Celtic society under pressure from outside would not have occurred. The weakening effect of constant internecine warfare would have been controlled. The disastrous over-indulgence in heady liquors, with its inevitable effect on society as a whole, would have been dealt with. So Celtic law, and the Celtic 'ideal' of behaviour, must always be seen as something desirable, but as something of which a great deal did not in fact apply in everyday life.

THE LAWS

The Irish laws consist of tracts the language of which was deliberately obscure and extremely technical. Until 1920 there was scarcely a single law tract that had been translated with any sort of reasonable accuracy. They were known as the 'Brehon Laws'; the judge was called *breitheamh*. Various scholars paved the way during the nineteenth century for the fine work that is now being done, especially by Professor Binchy, the greatest living expert of the law tracts. His work is making available to us information about early Celtic society (an ideal society, that is, for how far these complicated, obscure edicts were actually put into everyday practice we cannot know) which is of tremendous interest and importance in the task of piecing together the Celtic past and viewing it in human rather than purely academic terms. As Binchy says, there must have been much variation in local custom in the observation of the laws, but even so 'Irish law preserves in a semi-fossilised condition many primitive "Indo-European" institutions of which only faint traces survive in other legal systems derived from the same source.' The law tracts do probably all belong to the seventh century AD in their original written form, though some may be even earlier. All the traditional law of which they consist had been handed down orally in accordance with Celtic universal custom until at least the sixth century. The *filid*, 'prophets, seers', were the traditional custodians of legal lore. As the name 'seers' implies, these men were believed to have supernatural powers and wisdom which puts them on a par with the Druids themselves.

It seems probable that much of this orally transmitted lore was in verse form, which would facilitate learning. Even so, the task would be formidable, and to our present-day book-dependent minds virtually impossible. We know that poems were composed in syllabic metres as early as the seventh century.

The law was a science the secrets of which were closely and zealously guarded by the legal specialists. Even the earliest glossators found the language obscure and unintelligible. The traditional Irish law was, as we have seen, Indo-European in its origin and structure. Binchy says: 'Just as the Old Irish literary language was kept free from dialectal variations by constant intercourse between the men of learning from all parts of the country, so too the close relations that existed between the professional jurists of all schools preserved uniformity in the legal language.' Again, in showing the immense importance of the Irish law tracts in the field of comparative law, Binchy says: 'In this as in other points Irish law shows the characteristics of all early jurist-made systems. Besides the fictions of uniformity and continuity . . . we also find unreal schematism and passion for classification which meet us in the Hindu law books. In other words, the jurists, while their work undoubtedly rested on a basis of actual custom, tended to produce a symmetrical pattern, and in the interests of symmetry they sometimes generalised rules and institutions which in real life had a much more restricted ambit.'

It is extremely valuable to compare ancient Irish law with the Welsh laws, for even the differences are a guide to the extent to which Welsh law had been influenced by Roman legal concepts and terms. Welsh law, however, had the same origins as Irish law, that is in traditional lore which was worked on by later professional jurists. The pagan element in Irish law is strong, and so strong was the feeling against altering anything in these traditional codes of behaviour that Binchy says of them: 'The one important external influence on the system came with the conversion of Ireland to Christianity . . . but compared say with the Anglo-Saxon laws, the Irish tracts show on certain fundamental points an obstinate refusal to conform to Christian teaching.' In Ireland the very primitive system applied, whereby there was no public enforcement of private obligations. In Wales, however, the King—as the representative of the State—intervened in the public enforcement of edicts. In Ireland, distraint played a large role in the enacting of the law. The law tracts have elaborate details about the procedure to be carried out for the distraint of a defendant's property. By this means a person could be made to submit to arbitration. When this was agreed upon, the case was heard in the house of the judge, and both parties had lawyers to act on their behalf. Both parties had to find sureties to guarantee that they would accept and act upon the judge's verdict.

The whole system of Celtic law is too complex and complicated to allow of more than a few passing comments here. One very archaic and interesting feature in the procedure of the law was the use of fasting as a means of winning one's point. In some cases a plaintiff had to fast in front of the defendant's house; this more or less forced the defendant to agree to submitting to arbitration. The fast lasted from sunset to sunrise; the defendant must fast too, and if he wanted food he must offer it to the plaintiff also. He then had to pledge himself to accept arbitration or pay the amount demanded of him. If the defendant ignored the fast, and wouldn't pay, he lost his honour.

An interesting and archaic feature of Irish law was the fact that compensation for a wrong was estimated according to the social rank of the person who had suffered injury, and on the extent of the damage suffered. It was called *lóg-n-enech*, 'honour-price'. An example of the Welsh equivalent of this occurs in the Welsh story of *Branwen Daughter of Llŷr* in the *Mabinogion*. Mathol-wch, the Irish ruler, has had his horses maimed and ruined by Bran's brother, and he must have his due reparation: Bran says:

'Arise, Manawydan, son of Llŷr, and Hefeydd the Tall, and Unig Strong-shoulder, and go after him, and make known to him that he shall have a sound horse for each one of those spoiled. And along with that, as an atonement to him, he shall have a staff of silver that shall be as thick as his little finger and as tall as himself, and a plate of gold as broad as his face. And make known to him what kind of man did that, and how it was against my will that it was done, and it was my brother on the mother's side that did it, and how it would not be easy for me to put him to death or destroy him. But let him come to see me face to face, and I will make peace on those terms he himself may desire.' (*Jones, 28*)

The law tracts deal with such varied affairs as clientship, a fundamental and vital aspect of Celtic social organisation, as we have seen already; the five modes of procedures known as the 'Five Paths of Judgement'; suretyship; distraint; sick-maintenance; marriage—and so on. The laws governing marriage are of especial interest in that they show extremely archaic features which were unaffected by Christian standards. There was no difficulty about terminating a marriage by divorce; there is even some evidence of the custom of marriage for the year. If the two parties wished to terminate their union they were free to do so. Con-cubinage is, moreover, legally acceptable. A man could have a chief wife and a second wife. If the first wife attacked and injured the second wife, the former was not liable for damages; but the husband was entitled to compensation for injury done to her by anyone else. Surprisingly enough, since the institution of con-cubinage was a legal one, the second wife was called *adaltrach*, 'the adultress'. There are ten types of union listed in this tract on marriage, including permanent marriage and a temporary relationship. According to ancient Irish law, a daughter was per-mitted to inherit when there was no son.

THE 'FITNESS OF THINGS'

The Irish had various moral codes and attitudes to social behaviour which are in themselves extremely archaic; barbaric and crude though social intercourse must have been there were strong feelings of honourable conduct and 'the fitness of things'. We have seen how a defendant was expected to behave correctly and honourably when fasted against; there was another primitive practice known as the 'Act of Truth'. The basis of this was belief in the supernatural power of true uttterance. There are several instances of this in the Irish texts. One story tells of a legendary King of Ireland, Lugaid mac Con who ruled for seven years, from Tara. He took Cormac son of Art into his household as his foster-son; on one occasion sheep trespassed on his land and ate the Queen's woad. Lugaid said the sheep were then forfeit because they had trespassed. Although Cormac was only a small boy at the time he disagreed with this verdict: he said the shearing of the sheep, not their seizure was a suitable compensation for the shearing of the woad. As the woad would grow again on the plant, so would the wool grow on the sheep. 'That is the true judgement,' said all, 'and it is the son of the true Prince who has given it.' Immediately the side of the house in which the false judgement had been given, fell down the slope and became known as the 'Crooked Mound of Tara'. After that Lugaid was King in Tara for a year, 'and no grass grew, no leaves, and there was no grain'. After that he was dethroned by his people for he was a 'false prince'.

Again, in the story of the *Adventure of Cormac*, the King is approached by a warrior bearing a magical branch. This he gives to Cormac in return for the granting of three wishes; these turn out to be Cormac's daughter, his son, and finally his wife, Eithne. Cormac can bear no more and sets out with his company to find his family. He loses his followers in a thick mist, and he comes to an enclosure with a house of silver in it, half-thatched with birds' feathers. A handsome warrior meets him and a beautiful girl. In the evening a pig is killed and put on to roast. It could only be roasted if the truth were told for each of the four quarters. The warrior asks the man who had brought the pig to tell a story; he tells how he acquired the pig and also his axe and his stave. He also relates how the pig may be killed and eaten time and time again, but on the next day it would be alive and whole again. One quarter of the pig is then cooked. The warrior himself tells the next true story, and the second quarter of the pig is found to be cooked. The girl then tells a true story, and the third part of the pig is cooked. Cormac then tells his tale, how his wife and his son and his daughter have been taken from him. With this the fourth quarter of the pig is roasted. Once again the motif of the *truth* figures, when a gold cup is brought to the warrior and Cormac is astonished at its beauty. 'There is something more wonderful about it,' said the warrior, 'for if three lies are told over it, it breaks into three parts, and three truths make it whole again.' He tells three untruths and the cup breaks; then he tells three truths which recount the chastity of Eithne and Ailbe and Cairpre since they came there from Tara, and the cup becomes whole again. There are many other examples in the Irish texts of the belief in the power of truth, especially the royal truth. In the story of the birth of Cormac we learn that

> it was well with Ireland in the time of that King. It was not possible to drink the waters of her rivers on account of the spawn of her fish; it was not possible to travel her forests easily on account of the amount of their fruit; it was not easy to travel her plains on account of the amount of her honey, all of which had been granted him from heaven through the *truth* of his princedom. (*Dillon, 251*)

There is also an instance in the metrical *Dindshenchas* which states: 'Corn and milk in every stead, peace and fair weather for its sake, were granted to the heathen tribes of the Greeks, because they preserved truth.' This truth, known as the 'Justice of a Ruler' (*fírinne flátha*), had a parallel in the concept of 'Fair Play' (*fír fer*). This, as we have seen, was the right of a warrior, on challenging an opponent to single combat, to be met by a single opponent alone. Just as truth was considered to be a vital, magical force, so was the concept of taboo held in high esteem in early Celtic society. Taboo could either consist of the necessity of doing something specific or in a certain way in a given set of circumstances, or it could be the complete prohibition from doing a particular thing or things. Violation of one's taboo (geis) could lead to serious consequences and even to death. An example of such a taboo occurs in the *Táin*. Cú Chulainn, having obtained his name as a result of his having killed Culann's hound, must on no account taste the flesh of a dog. His doom is inevitable and his end close when he is tricked by hostile, supernatural forces into eating canine flesh and so violating his prohibition. Violation of one's taboos also led to loss of honour. The importance of honour is seen, for example, when, in the eleventh-century version of the *Táin*, Fer Diad is faced with the awful predicament whereby he must violate the bonds of foster-brotherhood and fight against Cú Chulainn, or endure the satires of the Druids and the satirists. This would result in his dying within nine days if he did not succumb immediately: 'For the sake of his *honour* Fer Diad came with them, for he deemed it better to fall by shafts of valour and prowess and bravery than by shafts of satire and reviling and reproach.'

In the story of *The Destruction of Da Derga's Hostel* we learn that Conaire, who was to become High King of Ireland, and whose father was a supernatural birdman, must never hunt birds. One day Conaire goes to Dublin in his chariot and sees a flock of huge birds which he tries to attack with his sling. They turned into armed men, and he is only protected by one warrior who says: 'I am Nemglan, King of thy father's birds; and thou hast been forbidden to cast at birds, for here there is no one that should not be dear to thee because of his father or mother.' The magic bird-man tells Conaire to go to Tara, for he is predestined to be the next King. The way in which the ancient Irish were supposed to have found out who was to be the rightful High King is interesting, and once again contains the concept of the power of truth:

A bull-feast was prepared by the men of Erin in order to determine their future King; that is, a bull was killed by them and thereof one man ate his fill and drank its broth, and a spell of truth was chanted over him in his bed. Whomsoever he would see in his sleep would be King, and the sleeper would perish if he uttered a falsehood.

(*Cross and Slover*, 97)

An example of the type of prohibitions and observances which appealed to these people then follows. The birdman tells Conaire that there will be a restraint of 'observance' on him when he becomes King:

'Birds shall be privileged, and this shall be your observance always: you shall not pass Tara on your right hand and Bregia on your left; you shall not hunt the crooked beasts of Cerna; and you shall not stay abroad from Tara for nine nights; and you shall not spend the night in a house from which firelight is visible outside after sunset and into which one can see from outside; and three red men shall not go before you into a red man's house; and plunder shall not be taken during your reign; the visit of one woman shall not come into your house after sunset; and you shall not settle a quarrel between two of your subjects.' (*Dillon, 27*)

This is a formidable list of observances and taboos; the allusions in several of them are obscure, and are of course of mythological significance, as we see later in the tale. The inevitable hostile forces which cause the steady violation of these observances, one after the other, set the scene for the King's downfall and doom. Again, Diarmuid, the romantic hero of the Fenian Cycle of Irish tales, whose life-span was bound up with that of a great boar, could on no account take part in a boar-hunt; when he does so, and hunts the huge, mythical boar of Ben Gulban, the boar attacks him, his weapons are useless, and he perishes. Other examples of the power of taboo are found in the same tale. Gráinne, the wife of Finn mac Cumaill, the legendary leader of one of the *fiana* (bands of warriors), has fallen in love with Diarmuid, who is one of Finn's men. He does not wish to be disloyal to his leader, but the girl says: 'I put you under *gessa* of destruction, Diarmuid, unless you take me from this house tonight before Finn and the kings of Ireland arise from their sleep.' Diarmuid asks Finn's son, Oisín, what he must do and Oisín says it is imperative that he observe the *gessa*. Osgar says: 'He is a wretched man who violates his *gessa*.'

Another ancient practice, having its roots in pagan religion, is the custom of swearing on the elements. The Celts feared nothing, even though the earth were to split under them, and the skies to fall down on them. They did not even fear the waves, although they regarded them as hostile, and would sometimes rush into the sea and fight with them and perish in preference to retreating. Cú Chulainn is supposed to have fought with the waves for seven days, and the Classical writers also refer to this custom amongst the Gauls. This foolhardy bravery was legendary and was, of course, partly due to their strong religious beliefs about the continued existence of a person after death, and the cheerful nature of the Otherworld.

When a youth came of an age to take arms he must be ceremonially initiated by receiving a shield and a spear from his lord, and a chariot. This ritual of the 'taking of arms' is described in interesting detail in the *Táin*. Cú Chulainn, although he is far too young to become an initiated warrior, overhears the Druid, Cathbad, telling his pupils that the boy who took arms on that day would be famous, but short-lived. He goes at once to his uncle, Conchobor, and demands weapons.

'What do you ask for little lad?' said Conchobor. 'I wish to take arms,' said the little boy. 'Who advised you lad?' said Conchobor. 'Cathbad the Druid,' said the little boy. 'He would not deceive you lad,' said Conchobor.

Then follows a fascinating account of the warrior-elect rejecting all the ordinary weapons which he is offered, one by one:

Conchobor gave him two spears, a sword and a shield. The little boy took and brandished the arms and shattered them into small pieces. Conchobor gave him two other spears and a shield and a sword. He shook and brandished, flourished and waved them, and shattered them into small pieces. As for the 14 suits of arms which Conchobor had in Emain for the youths and boys—for to whichever of them should take arms Conchobor would give equipment of battle and the youth would have victory in his valour thereafter—that little boy made fragments and small pieces of them all. 'Indeed these weapons are not good father Conchobor,' said the little boy. 'None of them suits me.' Conchobor gave him his own two spears and his shield and his sword. He shook and brandished and flourished and waved them so that the point of spears and sword touched the butt, and yet he did not break the weapons and they withstood him. 'These weapons are good indeed,' said the little boy. 'They are suited to me. I salute the King whose weapons and equipment these are. I salute the land from which he came.' Then Cathbad the Druid came into the tent and spoke. 'Is that boy then taking arms?' said Cathbad. 'He is indeed,' said Conchobor. 'Not by your mother's son would I wish arms to be taken today,' said Cathbad. 'Why is that? Is it not you who advised him?' said Conchobor. 'Not I indeed,' said Cathbad.

After some sharp words, the situation is accepted:

'Come little lad, mount the chariot now for it is the same good omen for you.' He mounted the chariot and the first chariot he mounted, he shook and swayed around him and shattered it to pieces. He mounted the second chariot and shattered it to pieces in the same way. He made fragments of the third chariot also. As for the 17 chariots which Conchobor had in Emain to serve the youths and boys, the little lad shattered them all to pieces and they withstood him not. 'These chariots are not good, father Conchobor,' said the little boy, 'none of these suits me.' 'Where is Ibar mac Riangabra?' asked Conchobor. 'Here,' answered Ibar. 'Harness my own two horses for yon boy and yoke my chariot.' The charioteer harnessed the horses and yoked the chariot. Then the little boy mounted the chariot. He rocked the chariot around him and it withstood him and did not break. 'This chariot is good indeed,' said the little boy, 'and it is my fitting chariot.' (*C. O'Rahilly, 163f.*)

After this fascinating archaic scene of the taking of arms by the future hero, Cú Chulainn persuades the charioteer to take him on a foray. Again, in the story of Mac Dathó's Pig, one of the leading Connacht heroes says: 'It is a custom amongst you Ulstermen that every youth who takes arms among you makes us the goal of his hockey-playing', thus implying that this is especially an Ulster custom. The importance of obtaining a set of arms from the correct person, and the inability of the youth to become an initiated warrior if he did not undergo this ritual, is stressed in the Welsh story of Math son of Mathonwy when Lleu's mother, the goddess Arianrhod, swears a destiny on her son: ' "Well," said she, "I will swear on this boy a destiny that he shall never bear arms until I myself equip him therewith." ' After that, we learn: 'And then Lleu Llaw Gyffes was reared till he could ride every horse and till he was perfected in feature, growth and stature. And then Gwydion saw by him that he was pining for want of horses and arms.' They then find Arianrhod and by magic and treachery they trick her into arming her son with her own hands, thus initiating him to warriorhood: ' "Lady," said he [Gwydion], "arm thou this youth, and I with the maidens, will arm myself." "That will I gladly." And she armed him gladly and at all points.'

THE INAUGURATION OF KINGS

Another very ancient ritual was connected with the selection and inauguration of the Irish kings. We have already looked at the ceremony of the bull-feast by means of which the true king was recognised by the tranced sleeper. The king in Celtic society, as elsewhere, was believed to be a sacred, semi-divine being; his ultimate ancestor was the eponymous tribal god. He was of immense importance to the moral and physical well-being of his people. In order to become ruler of his tribe, or group of tribes, the king-elect must be mated with the concept of sovereignty, clearly a fertility rite. This was known as *banais rígi*, 'royal marriage'. If the king himself should prove to be infertile, so would his people, his stocks and his land. In the story of *The Adventures of Art son of Conn* we learn:

> Conn the Hundred-Fighter son of Fedlimid Rechtmar . . . was once at Tara of the kings, the noble conspicuous dwelling, for a period of nine years, and there was nothing lacking to the men of Ireland during the time of this King, for, indeed, they used to reap the corn three times in the year. (*Cross and Slover, 491*)

However, when the Queen dies and Conn takes to wife an adultress from the Otherworld, one of the Tuatha Dé Danann (People of the Goddess Danu), things are very different. 'Conn and Becuma were a year together in Tara and there was neither corn nor milk in Ireland during that time.'

The king's person must be pure and unblemished in every aspect. In the story of the Second Battle of Moytura, the King of the Tuatha Dé Danann is Nuada, the equivalent of Nodons who was invoked at Lydney on the Severn. In the battle his hand is struck off and an artificial hand of silver is made for him by the god of medicine, Dian Cecht; this is mobile in every joint, but even so, he is now no longer perfect and must relinquish the kingship: 'A contention as to the sovereignty of the men of Ireland arose between the Tuatha Dé and their women; because Nuada, after his hand had been stricken off was disqualified to be king.' If the king, then, failed in any aspect of the qualities it was desirable he should possess, he must go, no matter how good a ruler he might be, or how beloved of his people. If his people made a decision which displeased him he must abide by it in any aspect of his personal life, even if it went against his deepest inclinations. There is a moving passage in the story of *Pwyll* in the *Mabinogion* which, although late, illustrates this. Pwyll has married Rhiannon, in origin a goddess, and they

> ruled the land prosperously that year and the next. And in the third year the men of the land began to feel heaviness of heart at seeing a man whom they loved as much as their lord and foster-brother without offspring; and they summoned him to them. The place where they met was Preseleu in Dyfed. 'Lord,' said they, 'we know you are not of an age with some of the men of this country, but our fear is lest you have no offspring of the wife you have; and so, take

another wife of whom you may have offspring. You will not last for ever', said they, 'and *though you desire* to remain thus, we will not *suffer it from you.* (*Jones, 17*)

The mating of the king at his inaugural rites was a symbol of his deep influence on fertility, both his own virility and that of everything else with which he must concern himself. There are many allusions, thinly disguised, in the Irish texts to the mating of the king-elect with a woman who later reveals herself to be the Sovereignty of Ireland, the territorial goddess. Several of the tales concern the adventures of a prince and his brothers who meet with a hideous hag. She asks each one in turn to have intercourse with her. Each one refuses with horror and abuse except the 'true' king, and he agrees. As he takes the repulsive creature in his arms she becomes the most beautiful girl man could ever conceive of. She then confers the sovereignty of Ireland upon him. She is in fact the immortal mate of the king who is himself to some degree immortal. In the story of *Baile in Scáil* (*The Phantom's Frenzy*), in which the phantom turns out to be the god Lugh, Conn of the Hundred Battles is invited to visit the domains of the god. There was a house with a ridge-pole of white gold, and they entered it. In a crystal chair a girl was seated; she had a crown of gold on her head. The phantom was also seated on his throne, and his beauty astounded all who saw it. The phantom spoke to them and said:

'I am not a phantom and I am not a spectre, and I have come after death to be honoured by you, and I am of the race of Adam. My name is Lugh son of Ethniu son of Smretha . . . and I have come to tell you the span of your sovereignty and of that of every prince that will come to you in Tara for ever.' (*Dillon, 1948, 109*)

The lovely girl is, of course, the Sovereignty of Ireland; she gives Conn food and ale. This is one of the many indications that the gods were believed to be deeply concerned with the choice and inauguration of the Irish kings. There is some very good evidence —although it has been hotly denied by some scholars—of the custom of the mating of the king during his inaugural rites with the territorial goddess in the form of a pure white mare. In India, where the practice was also known, the mating was symbolic; whereas in Ireland it was at one time evidently fully carried out, later becoming symbolic. There is a rite described by Giraldus

Cambrensis as apparently still pertaining in his day in one of the northern kingdoms, which is clearly a survival of this practice. It has been thought to have been a disgusting and shameful invention on the part of the Welsh writer in order to discredit the Irish. But early evidence is strong enough to make it quite clear that the observations of Giraldus were correct, even though he did not appreciate their ancient ritual origins. He describes the performance as a 'barbarous and abominable' rite. The tribe in question was an Ulster one, and the ritual was still practised in AD 1185 if the report given to Giraldus was correct. In front of the assembled tribe a white mare was led in, and the king went to it on all fours and mated with it.

> He who is to be inaugurated not as a prince but as a brute, not as a king but as an outlaw, comes before the people on all fours, confessing himself a beast with no less impudence than imprudence. The mare being immediately killed and cut in pieces and boiled, a bath is prepared for him from the broth. Sitting in this he eats the flesh which is brought to him, the people standing round and partaking of it also. He is also required to drink of the broth in which he is bathed, not drawing it in any vessel, nor even in his hand, but lapping it with his mouth. These unrighteous things being duly accomplished, his royal authority and dominion are ratified.
>
> (*Gir. Camb., Top. Hib., iii, xviii*)

The rite is paralleled by the Hindu horse-sacrifice on a similar occasion—here, however, it was the king's wife who united herself with the powers of fertility, not the king himself. The regular form of inauguration of a king, however, seems to have been the presentation to him of a white rod, as a token of kingship. This was given to the High King by his leading vassal king. The High King himself presented the symbolic rod to a vassal king.

Symbolic and magical stones were also connected with the royal inaugural ceremonies. According to antiquarian tradition the well-known Lia Fáil, 'Stone of Fál', for example, cried out when any legitimate King of Ireland stood on it. When the High King, Conn of the Hundred Battles, stepped on to it, it uttered a number of shrieks. These were interpreted by the Druids as representing the number of Conn's descendants who would be kings of Ireland. Various other sacred stones were used at these inaugurations, testifying to the widespread Celtic belief in the supernatural powers of certain stones.

All the evidence shows that, as in many ancient societies, the king or chieftain was regarded among the Celts as a semi-sacred being, beloved of the gods if chosen correctly, displeasing to them if wrongly selected; with consequent good or deleterious effects on the land and its fertility and the well-being of the tribe in general. His life was hemmed in with taboo. His inauguration and his subsequent activities were based on ritual and propitiation and the interpretation of the demands and preferences of the gods. The failing, ageing king would probably meet his death in a ritual manner before the loss of his powers could affect the fertility of his domain. There are hints of this in the early texts, but nothing so utterly pagan and repugnant to Christianity could receive anything more than overt suggestion by the monkish scribes.

LEARNING AND LITERACY

Throughout our survey of the everyday life of the Celtic peoples we have frequently had occasion to mention these aspects of the Celtic way of life. This is because they formed the foundation of all Celtic thought and action. We can devote this section to a brief look at them not merely as incidental features in the sum total of daily life and behaviour. We must glance at the *formal* nature of learning and its transmission, and the relationship between master and pupil and the methods of communication between the two. We are very limited here, because the scope of this study does not take us into the fully Christian period, whereas the writings in the vernacular originate in Christian times. We have no native records of the literatures of the Celts in Europe, although we may suspect from Classical sources that oral literary tradition must have been at least as rich as that of the insular Celts.

As a people, the Celts have always had a strong natural feeling for learning and intellectual exercise. It is an aspect of their temperament that has amazed and intrigued outsiders who have come into contact with them, and have found such a marked contrast between their frequently crude and often careless domestic arrangements and the refinement and elegance of their use of language and appreciation of linguistic subtlety. Even in modern times this teachability and appreciation of mental pursuits amazes people. Dr Johnson, in his famous tour of the Highlands of Scotland, comments on it constantly; and one can today carry on a conversation about literature and languages and philosophy with a Gaelic or Irish or Welsh postman or cottar which would put many a university-educated outsider to shame. The Celtic nobles may have spent much of their time in drunken revelry; the *literati* too were often drunk, with words, and they loved to use them in every subtle kind of manner, and give a variety of meanings to their utterances. They delight in alternating between terse, sharp, economical statements and flowery, adjective-packed, verbose descriptions, often to the point of tediousness. About Gaulish literature we have no information, but there is good reason to believe that it was as complex, as vital and as varied as the written insular material and the surviving oral tradition in the Celtic areas shows was the case for the British Isles.

The habit of praising the chieftain, so common in the vernacular tales, was also practised in Gaul. As we have seen, Athenaeus, quoting Posidonius, says:

> The Celts have in their company, even in war, as well as in peace, companions whom they call parasites. These men pronounce their praises before the whole assembly, and before each of the chieftains in turn. Their entertainers are called Bards. These are the poets who deliver eulogies in song. (*Tierney, 248*)

Even today, in the oral tradition of the Gaelic-speaking Highlands and Islands of Scotland, people remember and sing eulogies composed for past chieftains whose way of life cannot have been very dissimilar from that of the Iron Age chieftains with whom we are concerned here. Athenaeus, again quoting Posidonius, tells the story of the chieftain Louernius, who made a great feast:

> A Celtic poet who arrived too late met Louernius and composed a song magnifying his greatness and lamenting his own late arrival. Louernius was very pleased, and asked for a bag of gold and threw it to the poet who ran beside his chariot. The poet picked it up and sang another song saying that the very tracks made by his chariot on the earth gave gold and largesse to mankind. (*Tierney, 248*)

Diodorus Siculus says of the Gauls:

> In conversation they use very few words and speak in riddles, for the most part hinting at things and leaving a great deal to be under-

stood. They frequently exaggerate, with the aim of extolling themselves and diminishing the status of others. They are boasters and
threateners, and given to bombastic self-dramatisation, and yet they
are quick of mind and with good natural ability for learning.

All this fits in very well with what we know from written Irish
sources; the deliberately obscure language of the early law tracts
we have already commented upon.

The Irish *literati* were reputed to have a secret language known
as *bérla na filied*, only understood by those initiated into its secrets.
It is interesting that the hero Cú Chulainn was accomplished in
this, as was his wife Emer. Celtic heroes and heroines were no
mere physical beauties with empty heads. Their mental gifts must
be as fine and keen as must their bodies be beautiful and unblemished, according to the Celtic aesthetic preference. Strabo
says of the Gauls: 'On the other hand, if won over by gentle
persuasion, they willingly devote their energies to useful pursuits
and even take to a literary education.' Of the Druids, Caesar says:
'It is said they commit to memory immense amounts of poetry.
And so some of them continue their studies for 20 years. They
consider it improper to commit their studies to writing.' So we can
only deduce a flourishing oral literature of prose and poetry and
cult legend in Celtic Europe from such chance remarks, and from
the insular texts.

In Ireland, although the bard with his praise-poetry for the
kings and nobles was an important person in society, the *fili* was
even more eminent. This word came to mean 'poet', but in origin
it had more of the meaning of 'seer'; and at one time the *fili* may
have had some of the attributes of the Druid. The *fili* could practise
divination by means of various rites. He was also accredited with
the supernatural powers of blemishing, or causing death, by
satire. So originally, in the fully pagan society, the *fili* must have
had religious as well as secular functions. It took him up to 12
years to learn his craft. We do not know whether these highly
specialised poets and wise men usurped some of the Druids'
functions after the coming of Christianity, or if this took place at
an earlier date. The *filid*, like the bards, were trained in schools.
As Jackson points out, the training, which was oral and based on
the question and answer principle, was done by the master
intoning what had to be learnt and the pupils then repeating it all
together. This is implied by the fact that the Old Irish verb 'to

teach', *for-cain*, does in fact mean 'to sing over'. The *filid* learned to compose in the various poetic metres. They would have had to master things like the genealogies, antiquarian traditions and the heroic tales, as well as their own magical accomplishments. It is an astonishing fact that these bardic schools continued to flourish in Ireland until the seventeenth century, when the old Gaelic world broke up under external pressure. The pupils lay on their beds in a dark room composing verses which were later corrected by the master. The qualified *fili* not only praised his own lord, he was free to travel and praise other nobles; and he expected to be handsomely rewarded for his panegyric utterances.

The *ollam* had a high rank in law, being the highest class of poet. He could legally travel with a retinue of 24 men, and expect all to receive the hospitality of the host. His rank in law was in fact equal to that of a petty king, an indication of his power. The poets were free to travel and were protected by law; but their greatest protection was in fact their power of satire, and the people's belief in it, and fear of its results. We have seen how in the *Táin*, when Medb wishes Fer Diad to fight in single combat against his friend and foster-brother, Cú Chulainn:

> Then Medb sent the Druids and satirists and harsh bards for Fer Diad, that they might make against him three satires to stay him and three lampoons, and that they might raise on his face three blisters, shame, blemish and disgrace, so that he might die before the end of nine days if he did not succumb at once. (*C. O'Rahilly, 212*)

Again, in the *Táin*, we learn of the protection and free access to different tribal regions granted to the *literati*; Cú Chulainn asks Ibar the charioteer if he knows why the ford is called Áth na Foraire:

> 'I do indeed,' said Ibar, 'a goodly warrior of the Ulstermen is always there, keeping watch and ward so that no warriors or strangers come to Ulster to challenge them to battle, and so that he may be the champion to give battle on behalf of the whole province. And if poets leave Ulstermen and the Province unsatisfied, that he may be the one to give them treasures and valuables for the honour of the province. If poets come into the land, that he may be the man who will be their surety until they reach Conchobor's couch, and that their poems and songs may be the first to be recited in Emain on their arrival. (*C. O'Rahilly, 165*)

So the poets and prophets were honoured; and the noblemen would go a long way to avoid offending them, thereby winning their reputation for generosity and fit behaviour.

The Druids taught in schools also, about druidic lore, how to interpret the omens, and various other aspects of their calling. In the *Táin* we learn that 'Cathbad the Druid was teaching his pupils to the north-east of Emain, and eight pupils of the class of druidic learning were with him. One of them asked his teacher what omen and presage was for that day, whether it was good or whether it was ill.'

There is evidence for a limited literacy amongst the learned and merchant classes. The Classics imply this; Caesar actually states: 'They consider it improper to entrust their studies to writing, although they use the Greek alphabet in nearly everything else, in their public and private accounts.'

There are inscriptions from south Gaul in Gaulish, but using Greek characters; there are also the Celtic coin inscriptions, the Coligny Calendar, discussed below, and odd items such as the iron sword from Switzerland, dating to the first century B C, having the name Korisios in Greek characters stamped on it (*1*); there is also some indication of a limited literacy amongst certain of the Celts at least by the presence of graffiti in Roman letters dating to the period before the Roman Conquest, on some pottery from Colchester, the Belgic *oppidum* of Camulodunum. The Druids were much concerned with calendrical computation; the various Classical writers comment on this, and Pliny tells us that the Druids measured their months and years by the moon:

> The mistletoe, however, is found but rarely upon the oak; and when found, is gathered with due religious ceremony, if possible on the sixth day of the moon (for it is by the moon that they measure their months and years and also their *ages* of 30 years). (*Kendrick, 89*)

Their mastery of calendrical calculation is evidenced by the discovery, in fragmentary condition, of the remarkable Coligny Calendar; this provides vital information about one aspect of Celtic intellectual achievement. It consists of the remains of a huge bronze plate, engraved with a calendar of 62 consecutive lunar months. The language used is Gaulish, many of the words used occur in abbreviated form, but the numerals and the lettering are Roman. It reckons by nights, in true Celtic fashion, and marks

38 Part of the Coligny Calendar, a bronze plate found at Bourg, Ain, France

lucky and unlucky days. Of this habit of reckoning Caesar says: 'For this reason they count periods of time not by the number of days but by the number of nights; and in reckoning birthdays and the new moon and new year their unit of reckoning is the night followed by the day.' There are certain place-names which occur on the Continent, as well as personal names, the words on the Coligny Calendar (*38*), and some inscriptions in Gaulish which testify to a certain literacy in the native language and, although they indicate little of the grammatical structure, they do convey some idea of the Celtic sound-system.

The earliest Irish written documents, which really fall outwith our scope here, are inscriptions in an alphabet known as the *ogam* script (*39*). This is based on the Latin alphabet; each letter is named from a plant or tree. For example, C is *coll*, 'holly'; D is *daur*, 'oak', and so on. It would seem to have been developed in Ireland in immediately pre-Christian times. It was, as Dillon points out, a ceremonial script; it is only found on commemorative stones. In the heroic tales it is connected with funerary rites, or with mysterious messages. In the *Táin* we learn that:

Sualtaim went with warnings to the Ulstermen. Cú Chulainn went into the wood and cut a prime oak sapling, whole and entire, with one stroke and standing on one leg and using but one hand and one eye, he twisted it into a ring and put an ogam inscription on the peg of the ring and put the ring round the narrow part of the standing stone at Árd Cuillen. He forced the ring down until it reached the thick part of the stone. After that Cú Chulainn went to his tryst. . . . The nobles of Ireland came to the pillar stone and began to survey the grazing which the horses had made round the stone and to gaze at the barbaric ring which the royal hero had left round the stone. And Ailill took the ring in his hand and gave it to Fergus and Fergus read out the ogam inscription that was in the peg of the ring and told the men of Ireland what the inscription meant. And as he began to tell them he made the lay:

'This is a ring. What is its meaning for us? What is its secret message? And how many put it here? Was it one man or many?'

(C. O'Rahilly, 150)

Some ogam inscriptions are pre-Christian, some Christian; we cannot date them to a period earlier than the end of the fourth century AD. The commemorative ones tend to go back to an eponymous divine ancestor. Some 300 inscriptions are known.

The vernacular literatures of Ireland and Wales belong to the fully Christian period in their written form. And although at present a few poems in Ireland do go back to as early as the sixth century AD while the famous British (or Scottish) poem, the *Gododdin*, may date in manuscript form to the late eighth century AD all these, as literature, are too late for comment here. We are concerned only with the world of the pagan Celts, an essentially non-literate world as far as the transmission of traditional lore was concerned, but a world deeply conscious of, and preoccupied with, literature and intellectual concepts; but the transmission of these ideas and native traditions was essentially oral, perhaps to an even greater extent in Ireland than elsewhere. However, a considerable amount of the oral repertoire of the pagan Celtic world, committed to writing as it was in Christian times and in a fully Christian milieu, does contain pagan motifs and mythological legends and descriptions of a material culture which are essentially barbaric and non-Christian; for this reason we use the early texts comparatively with the other sources of evidence for the pagan Celts to give us some additional information about the Iron Age world. But as *literature* they come outside the range of our investigation. It is their contents, rather than their form and structure that concern us here. There was no literature as we think of it in the

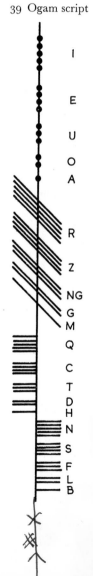

39 Ogam script

pagan Celtic world: only an oral literature, the richness and complexity of which can hardly be comprehended by us today, living as we do in our world of books and radio, of television, and with computers to do our reckoning for us.

The rich literary tradition of Ireland, then, takes much of its inspiration, as well as a good deal of its matter, from the pagan world; but it belongs in form and transmission to a later, Christian era, rather than to the world of the La Tène chieftains with their privileged circle of Druids and bards, seers and harpers, *filid* and 'men of art'. The learning and the literature of the early Celts was based on the oral tradition; the master sang what was to be learned, the class intoned it until it knew it off by heart; the Druids consulted the omens for their knowledge, not the books. And although the literature was orally transmitted, there is little evidence for improvisation. Even in a present-day Gaelic-speaking gathering, any change in a single word by the story-teller is noticed and commented on by the avid listeners, as familiar with the tale as the teller himself.

The early Celts were non-literate; and it is this great background of oral knowledge, of intricately-worked-out legal codes, of calendrical skill and of tale and poetry, which made the imposition of Christianity on a society already so highly organised in this respect, so comparatively easy and painless.

6

The Religion of the Pagan Celts

If these last chapters of the book are, proportionately, the longest, it is because religion and art—together with learning—made up so much of the total background to the life of the Celtic aristocracy. We have considerably less knowledge of the lower social orders and their day to day lives, spiritual and material; much of this can only be surmised. The literatures of the early Celtic world, alike with the Classical comments on the barbarians, are only concerned with the thoughts and activities of the learned and landed members of the community. The tangible remains of the Celts, as revealed by the discipline of archaeology, are also illustrative of the more prosperous aspects of their society—of the graves, the weapons and personal ornaments, the horse-trappings; of the homes and fortifications of the wealthy aristocracy. The non-free members of the populace and the lowest of the free orders, had few, if any, vessels of pottery, or objects made from metal to leave behind them; their humble dwelling-places would require little in the way of permanent foundations which would leave post-holes and so on to edify the archaeologists. The situation would not seem to have been so very different in the Highlands of Scotland in the eighteenth century, for writing of his tour there with Dr Johnson, Boswell remarks:

> When we had advanced a good way by the side of Lochness, I perceived a little hut, with an old looking woman at the door of it. I thought here might be a scene that would amuse Dr Johnson; so I mentioned it to him. 'Let's go in,' said he. We dismounted, and we and our guides entered the hut. It was a wretched little hovel of earth only, I think, and for a window had only a small hole, which was stopped with a piece of turf, that was taken out occasionally to let in light. In the middle of the room or space which we entered, was

a fire of peat, the smoke going out at a hole in the roof. She had a pot upon it, with goat's flesh, boiling.

One feels such a scene could have been witnessed in the Iron Age world, and the lower orders must have known just such a humble, impermanent dwelling, and paucity of material goods. In spite of the essentially limited nature of the evidence for anything other than the aristocratic element in Celtic society, there are certain factors—especially those connected with the survival of the Celtic culture in the periphery of the Western world—which suggest that despite the lowly nature of their dwellings and lack of possessions, the humbler members of the community possessed, in common with their modern counterparts, and with their social superiors, a deep reverence for the arts, for intellect and for learning; and for the gods and the ritual attendant upon them. They may, and undoubtedly did, invoke local spirits and elemental forces which they believed to control their own small destinies, over and above the great deities of the upper classes and the high-born priests who interceded with the gods on behalf of the tribe in general. They may well have observed special ritual days, and have performed sacred rites known only to themselves and those of their social standing; they may have sacrificed in times of need in their own particular way, and have had firm faith in the power of the water of very local venerated wells to aid the sick or make fertile the sterile. But all the evidence points to their having also participated in their *tribal* capacity in the great ritual gatherings, and to their presence at the vital sacrifices upon which the well-being of the people depended. Caesar himself comments:

> When a private person or a tribe disobeys their ruling they ban them from attending sacrifices. This is their harshest penalty. Men placed under this ban are treated as impious wretches; all avoid them, fleeing their company and conversation, lest their contact bring misfortune upon them; they are denied legal rights and can hold no official dignity. (*Tierney, 271*)

What we know of the present-day cottar and crofter in the remaining Celtic regions does then suggest very strongly that their similarly placed ancestors in the pagan Celtic world had a comparable reverence for the mind and the spirit and all their cultural manifestations—a regard which the humble nature of their material circumstances could in no way influence. For labourer and landowner alike the great gods and semi-divine heroes could only have been conceived of in certain intellectual terms, limited though these may have been. Strength and magic they might have, but intellectual powers were vital. The buffoon, the empty-headed handsome hero, the lovely but stupid goddess, these could not have been tolerated in Celtic society at any level. It has often been suggested that the Dagda was a sort of amiable fool, but there is no real evidence for this. Hostile or humorous *literati* bent on reducing a powerful tribal god to the status of a good-natured buffoon could be responsible for such an impression.

The gods and heroes alike were thought of as being on the whole intellectual, deeply versed in the native learning, poets and prophets, story-tellers and craftsmen, magicians, healers, warriors. In short, equipped generally with every quality admired and desired by the Celtic peoples themselves. They were the divine reflection of all that was enviable and unattainable in a human society.

Religion and superstition thus played a fundamental and profound role in the *everyday* life of the Celts. This is, in fact, the key to any understanding of their distinctive character. Caesar says: 'The whole Gallic people is exceedingly given to religious superstition.' All the evidence supports his statement, and we have little need to seek for underlying political bias here. Perhaps even more than other ancient peoples, the Celts were so completely engrossed with, and preoccupied by, their religion and its  expression that it was constantly and positively to the forefront of their lives. The deities and the Otherworld in which they were believed to reside—when they were not intruding upon the world of men as they frequently did—were not mere academic concepts to be remembered at convenient intervals, on feast-days or when a great victory was to be celebrated, at times of national sacrifice, or distress, either tribal or personal, or when something special was desired. They were ever-present, sometimes menacing, always dangerous. When placated, helpful and generous; when offended, vengeful and without mercy. The everyday life of the Celts included the supernatural equally with the natural, the divine with the mundane; for them the Otherworld was as real as the tangible physical world and as ever-present.

It must be stressed from the start that a knowledge of pagan Celtic religion is no easy thing to acquire. Just as the elements from which it is ultimately derived are diverse and elusive, so is the source material for its study varied—unequal in both quality and time; scant and scattered. The whole of the everyday life of the early Celts, the nature of their social attitudes and their tribal structure, their laws and their distinctive art style must be studied in order to further an understanding of the rules and prohibitions which governed their religious behaviour. Early Celtic society was essentially decentralised. The tribal system which characterised it produced very local developments, but always within the wider whole. We know that at the height of their power the Celts occupied very considerable tracts of Europe. Their territory stretched, as we have seen, from the Atlantic in the west to the Black Sea in the east; from the Baltic in the north to the Mediterranean in the south. But, in spite of these tremendous divergencies and the long period of time that elapsed between the formation of the recognisable Celtic world and the year AD 500—in spite of tribal peculiarities and preferences, and probably variation of linguistic dialects and economic systems throughout the whole region, as well as between the Continent and the British Isles—in spite of all this, it is indeed possible to speak in terms of *Celtic* religion, though not of a religious *system*; of a similarity of ritual, a uniformity of cult types; of the same blending of natural and supernatural—all these indicate a basic religious homogeneity which is indeed remarkable.

There are various sources of evidence for pagan Celtic religion, and the fragmentary nature of these is made additionally hazardous by the problem of relating one to the other and demonstrating any convincing link. However, by bringing a variety of disciplines and comparanda to bear, a fairly general idea of the nature of Celtic belief and ritual can be obtained. First of all we must inquire into the main sources for pagan Celtic religion. The most important source of all is lacking—texts written in their own language or in a Classical tongue by the Celts themselves, which would provide the Celtic viewpoint from *within* the society. These simply do not exist. The Celts did not care to commit their laws, genealogies, history, poetry or religious precepts to writing. They regarded them in a semi-sacred light. Some Celts certainly used Greek for business transactions, as we have seen. There is no doubt, however, that the Celts were unwilling that their traditional lore and learning should become available to blasphemous outsiders; the secrets were jealously guarded by those responsible for their preservation and perpetuation. Moreover, the cultivation of an oral memory is one of the most characteristic features of their culture, and still persists and is held in high honour in the Celtic-speaking areas of the modern world.

All these traditional disciplines, then, were required to be handed on orally from master to pupil, from generation to generation. A Druid-elect, we now know, took some 20 years to master and fully assimilate the secrets of his calling. Likewise, in Ireland, a *fili* ('poet', 'seer'), was required to study for from seven to 12 years in order to master orally the complex disciplines with which he was concerned. The oral tradition and its persistence is one of the most striking characteristics of the culture of the Celts. Ireland has no classical texts to aid its archaeological repertoire in a study of religion, but it has its vernacular literature, as has Wales; and although the actual writing down of the tales and mythological episodes is comparatively late—from the seventh to eighth centuries on—they clearly refer to events of a much greater archaism than the period in which they were given literary form.

SOURCES

As a result of this lack of direct textual evidence on the part of the Celts themselves, we are driven to seek elsewhere for such information as we can assemble. This is, in the main, threefold and must be handled with great caution. When we find that the various sources of information combine to support each other we are on comparatively safe ground.

In one sense, the most reliable of the three sources is archaeology, but this is essentially limited and lacks the detail provided by the written word. Another, the Classical writers, provides fascinating commentaries on aspects of Celtic religious life; but it cannot always be clear to what period they are referring or whether they are going by hearsay alone, or have had actual experience of the practices they record. The remaining source, the vernacular literatures, are the most dramatic and detailed evidence for pagan Celtic religion; but they are so heavily overlaid both by interpolations on the part of the Christian scribes and by international folk-tale and folklore motifs that they require a lot of judicious handling, and the temptation to interpret freely must be firmly checked. By and large, there is enough evidence for Celtic religion to allow a fairly comprehensive and convincing picture to be constructed from the numerous fragments of information at our disposal. And it is possible, to some extent, to determine what is universal in their religious attitudes and what is essentially their own peculiarly Celtic and individual mode of expressing belief in the supernatural powers.

Having seen something of the nature of the source material, and having ascertained that the Celts did in fact have a religion of which something can be envisaged by using these diverse disciplines and materials, we now want to know something of the religion itself—what is most typical about it, what are some of the fundamental features and cults?

The Celts had places in which they invoked the deities, and they also had priests to intercede with the gods on behalf of the tribe. They had their sacred days and festive periods, and cult legends which explained the origins of these. As these are the aspects of religious practice upon which all else depends, it will be useful to try to get some general idea of them first, before proceeding to consider the actual gods and goddesses themselves.

TEMPLES, SHRINES AND SANCTUARIES

In recent years archaeological excavation has revealed certain structures which have completely changed earlier ideas about the nature of pagan Celtic temples and places of worship. It had been generally thought that, with a very few exceptions such as the sophisticated temples built in the Mediterranean fashion at Roquepertuse and Entremont near the mouth of the Rhône, the Celts did not use anything in the nature of built temples for their religious activities. The priests, the Druids, were believed to have carried out their ritual practices and to have made offering to the gods only in natural places, without structures—in groves of trees made sacred by long association with the gods, for example, or beside sacred wells whose waters contained distinctive virtues and through which access to the patron deity could be gained. Later, under the aegis of the Christian Church, these local divinities were replaced by local saints, often bearing the same name as their pagan originals; and the well-worship continued undisturbed. The tops of venerated hills, too, or the precincts of burial mounds associated with some divine ancestor were also favoured places: but built structures were not believed to have been used. Now, a series of field monuments is beginning to be recognised and dis-

closed which represent the constructed sanctuaries of the pagan
Celts. Many of these have been found in Europe, and some in
Britain. Further investigations and excavations, and the re-
examination of the results of earlier excavations will undoubtedly
bring many more to light and, in some instances, will indicate that
erroneous interpretations of the purpose of such structures has in
fact concealed their real significance; there are probably many
more in the British Isles, for example, than would at present
appear to be the case.

These structures are rectilinear earthworks, known in Europe
as *viereckschanzen,* 'square enclosures'. In the main they seem to
date to the first century B C, and culturally to go back to the square
Iron Age burial enclosures and forward to the Gallo-Roman

40 Plans of 'viereckschanzen', pagan earthwork precincts

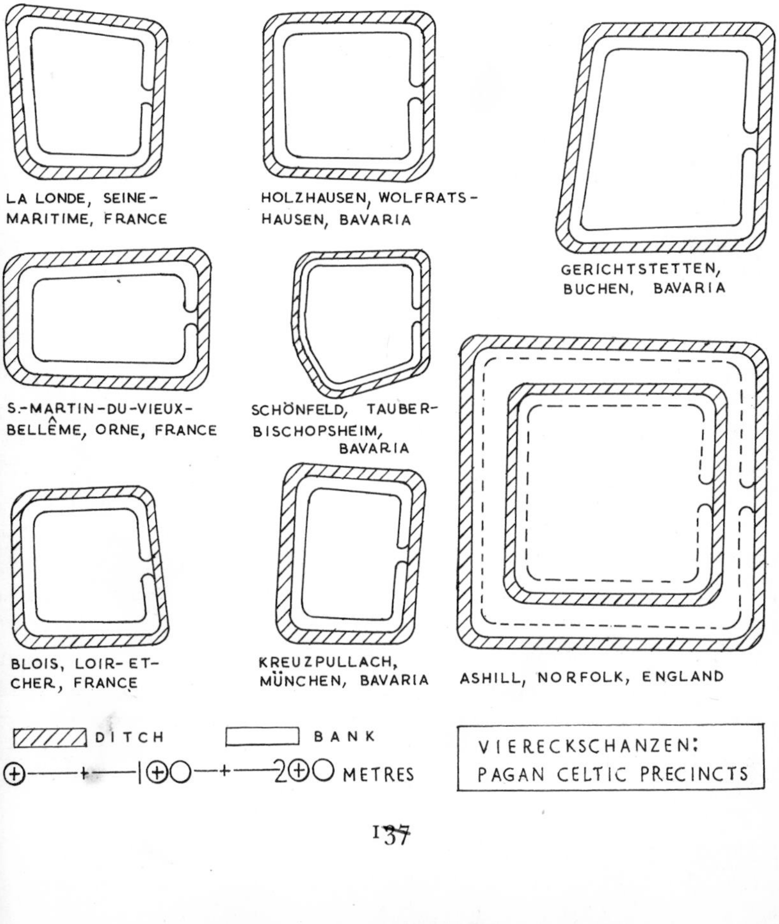

LA LONDE, SEINE-
MARITIME, FRANCE

HOLZHAUSEN, WOLFRATS-
HAUSEN, BAVARIA

GERICHTSTETTEN,
BUCHEN, BAVARIA

S.-MARTIN-DU-VIEUX-
BELLÊME, ORNE, FRANCE

SCHÖNFELD, TAUBER-
BISCHOPSHEIM,
BAVARIA

BLOIS, LOIR-ET-
CHER, FRANCE

KREUZPULLACH,
MÜNCHEN, BAVARIA

ASHILL, NORFOLK, ENGLAND

▨▨▨ DITCH   ▭ BANK

⊕——+——|⊕O—+—2⊕O METRES

VIERECKSCHANZEN:
PAGAN CELTIC PRECINCTS

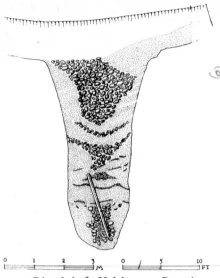

temples, built usually of stone and square or circular on plan. Some *viereckschanzen* contain pits or offering-shafts, like the remarkable examples at Holzhausen, in Bavaria (*40, 41*). Here two earthworks, set close together, were found to have timber palisades underneath; the enclosures contained deep shafts in which traces of offerings were found, including flesh and blood, presumably sacrificial. In one of these enclosures traces of a timber-built temple were found.

41 Ritual shaft, Holzhausen, Bavaria

Many deep shafts, mostly circular in section, have been found in Britain, some of them exposed in cuttings when the railways were being created in the last century. Much damage and waste resulted from unscientific recording and digging, and traces of associated buildings or earthworks were often ignored, or so imprecisely described as to render virtually useless most of the information given. The shaft excavated at Wilsford, Wiltshire (Ashbee, 1963) has been dated by radio-carbon to the fourteenth century B C, indicating that this type of religious structure and focus for ritual had an ancestry which pre-dated the Celts themselves by a long way. This gives rise to new thoughts on the origins of the Celtic priests, the Druids, who certainly used this kind of shrine in Celtic times.

An oblique reference in Athenaeus, which we have already considered in another context, is suggestive of these rectangular religious enclosures.

Posidonius again, when telling of the wealth of Louernius, father of Bituis, who was dethroned by the Romans, says that in an attempt to win popular favour he rode in a chariot over the plains distributing gold and silver to the tens of thousands of Celts who followed him. Moreover *he made a square enclosure* one and a half miles each way, within which he filled vats with expensive liquor, and prepared so great a quantity of food that for many days all who wished could enter and enjoy the feast prepared, being served without a break by the attendants. (*Tierney, 248*)

We know from Irish sources that Celtic ritual gatherings were accompanied by lavish feasting and drinking, and that games and races and marketing of wares played an integral part in the solemn religious festivals. One of the most exciting and impressive discoveries made in recent years was the excavation in 1956 of a remarkable Celtic sanctuary at Libenice, near Kolin, in Bohemia (42). A long ditched and banked enclosure was found to contain evidence for sacrifice, infant and animal, a human skull from which libations may have been poured, a platform for sacrifice, pits containing bones, and great quantities of ritually smashed pottery; two twisted bronze torcs would seem originally to have encircled the necks of two great wooden idols of which only the post-holes were found to have survived. The burial of an elderly woman, perhaps the priestess of the shrine, was found, together with brooches, pottery, and other objects which make the sanctuary datable to the third century BC. A much earlier, but comparable structure was found at Aulnay-aux-Planches in the Marne; it belongs to the Urnfield culture, and is datable to the eleventh century BC. It is also possible that the long enclosure known as the 'Banqueting Hall' on the Hill of Tara, one of the most important sacred places in early Ireland, is a further example of some such structure. These various enclosures are followed, on the one hand, by the stone Romano-Celtic temples, and on the other, by the enclosed Roman cemeteries of Gaul and Britain. The evidence, then, serves to indicate that, far from worshipping their gods in groves and other features of the countryside alone, the Celts did in fact have a variety of built structures

42 Model of La Tène-period sanctuary at Libenice, Kolin, Bohemia

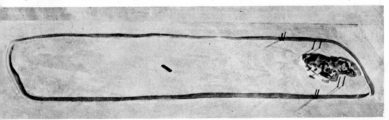

of some sort, in which their rites were performed; and there is no doubt that future archaeological researches on the Continent and in the British Isles will bring many more to light. There is also quite a body of evidence for wooden temples, constructed within these banked, earthen enclosures.

The Celtic word for 'sanctuary' was *nemeton*; there is no reason to suppose that the term did not include these earthworks, as well as referring to the clearings in a grove which also served as sacred places. The word appears in Old Irish as *nemed* and *fidnemed*, 'sacred grove'. Place-name evidence shows that the word *nemeton* was widely in use in the Celtic world. In the sixth century AD Fortunatus mentions a place called Vernemet(on), 'Great Shrine', and there was a place of this name in Britain, somewhere between Lincoln and Leicester. Nemetodurum is the early name for Nanterre, and a place known as Nemetobriga occurs in Spain. Drunemeton, 'Oak Sanctuary', which was both the sanctuary and the meeting-place of the Galatians, is recorded, and several others. In Britain there are records of a place called Medione-meton, 'Central Shrine', somewhere in Scotland,* and at Buxton in Derbyshire a sacred spring was known as Aquae Arnemetiae, 'The Waters of the Goddess Arnemetia', the goddess of the springs and sacred grove.

The Celts, then, did not only venerate their deities and perform their propitiatory rites in sacred clearings in hallowed groves. They constructed earthworks of various kinds in which were either timber-built temples, or some focal point for sacrifice and propitiation of the gods, such as a great ritual pole or pillar, a shaft or pit for the disposal of the remains of the victims, animal and human, and a repository for votive offerings of other kinds; and no doubt in most cases there would be some sort of crude hut of wood or wickerwork for the use of the priest and the housing of his insignia and ritual objects.

THE DRUIDS

Such were the places in which the Celts worshipped; now we must try to ascertain who it was who interceded between the gods and their devotees. Some at least of the Celtic priests were known as 'Druids', and we have already considered this order in the con-

* For a discussion of the probable siting of Medionemeton see Feachem, 1969.

text of their place in society and their role as preservers of the ancient tradition. Now we must consider them in the context of religion, as priests. Most people are familiar with the term 'Druid', and envisage the romantic Celtic priests who performed the sacred rites so graphically described by Pliny:

> They call the mistletoe by a name meaning the all-healing. Having made preparation for sacrifice and a banquet beneath the trees, they bring thither two white bulls, whose horns are bound then for the first time. Clad in a white robe, the priest ascends the tree and cuts the mistletoe with a golden sickle, and it is received by others in a white cloak. Then they kill the victims, praying that God will render this gift of his propitious to those to whom he has granted it. They believe that the mistletoe, taken in drink, imparts fertility to barren animals, and that it is an antidote for all poisons. Such are the religious feelings that are entertained towards trifling things by many peoples. (*Kendrick, 89*)

One wonders whether the presence of enigmatic knobbed horns on bulls in Celtic religious iconography does not indicate that the horns have been bound in preparation for sacrifice, and show that the beasts belong to the god, or are the god himself in animal form. It is also interesting to note that the word for mistletoe in modern Irish and Scottish Gaelic, *uil-ìoc* has the meaning of 'all-healing'. Pliny's account of this ritual attendant on the sacrifice of the bulls has greatly coloured subsequent attitudes to the question of the Celtic priesthood so that the limitations of our real knowledge of the Druids has been obscured, and fancy has, to a very great extent, been allowed to colour fact. The truth is, that apart from certain Classical comments of a limited nature, on this pagan priestly order, and some rather vague references in the vernacular tradition, we really know very little about the Druids. We do not know whether they were common to the entire Celtic world; whether they were the only important priests; whether they functioned in a particular period-of time. All we do know is that at some period in their history some of the Celtic peoples had powerful priests of this name, who kept the often hostile forces of the Otherworld at bay, and knew the correct ritual which could canalise these powers for the good and benefit of mankind in general and the tribe in particular. For the most comprehensive analysis of the nature of Druidism see Piggott, 1968.

The pre-eminence given to the Druids in modern times stems entirely from the activities of antiquarian writers dating from the sixteenth century onwards. The whole cult of Druids was bound up with the concept of the Noble Savage, and from a slight factual basis the fanciful theory was constructed, ending in the modern Druidic cult which operates at Stonehenge. There is not the slightest evidence that the pagan priests of the early Celtic peoples were ever associated with this Neolithic-Bronze Age monument although, of course, their direct predecessors may well have been. Such modern gatherings as the Eisteddfod, the annual Welsh festival of music and native culture, and other such festivals throughout the surviving Celtic world, have served to perpetuate the image of the idealised *Druid*, but it is an essentially false image, based on *revival* rather than *survival*.

So powerful was the influence of the philosophical antiquarians that there is hardly a henge monument or a Neolithic or Bronze Age antiquity in the country which has not been accredited with a Druidic origin or association. We find Druid's Circles, Seats, Mounds, Stones and so forth throughout the British Isles especially in the remaining Celtic areas. Dr Johnson had a very perspicacious comment to make on the first of these that he viewed:

> About three miles beyond Inverness we saw, just by the road, a very complete specimen of what is called a Druids' Temple. There was a double circle, one of very large, the other of smaller stones. Dr Johnson justly observed, that, 'to go and see one druidical temple is only to see that it is nothing, for there is neither art nor power in it: and seeing one is quite enough'.

The Celts themselves do not comment on their own priesthood in pre-Christian times. The only references to the Druids in Ireland are, therefore, in post-pagan times, and it is not clear whether the character of the Druids which emerges there is accurate, or merely due to the unsympathetic attitude of a hostile and innovating priesthood. In some instances, the Druids, who are referred to constantly, are given a role of dignity and power—in some instances, indeed, they are accorded a pre-eminence over the king himself. In the *Táin*, the Druid Cathbad is described as being the father of the King, Conchobar mac Nessa, himself. Cathbad is referred to as being in charge of a group of pupils whom he instructs in druidic learning. He is portrayed, according to Irish tradition, in his role of instructor of the young in the religious lore of the tribe, and the nature of the omens by which it may be made favourable. This concurs with the picture Caesar draws of the Celtic priests in the first century BC: 'The Druids are concerned with the worship of the gods, look after public and private sacrifice, and expound religious matters; a large number of young men flock to them for training, and hold them in high honour.'

In one of the earliest of the Old Irish tales, *The Exile of the Sons of Uisliu*, the drama of the prenatal screaming of the fateful girl Deirdre, within her mother's womb, has to be explained by the prophetic powers of the Druid Cathbad. After the portentous wail has occurred, and terrified the festive gathering, the mother-to-be rushes to the Druid and implores him in the following terms to explain the phenomenon: 'Listen to Cathbad of the comely face, a prince,* a diadem great and mighty, who is magnified through the wizardries of Druids, since I myself have not wise words.' Cathbad 'thereafter put his hand on the stomach of the woman so that the infant resounded under his hand. "True it is," he said, "that a girl is there, and her name will be Deirdriu, and concerning her there will be evil." ' Afterwards a girl-child is born, and her life does in fact follow the course prophesied by the Druid.

These are the dignified and powerful aspects of the Druids according to the Irish tradition. Other references are different, and less flattering. One very impressive account of a Druid has a certain shamanistic flavour. It concerns the powerful Druid Mog Ruith; at least one Celtic mythologist has regarded him as being in origin the sun-god. While this seems to be going much further than the evidence permits, he is nevertheless accredited with being a powerful sorcerer, and with the ability of causing a tempest or creating a cloud by a mere breath. In the story of *The Siege of Druim Damhghaire* he wears an *énchennach*, a 'bird-dress', which is described in the following terms: 'Mog Ruith's skin of the horn-less, dun-coloured bull was brought to him then, and his speckled bird-dress with its winged flying, and his druidic gear besides. And he rose up, in company with the fire, into the air and the heavens.'

Another account of the Druids from the Irish vernacular

* Caesar, as we have seen, notes the fact that the Druids are recruited from the aristocracy; they and the 'knights' constitute the Celtic upper classes.

tradition portrays them as humorous characters, and leaves them with less dignity than their antiquarian admirers would have cared for. This may, however, be due to confusion with the word *drúith*, 'a fool'. In the tale *The Intoxication of the Ulstermen*, which is full of mythological motifs and situations, the Queen, Medb, in origin an Irish goddess, is guarded by two Druids, Crom Deroil and Crom Darail. They are standing on a wall arguing about what they can see approaching them. One thinks a great host is drawing near, and the other contends that these things are merely part of the natural, living landscape. But it is in fact a host which bursts upon them:

> Not long were they there, the two watchers and the two Druids, when a full, fiery rush of the first band broke hither past the glen. Such was the fury with which they advanced that there was not left a spear on a rack nor a shield on a spike, nor a sword in an armoury, that did not fall down. One would think it was the sea that had come over the walls, and over the recesses of the world to them. The forms of countenances were changed, and there was chattering of teeth in Tara-Luachra. The two Druids fell in fits and faintings and in paroxysms; one of them, Crom Darail, over the wall outside, and Crom Deroil over the wall inside. And notwithstanding, Crom Deroil got up, and cast an eye over the first band that came into the green.

The Druidic Order may have continued to hold some kind of power until well into Christian times in the Goedelic world at least, for there is no reason to suppose that, with the coming of Christianity the pagan cults and all their attendant paraphernalia and personalities died out overnight, as it were. In Scotland, St Columba is alleged to have encountered a Druid, named Broichan, near Inverness, in the seventh century AD. The Order probably carried on for some time into the Christian era, though without its former religious powers and political influence; perhaps only in the role of magicians and sorcerers.

But their earlier powers in at least some parts of the ancient world cannot be disputed. Caesar cannot have been very far wrong when he noted (in extension to the quotation on p. 143):

> For they have the right to decide nearly all public and private disputes, and they also pass judgement and decide rewards and penalties in criminal and murder cases, and in disputes regarding legacies and boundaries. . . . It is thought that this system of training

was invented in Britain, and taken over from there to Gaul, and at the present time diligent students of the matter mostly travel there to study it. (*Tierney, 271*)

Pliny, moreover, mentions the august nature of Druidism in the British Isles. He also comments: 'At the present day Britannia is still fascinated by magic, and performs its rites with so much ceremony that it almost seems as though it was she who had imparted the cult to the Persians.'

Caesar does not mention them in his account of Britain. Such an episode as the Boudiccan rebellion, and the references to religious observation and practice connected with it, give the impression that something very similar to Druidism was in operation during the first century AD, however, at least in some parts of Britain. There is in fact only one actual reference to Druids in Britain by any Classical author. In describing the attack by the Roman Governor Paulinus on the Druidic stronghold in Anglesey in AD 61, Tacitus says:

On the shore stood the opposing army with its dense array of armed warriors, while between the ranks dashed women in black attire like the Furies, with hair dishevelled, waving brands. All round the Druids, lifting up their hands to heaven and pouring forth dreadful imprecations, scared our soldiers by the unfamiliar sight so that, as if their limbs were paralysed, they stood motionless and exposed to wounds. Then, urged by their general's appeal and mutual encouragements not to quail before a troop of frenzied women, the Romans bore the standards onwards, smote down all resistance, and wrapped the foe in the flame of his own brands. A force was set over the conquered, and the sacred groves, devoted to inhuman superstitions, were destroyed. The Druids indeed deemed it a duty to cover their altars with the blood of captives and to consult their deities through human entrails. (*Annals, XIV, 30*)

We know that the Druidic stronghold on Anglesey may have been bound up with economic, equally with religious concerns, which might account for the fanatical resistence to Roman pressure. Further archaeological excavation together with a classification of certain cult figures at present in Anglesey, which have not been studied in this context, may help to cast more light on the nature of Druidism here, and perhaps in Britain as a whole.

That female Druids, or Druidesses as we may call them, also played a part in pagan Celtic religion, is suggested by the Classics, and is supported by the insular texts. Vopiscus, although somewhat dubious as a source, has some interesting comments:

> When Diocletian, so my grandfather told me, was sojourning in a tavern in the land of the Tongri in Gaul, at the time when he was still of humble rank in the army, and had occasion to settle the daily account for his keep, with a certain Druidess, this woman said to him, 'You are far too greedy and far too economical, O Diocletian.' Whereto he replied, jestingly, 'I will be more liberal when I am an emperor', to which the Druidess answered, 'Laugh not, Diocletian, for when you have killed The Boar you will indeed be emperor.'
> (*Numerianis, XIV*)

Also, referring to the prophetic powers of the Druidic Order, and mentioning its female element again, Vopiscus recounts:

> He [Asclepiodotus] used to say that on a certain occasion Aurelian consulted the Gaulish Druidesses to find out whether his descendants would remain in possession of the imperial crown. These women told him that no name would become more illustrious in the State annals than that of the line of Claudius. It is true, of course, that the present emperor Constantius is of the same stock, and I think that his descendants will assuredly attain to the glory foretold by the Druidesses. (*Aurelianus, XLIII, 4, 5*)

We have already seen the prophetic powers attributed to the female seer, Fedelm, in the *Táin*; and there is every reason to believe that there was a certain female influence present in the Druidic Order in some areas and at some stages, at least.

IDOLS, IMAGES AND VOTIVE OFFERINGS

We have seen something of the temples and sanctuaries of the Celts and that the Druids were priests to at least some of the Celts. The next question is whether, in pre-Roman times, cult images were fashioned—did the Celts worship their deities in tangible form, or were they always merely concerned with abstract concepts of divinity? All the evidence suggests that they had images and idols of various kinds in abundance. In the first instance, many of these must have been fashioned of oak heart-wood; the great cache of some 190 wooden objects from the site of the Temple of Sequana at the source of the River Seine, all of oak heart-wood, provides striking evidence of this, as do many other cult objects in wood from Denmark, with its remarkable Celtic influence, France and the British Isles. The very large number that has in fact been preserved is indicative of the great quantities of such objects which must have been in existence at one time or another. Wood, then, would seem to have been the favourite material from which idols were fashioned; and because the Celts venerated the oak above all trees, this would be a natural first choice. The word *druid* is believed by some philologists to be connected with the Celtic word for an oak, itself related to the Greek word for an oak, *drus*. The second syllable is supposedly connected with the Indo-European

43 Five of the 190 objects, all of oak heart-wood, found in the sanctuary of Sequana at the source of the river Seine, Côte-d'Or, France

44 Pillar from Pfalzfeld, Hunsrück, Germany

root *wid*, meaning 'to know', giving a meaning such as 'the wise man who worships the oak'. Maximus of Tyre says that the Celts represented Zeus (meaning their own equivalent of the Classical god) by means of a high oak tree. Caesar refers to Mercury as having the largest number of images in Gaul, referring once again to the native gods assimilated to him in Roman times. All these things indicate that, far from being aniconic as has often been claimed for Celtic religion, the reverse was in fact the case.

It is, however, apparent that images fashioned from stone were less popular; and although these are known in limited numbers from as early as the sixth century BC at least, it is only under the aegis of the Roman world from the first century BC onwards that sculpting in stone became widely popular. But there is much evidence to show that stones themselves, whether decorated in the Celtic manner, as at Turoe or Castlestrange in Ireland, (or the St Goar pillar in Germany) or whether merely as blocks of stone or standing stones, were venerated in their own right, and were believed to possess strange powers (*44*). Stones were, as we have seen, often set up at tribal boundaries. The Lia Fáil, the great inauguration stone of ancient Ireland, screamed when a rightful ruler of Ireland stood on it. And there are countless stories in the Old Irish tradition telling of the powers of sacred stones. Today, in modern Celtic folk-belief, certain stones are accredited with supernatural powers, and the use of stones in black magic and allied practices is still remembered in isolated parts of the existing Celtic world. There is a reference to a stone idol, called Cenn Cróich or 'Cromm Cruaich' (in modern folk legend Crom Dubh), and his eleven companions in the Irish *Dindshenchas* (stories used to account for the origins of certain important place-names). Although this legend cannot necessarily be taken at its face value *in toto*, there are aspects of it which cohere convincingly with the overall pattern of Celtic belief in so far as we can comprehend it. Moreover, the fact that the idol was alleged to have stood at Mag Slecht, 'Plain of Prostrations' in the north-west corner of County Cavan, which would seem to have contained a large cult area of first importance in pagan times, strengthens its basic validity. The legend tells how:

> Here used to stand a lofty idol, that saw many a fight, whose name was Cromm Cruaich; it caused every tribe to live without peace. . . . He was their god the wizened Cromm, hidden by many mists: as for the folk that believed in him, the eternal kingdom beyond every haven shall not be theirs. . . . Ranged in ranks stood idols of stone four times three; to beguile the hosts grievously the figure of Cromm was formed of gold. Since the kingship of Héremón, bounteous chief, worship was paid to stones till the coming of noble Patrick to Ard Macha. He plied upon Cromm a sledge, from top to toe; with no paltry prowess he ousted the strengthless goblin that stood there.
>
> (*Gwynn, XI, 19 ff.*)

This graphic account of the overthrowing of the idols of the heathen by the Christian Church would perhaps help to account for the paucity of stone sculptures in the pre-Roman Celtic world.

Cromm or Cenn Cruaich is still apparently known as Crom Dubh in Irish folk-tradition. Máire MacNeill, amongst others, discusses legends about this cult figure in relation to the great calendar festival of Lughnasa. Another stone idol is described in the Irish Martyrology of Oengus: 'Clochar, that is a stone of gold, that is a stone encased in gold which the heathen had for worship; and a demon, Cermand Cestach by name, used to speak out of it, and it was the chief idol of the north.'

Another idol, this time allegedly belonging to the British, is called Etharún. The name may contain the same root as that found in the name of the great Gaulish god-with-the-wheel, Taranis, traces of whose cult are in fact discernible in Britain. Not only were gods or demons believed to inhabit stones and to make utterances from them; weapons likewise were supposed to be the dwelling-place of spirits; the sacred weapons of the gods and the semi-divine heroes were capable, according to popular belief, of acting and speaking independently of their owners through the machinations of the supernatural forces by which they were controlled. In the *Táin*, we learn how Sualtaim, Cú Chulainn's earthly father, perishes by his own shield: he has violated the taboo whereby no one could speak before the Druid:

> Sualtaim went his way in anger and wrath since he got not the answer which sufficed him from the Ulstermen. Then the Líath Macha reared under Sualtaim and came forward opposite Emain, and his own shield turned on Sualtaim and its rim cut off his head. The horse itself turned back again into Emain, with the shield on the horse and the head on the shield. And Sualtaim's head spoke the same words, 'Men are slain, women carried off, cattle driven away, O Ulstermen.' (*C. O'Rahilly, 247*)

The number of small votive weapons, such as spears, swords and shields, found in ritual contexts in Britain and on the Continent, are suggestive of the supernatural powers which were believed to inhabit them. Some of these miniature arms had been deliberately broken, no doubt in accordance with current ritual and belief. Daggers having anthropoid hilts (*45*), no doubt portrayals of the spirit or deity which was believed to lie within them, or responsible for their origin, are a further source of evidence for the worship accorded to such objects in the ancient Celtic world.

45 Anthropoid hilt of short sword, North Grimston, Yorkshire E. R.

La Tène art, as we shall see in the next chapter, is another repository for cult symbols, all of which are subtly woven into the overall flowing pattern of curves and spirals and stylised foliage and plant design; the torc (neck ornament) itself was clearly a magical badge, worn by gods and heroes alike. Many of the elaborate horse-trappings and helmet decorations can be seen to display the insignia of magical power, and evil-averting properties. Far from being ignorant of the worship of idols and anthropomorphic images, the Celts can be shown to have had their full share of these. But, with their usual indirect mode of expressing their beliefs and ideas, these are not always obvious, and only a study of their total culture and everyday attitudes can reveal the subtle religious and superstitious import of much that at first sight would seem to be straightforward and mundane.

FESTIVALS AND RITUAL GATHERINGS

We have looked at the sanctuaries and sacred places of the Celts, and have found these to have been numerous, although many have only been recognised as such in recent years, and many more certainly still await identification. We have glanced at those whose responsibility it was to intercede with the gods on behalf of mankind, and have found that certain of the Celts at least had priests, known as Druids; and there is evidence for other priests of different names, although we know nothing of their significance, or their relationship to the Druidic Order. We have seen that idols and images abound; and as research and knowledge progress, more of these will no doubt be found, or recognised from literary contexts. Finally, what were the occasions upon which all these things were used? What were the rituals carried out by these priests, in the sanctuaries, where many of the idols and the other religious paraphernalia were employed?

The Celts celebrated certain fundamental calendar festivals. As we have seen, the period of the Celtic day was marked by the night. The Celtic year was divided into four main parts in Ireland, and it is likely that this applied to the rest of the Celtic world as well. Each part of the year was preceded by a great religious festival commemorating some cult legend. The festival was accompanied by feasting and merry-making, by fairs and marketing, games and sport, and by solemn religious observances and in Gaul at least the sacrifice of humans as well as beasts. This custom was abhorrent to the Romans, who had long since given up the practice of human sacrifice by the time they came into close contact with the pagan Celtic world.

The first of the ritual divisions of our calendar year occurred on 1 February. It was a feast apparently sacred to the goddess Brigit, later taken over by St Brigid, her Christian successor. This powerful goddess is also found as Brigantia, patron deity of north Britain. Dedications and names on the Continent demonstrate her presence there too. She is likely to have been one of the more universal deities of the pagan Celtic world. The feast, known as Imbolc (or Oímelg) is somewhat obscure, but it seems to have been connected with the coming into milk of the ewes, and was, therefore, essentially a pastoral festival. In later Christian tradition, St Brigid's association with sheep and a pastoral economy, and with fertility in general, are noteworthy, and would seem clearly to be a carry-over from her pagan predecessor's role.

The second festival, Beltaine, took place on 1 May. It may have been connected with the worship of the ancient Celtic god Belenos, who is known from some 31 inscriptions which occur in north Italy, south-eastern Gaul and in Noricum. There are also epigraphic traces of his cult in the British Isles, and some evidence from the literary tradition to suggest that knowledge of this deity continued into the later Celtic world in some vestigial form. Beli Mawr, who figures in the *Mabinogion* as a powerful King of Britain, seems in fact to have been regarded as the ancestor-deity of the aristocracy of early Wales, and may be identical in origin with Belenos himself. The power and influence of this early pastoral god would thus account for the popularity and longevity of his festival, which still continues vestigially in parts of the Scottish Highlands at least. According to the ninth-century Irish glossator Cormac, Beltaine comes from *Bel-tene*, 'a goodly fire'. It was the festival connected with the promotion of fertility, and was much concerned with magical rites to encourage the growth of cattle and crops. Bonfires were kindled and the cattle driven through the flames for the purposes of purification. According to Cormac again, two fires were lit by Druids, and the beasts driven between them. Sacrifice no doubt took place at all these festivals. Beltaine was also known as Cétshamain.

The third seasonal festival, too, was widespread throughout the Celtic world, and traces of it still survive in modern Celtic folk-custom. Occurring on 1 August, the Feast of Lughnasa was essentially an agrarian feast, having to do with the harvesting of the crops rather than with the pastoral economy. It was closely connected with the god Lugus in Gaul (Lugh in Ireland, Lleu in Wales), a powerful god with a widespread cult orbit, who may have been introduced into Ireland by later Celtic settlers. In Roman Gaul the Feast of Augustus was celebrated at Lyon

(Lugudunum) on this date, and it seems clear that this replaced the old festival in honour of the Celtic god, whose fortress it was alleged to have been. Lughnasa was a festival of great significance in Ireland, as the surviving folklore demonstrates. The feast was sometimes called Brón Trogain, 'Trogain's Sorrow', and this may perhaps have been an older name than Lughnasa. In Ireland two great assemblies were traditionally held on Lughnasa, both associated with powerful goddesses. One assembly was Oenach Tailten, the other Oenach Carmain. The location of Oenach Tailten was at Teltown, in County Meath. There are two stories which account for the origin of the feast. One states that it was established by the god Lugh in honour of his foster-mother Tailtiu, who died there on 1 August. We have already seen how important the system of fosterage was in Celtic society, and how, ideally, foster-parents were treated with honour and devotion. This arrangement was clearly also supposed to apply to the society of the gods.

The Feast of Lughnasa traditionally lasted for a month, 15 days before 1 August and 15 days after. Other traditions report that Lugh founded the Feast of Tailte in order to commemorate his two wives Nas and Búi. In Ulster Lughnasa was held at Emain Macha; in Leinster at Carman. Carman was reputed to have been the mother of three sons; the mother laid waste to Ireland in company with her sons, she using magic and sorcery in true feminine fashion, they using power and arms. The sons were finally overcome and compelled to leave Ireland, and Carman remained behind as a hostage together 'with the seven things they worshipped'. She died of grief, and the feast was held in her honour afterwards in accordance with her wishes.

The fourth festival—which was in fact the first in the Celtic year since it marked its beginning—was that of Samain, perhaps the most important of the four, when the Otherworld became visible to mankind, and all the forces of the supernatural were let loose upon the human world. It was a time of great danger and spiritual vulnerability. It was celebrated on the night preceding 1 November, and on that day itself. It is the significant feast in the Old Irish tales, and most things of mythological importance and ritual significance were alleged to have occurred then. It was the end of one pastoral year and the beginning of the next, and there is no doubt that sacrifices were made to propitiate the forces of the Otherworld and to keep the hostile elements at bay.

At Samain the Dagda, the tribal god of Ireland, ritually mated with the Mórrígan, the raven-war-goddess, whose influence on the battlefield was by magical interference during the fray rather than by the strength of weapons. Her prognostic powers are emphasised throughout the early tradition. She was a good friend and a ruthless enemy.

On another occasion the Dagda mates with the river-goddess, patroness of the River Boyne.

The Festival of Samain is still carried out in the isolated Celtic areas where, until very recently, a fairly complicated ritual was observed. It was a night of divination and magic, where the correct ritual must be performed in order to pacify the supernatural forces which were believed to be everywhere in the world of men at that time.

There were, of course, other religious festivals which were celebrated in the ancient Celtic world. There was the Festival of Tea, divine patroness of the Assembly of Tara, one of the great sacred places of Ireland; she too was held captive, like Carman and Tailtiu. Tlachtga, likewise, patroness of the feast, was reputed to have given birth to three sons at a single birth—a typical Celtic mythological motif—each having a different father. Like the goddess Macha, she died in childbed. These ancient goddesses thus clearly played their part in the ritual festivals of the ancient Celtic calendar.

THE SEVERED HUMAN HEAD

Moving from sanctuaries and shrines, priests and idols, periodic festivals and ritual gatherings, we come now to consider the nature of the actual deities for whom this framework for the enactment of the religious observances was constructed. But, before going on to look at the nature of some of the individual deities and their cults, one can perhaps bridge the gap as it were by considering a symbol which, in its way, sums up the whole of pagan Celtic religion and is as representative of it as is, for example, the sign of the Cross in Christian contexts. This is the symbol of the severed human head; in all its various modes of iconographic representation and verbal presentation, one may find the hard core of Celtic religion. It is indeed an expression of 'a part for the whole', a kind of shorthand symbol for the entire religious outlook of the pagan Celts. It is, as it happens, the best documented of all the cults, being fully attested to not only by the three early sources of evidence which we are using here, but having such a longevity of tradition as to continue down to the present day in superstitious and folklore contexts in the surviving Celtic regions. The Celts, like many other barbarian peoples, hunted human heads. We know this from the skulls found in Celtic hill-forts; in some cases, the nails from which they were suspended on the gateway or on posts round the ramparts were still present. These severed heads would serve as trophies testifying to the military prowess of their owners; and, at the same time, the powers, believed to be inherent in the human head, would act protectively and keep evil from the fortress or the home, while ensuring positive good luck and success. Diodorus Siculus comments on the custom of decapitating their enemies amongst the Gauls, and describes how they nailed them up on their houses or embalmed them in oil and regarded them as priceless treasures. His testimony as to the importance of the head in Celtic everyday and spiritual life is supported by an observation by Livy: 'The consuls got no report of the disaster till some Gallic horsemen came in sight, with heads hanging at their horses' breasts, or fixed on their lances, and singing their customary song of triumphs.'

Livy likewise describes the placing in a temple of the head of a prized enemy chieftain by the tribe, the Boii, in 216 BC. Human skulls were displayed in skull-niches at the great temples at Roquepertuse and Entremont, further testifying to the correct observations of the Classics. Livy, moreover, remarks upon the Celtic custom of decorating human heads with gold and using them as drinking cups, and this may have been the function of the human skull found in the sanctuary at Libenice. There are many instances of heads being used in these ways in the vernacular literatures. Straightforward head-hunting occurs regularly in the Ulster Cycle of Irish stories as well as elsewhere. In the *Táin,* after his first skirmish since his taking of arms, Cú Chulainn returns to Emain Macha with a flock of swans, wild deer, and three severed heads. Later in the *Táin*, he is described as having 'nine heads in one hand and ten in the other, and these he brandished at the hosts in token of his valour and prowess'. It seems unlikely that the hosts would wish to question him on that score.

Several heroic or divine characters are referred to as never sitting down at a feast without having a severed head before them on the table. The Celts believed that the human head was the seat of the soul, the essence of being. It symbolised divinity itself, and was the possessor of every desirable quality. It could remain alive after the death of the body; it could avert evil and convey prophetic information; it could move and act and speak and sing; it could tell tales and entertain; it presided over the Otherworld feast. In some cases it was used representationally to portray some individual divinity or cult; in others, it was used symbolically to express religious feeling in general.

The most impressive piece of literary evidence for the belief in the powers of the severed head occurs in the story of Branwen in the *Mabinogion*. In this tale, concerning the ill-fated sister of Bran the Blessed, 'The Blessed Raven' (possibly in origin a powerful Celtic god), the magical severed head of the euhemerised deity plays an important role. Bran is described as being so vast in size that no house could ever be constructed large enough to contain him—a sure indication of his supernatural nature; after a disastrous sortie to Ireland he is wounded and on his request his head is struck off by his surviving followers; before they do this he prophesies future events for them, and instructs them on what to do and how to behave in order to avoid disaster and disillusionment. His severed head continues to live after Bran's decapitation. His men take it with them into an Otherworld region, where they feast and make merry for a considerable period of enchanted time, having no awareness of where they really are or any memory of the sufferings they have endured. The head entertains them and provides magnificent hospitality and companionship:

> There they passed the fourscore years so that they were not aware of having ever spent a time more joyous and delightful than that. It was not more irksome having the head with them than when Bran the Blessed had been with them alive. And because of those fourscore years it was called the Assembly of the Wondrous Head.
>
> (*Jones, 39*)

Finally, one of his followers ignores a warning given to them by Bran, and opens a forbidden door. All the magic vanishes and they are once more reminded of what has transpired. Acting again on Bran's instructions, they take the head to London, and bury it there. It acts as a talisman, keeping all evil and plague away from the country until it is disinterred. Then its powers cease. There are several parallels in the Irish tradition, in which a severed head presides at a feast or gives entertainment to the company.

Archaeology provides full corroboration for this most important cult amongst the pagan Celtic peoples. Hundreds of heads were fashioned from stone; as many or more must have been made from wood, but the proportion of those which survive is necessarily less than that of stone examples. La Tène art uses the human head or mask as a constantly recurring motif, and here, as in the later stone examples, various cult features such as horns, leaf crowns or multiple heads can be distinguished. These heads would no doubt have been accredited with magical, evil-averting powers; and some were portrayals of an individual god or goddess.

The Celts had firm belief in the magical powers of the number three. Their divinities, according to their cult legends, were often alleged to have been born with two others of the same name at the same birth. Certain mythological characters are described as having three heads. Three-faced heads (*46*) were sculpted in the Celtic countries in Roman times, no doubt further testifying to the sacred power of three. Several of these have been found in Britain. Other heads are janiform (*47*), perhaps reflecting some concept such as the power of the god to look forwards into the Otherworld and backwards into the world of mankind. Sometimes the heads are horned, and must be related to the cult of horned gods in

46 Two of the faces of the tricephalos found on Corleck Hill, Co. Cavan, Ireland

47 Basalt lava janiform head, Leichlingen, Rhineland, Germany

48 Horned head from Starkenburg, Germany

general (*48*). Sometimes they have no ears, sometimes exaggerated ears, or slots for the insertion of animal ears. The eyes are usually emphasised, sometimes one is larger than the other, sometime one or both have several pupils. The faces are usually mask-like and expressionless, quite unlike a portrait head from the Classical world. This great corpus of heads, and the evidence for many more which must have existed at one stage, in both wood and stone, as well as in metal (*63*), provides a great additional source of evidence for the fundamental and vital role of the human head in pagan Celtic religion at all stages and in every tribal region. The Celts can truly be said to have venerated a god-head, symbolic of all their religious belief.

DEITIES AND CULTS

We must now look at the *type* of deities the Celts venerated; for although there is a marked basic homogeneity of religious attitude and ritual practice, there is also a clear tendency to envisage the gods and goddesses as divine types within their own particular cult orbits. In this way, although there are literally hundreds of divine names from the epigraphy and the literary traditions—

some recurrent and found throughout the pagan Celtic world, others appearing only once or twice—there is a limited number of divine types; and it is clear that the same *type* of deity was venerated over a wide region, even though he or she may have had different names and slightly differing cult legends according to tribal distribution and preference.

Before we examine some of the more outstanding of these cults, it is necessary to say something of the *order* of the Celtic divinities as far as the evidence at present available allows this. There would not seem to have been any ordinary clear-cut pantheon, any rigid segregation of gods and goddesses into specific functions or departments. There are certain deities whose appearances in epigraphy and literature suggest an influence more profound, perhaps, than that of those who are commemorated only once or twice, and this would possibly justify us in thinking in terms of a certain hierarchy of divinities. But even so these are all-purpose gods and goddesses as well as having some special sphere with which they are fundamentally concerned.

The Celtic deities in general would seem to have been thought of as being good all-round characters. The tribal god, no matter what his name may have been in the different regions, was an absolutely basic Celtic god-type. Each tribe would have its own divine father. He would be thought of as the ancestor of the people, the father of the king or chief in whom so much divine power was believed to reside. Just as the god was responsible for the general well-being of the tribe, for the fertility of its stock and of the people themselves—for good harvests and the absence of plague and disaster, for well-chosen laws and just legal decisions— even so was the king. A blemished king, or one who was proved to be morally corrupt, could do nothing but harm to the tribe; a good reign ensured good weather and crops, everything that was beneficial to the people. Like the king, the father-god would preside over justice and the laws in times of peace. He would take up arms and lead his people into battle in times of war. Caesar says: 'The Gauls all assert their descent from Dis Pater, and say that it is the Druidic belief.' This Celtic equivalent of Dis Pater, the divine ancestor god, is undoubtedly the universal tribal god represented by the Dagda, 'Good God', in Irish tradition—the great, powerful, club-wielding, cauldron-bearing warrior, mate of the mighty Morrígan, the raven-war-goddess, and of Boand, eponymous goddess of the River Boyne. His equivalent in Gaul would seem to have been such a figure amongst others, as Sucellos, 'the Good Striker', who, with his mallet and patera attributes, bears such close resemblance to the verbal descriptions of the Dagda.

The tribal god was mated to the earth-goddess, whatever her name may have been according to the different regions and traditions. As we have seen, one of the Dagda's mates was the powerful war-goddess who took on crow or raven form at will, and who influenced the outcome of battle by means of her magical and prognostic powers. A further link between the Gaulish Sucellos and the Irish Dagda as tribal fathers is the fact that the Gaulish god's consort is Nantosvelta, 'She of the Winding Stream', whose attribute is in fact the raven.

We can, then, envisage Celtic divine society as being composed of a basic all-purpose tribal god, the divine counterpart of the king or chieftain, with the earth-mother as his consort, she being concerned with the fertility of the land, the crops and the stock and taking an active part in battle against the tribal enemies using incantations and magical spells rather than weapons to bring about victory. Over and above this fundamental divine couple there is evidence for gods having rather more closely defined spheres of influence, such as one finds in human society. A smith-god, a divine healer, a god specially concerned with the literary arts, a patron deity of some powerful well or river. But the all-purpose god could also turn his hand to any of these skills if necessary, and there must have been a good deal of overlapping of sphere.

It would appear, then, that the Celts envisaged the divine social order as being similar to that of the tribal hierarchy. There is also some evidence for a group of 'higher' deities than the gods of the tribe, namely the gods of the divinities themselves. Certain of the goddesses would seem to have occupied at some stage at least the position of the 'mother of the gods'. There are various shadowy but powerful beings, such as Anu or Danu; Brigit or Brigantia; or the Welsh Dôn, who would have seemed to have fulfilled such a role. Anu is 'she who nurtures well the gods'; perhaps identical with Danu she has her equivalent in the Welsh Dôn. Brigit is the pagan goddess, mother in some legends of the gods Brian, Iucha, and Iucharba. According to other traditions it is Danu who is the mother of these three, the 'Men of the Three Gods' (*fir tr ndea*) as they were called. Brigit comes into full fruition not as the riple daughter of the tribal god, the Dagda (for she was one of hree sisters named Brigit), but as the early Christian evangelising aint, Brigit of Kildare, round whose sacred, perpetually burning ire nine virgins kept constant watch. Her British equivalent is of course Brigantia, 'the High One', who gave her name to the erritory of Roman Britain equivalent to the present-day six northern counties of England, and to the powerful confederation of tribes, the Brigantes, who occupied this area.

All these powerful female deities, whether they are in fact ultimately the same divinity, or the same basic concept of the divine mother, suggest that over and above the tribal god and his consort—the earth-mother of the tribe—there was indeed a group of higher deities, those who nurtured the gods themselves and whose sons were superior even to the tribal deities.

Other vague, ill-defined, but potentially exciting goddesses may perhaps be detected in the literary references to the female champions who train Cú Chulainn in the invincible tricks of single combat which were to serve him in such good stead in times of stress. Scáthach, who is alleged to grant Cú Chulainn, hero of the Ulster Cycle, three wishes under duress, is a great warrior-queen of the type of the early Irish divine queen Medb, 'She who Intoxicates'. She grants the hero her daughter, a first-class instruction in military strategy, and a prognostication of his future. He then goes on to overcome her enemy, another powerful female, Aífe, who rides independently in her chariot and is arrogantly indifferent to the world of men. The Ulster hero conquers her by superior strategy, and obtains three wishes from her too, one of which is that she will not only make peace with Scathach but will sleep with him and bear him a son. This does in fact take place, and the son to whom she gives birth is the son whom Cú Chulainn, at a later stage in his career, fails to recognise, and slays in single combat before he is made aware of his relationship to the youthful combatant.

All of these powerful warrior-goddess-queens, then, can be thought of as being related in some way to each other, and all may in fact represent the concept of the goddess over and above the tribe, the great goddess of the gods themselves.

With this basic organisation of the pagan Celtic Otherworld in mind, with its division of deities into tribal god and earth-mother and then all the gods and goddesses of various, more specific functions, we must next glance at some of the individual cults

49 Antlered God, CORINIVM,
Cirencester, Gloucestershire

with which these deitie
were concerned, no matte
by which particular name
they were invoked. We
have seen that the cult o
the severed human head
was one vital to Celti
religion, and one which
was used to express every
aspect of Celtic religiou
attitude. With the reser
vation in mind that thi
symbol could alone stand
for any of the numerou
separate cults of which
their mythology was com
posed, we must now make
an outline sketch of some
of the more typical cults
and the types of deities with which they were concerned.

The Celts venerated animals to a great degree, as we shall se
presently. For this reason it is not surprising that one of the bes
attested of their god-types throughout the pagan Celtic world i
the horned god. There are two main types of horned deity. The
first is an antlered god, known from one inscription by the name
of (C)ernunnos, 'the Horned One'. There is early evidence for hi
cult throughout the Celtic world, and there is a remarkable con
sistency of appearance. He bears stag antlers (49), and is often ac
companied by the stag, his cult animal *par excellence*. He frequently
wears the torc, the sacred neck-ornament, about his throat, and
sometimes carries one. His regular companion is the mysteriou
ram-headed or horned serpent. This creature also appears with
the native equivalent of Mars. The stag-god is often portrayed i
a squatting posture, perhaps reminiscent of the sitting habits o
the Gauls, who did not use chairs but squatted on the floor. Hi
cult was obviously widely distributed in the Celtic regions, and he
may have been a deity especially venerated by the Druids. There
are convincing traces of him in the literary traditions of both
Wales and Ireland; and the fact that in later Christian illuminated
manuscripts he has become symbolic of the devil and anti
Christian forces is indicative of his fundamental importance i

Celtic religion. He is frequently portrayed as lord of the animals as, for example, on the Gundestrup cauldron, where he sits holding the ram-horned serpent by the neck and flanked by a wolf and a bear; a variety of other animals fill the background. Unlike the second type of horned deity, the antlered god is always portrayed in a pacific role, and his whole cult is suggestive of fertility and agricultural and commercial prosperity. There is a dignity and refinement about it which is suggestive of great antiquity and importance.

The second type of horned god, also found throughout the Celtic world, is that of a bull-horned or ram-horned god. He is infinitely cruder than his antlered counterpart, but does share some features in common with him. There are times when these two cults would seem to overlap. Both, for example, are brought into association with the Roman Mercury. Mercury's connection with economic prosperity would be a reason for the Celtic antlered god to be likened in Roman times to the Classical god. Moreover, in his earlier role as protector of flocks and herds, Mercury would naturally be comparable to the antlered god as lord of the animals and to the bull- or ram-horned god with his emphatically pastoralist connections. The bull-horned god is nameless; he may have been any one of the deities worshipped locally in Gaul, or in north Britain, where the evidence for his cult is particularly impressive. He is very much a god of war (*50*). Sometimes he appears in the native iconography as a horned head, in most typical native fashion. Most frequently he is figured as a naked, phallic warrior, bearing a spear and shield. Sometimes he is likened to Mars, sometimes to Mercury. Again, he may be linked with Silvanus as a crude woodland deity, phallic but unarmed. As

50 Horned warrior-god from ALVANA Maryport, Cumberland

a god of ceaselessly warring pastoral tribes he was, of course, a fitting expression of their fundamental attitudes and desires—a powerful fighter, a protector of flocks and herds, a bestower of virility and fertility on man and beast.

We have seen that the tribal god was essentially a powerful warrior, and no matter what his pacific spheres of influence and activity were, once the tribe was placed in danger of invasion by hostile forces, or was ready to set out on an expedition of conquest, then the father-god assumed his role of leader in battle, and became the divine ideal for human stamina and endurance. Since the Celts were a restless, mobile people, given to personal adornment rather than to permanent homes and elaborate permanent religious structures, they would probably take with them some amulet or idol which was readily portable and especially symbolic of, or sacred to, the divine warrior. This must often have been a head fashioned from stone or wood, or a small wooden idol, or perhaps even a stone or a sacred weapon, from which the god would speak and inspirit the soldiers. It is natural that the Celtic gods must have appeared to be overwhelmingly aggressive when the Romans first came into contact with them, and for this reason the native tribal god would tend to become equated with Mars, the Roman god of war. Once the strife and tension had lessened, and life had become more pacific and settled under Roman rule, the original portrayal of the native god as Mars would tend to remain. But we know that in many instances, largely on account of other attributes and dedications which appear in the iconographic repertoire, this warrior-god was more closely concerned with such things as healing waters and agricultural fertility, or figured as a very local protective power, guardian of the native cultural tradition, in the form of the *genius loci*.

In the northern regions of Britain, where the military aspect of the Roman Conquest was always dominant, the war-god— frequently in the form of the bull- or ram-horned god—would be represented by Mars solely in his role as war-god. Only one northern deity, namely Mars Condatis, 'Mars of the Watersmeet', commemorated at Chester le Street and Piercebridge in County Durham, is suggestive of concern with the powers of a sacred stream or river, and this is reminiscent of the role of Mars in many parts of Gaul and in south-west England. The gods equated with Mars in this south-western region of Britain, then, were largely concerned with healing, and it is interesting to note that the Irish deities were likewise skilled in this respect. Lugh mac Eithlenn, one of the Tuatha Dé Danaan ('People of the Goddess Danu') of early Irish tradition, who is the brilliant skilled warrior as well as being gifted in a great variety of other crafts, is allegedly the divine father of the great hero Cú Chulainn. When Cú Chulainn is almost fatally wounded in the *Táin*, Lugh comes to him in the guise of a warrior, but invisible to all but the hero. He sings magic chants over his son so as to induce sleep, and then fills his terrible wounds with sacred herbs and plants, and with charms and incantations he heals the wounded hero, and makes him whole again and able to fight.

To a warlike people such as we know the Celts to have been, the god in his role as warrior would have been of supreme importance in the mythology and later iconographic repertoire. The cult of weapons is also relevant here. As we have seen, many of the early Irish tales tell of how certain venerated swords or shields or spears had been fashioned by the gods themselves, or acquired by deities and brought to Ireland.

The Celtic goddesses were, on the whole, powerful female deities. Basically, they were concerned with the earth, with fertility of both crops and stock, with the sexual pleasures, and with war in its magical aspects. The concept of the female deity in triadic form would seem to have been fundamental to pagan Celtic belief. The basic iconographic form of the tribal mother was the group of three mother-goddesses, the triple *matres*, known from both the Gallo-Roman and the Romano-British world. The maternal aspects of the tribal goddess being of supreme importance, it is not surprising to find that she was expressed in sculptural terms as a mother-goddess, nurturing her young or having them on her lap, or playing with them in some way. The maternal and sexual concerns of the Celtic goddesses were thus always very much in evidence. But over and above this basic function of the tribal mother certain specific spheres of influence can be detected. For example, the triple raven-war-goddess, the three Mórrígna, although their sexual aspect was very clear, were more concerned with battle itself, with prognostication and with shape-shifting. Other goddesses, like Flidais, probably a woodland goddess, would seem to have been, like Cernunnos and other deities, especially concerned with the mastery of the woodland beasts—the native equivalent of Diana. They led the chase, drove their chariots through the untamed woodlands, and protected and made prolific the flocks and herds. Flidais was mated to the great hero Fergus mac Roich, 'Fergus son of Great Horse'. Only she could fully satisfy him sexually.

Other great goddesses known from the early Irish tradition include Medb herself, with her endless repertoire of husbands and lovers; the great goddesses of healing springs and wells; ill-defined female deities such as the British goddess Ratis, 'Goddess of the Fortress'; Latis, 'Goddess of the Pool' (or 'of Beer'); and so on. Coventina, the nymph goddess of north Britain, whose dedications are numerous and who had her cult centre at Carrawburgh (Brocolitia), on Hadrian's Wall, in Northumberland, is another deity of whom we know little. The richness and complexity of the votive deposit in her sacred well indicates the veneration which was accorded to her. Traces of her name on the Continent suggest that she may have had a wider cult orbit than would at first appear to have been the case.

At Bath, Somerset (Aquae Sulis), another great native spring goddess had her cult adopted by the Romans. Sulis, the goddess of the hot healing springs there, became equated with the Classical Minerva. The iconography of the Roman baths shows imagery which is at once Classical and native; but one feels that the Classical representations exist primarily in order to give tangible form to the native beliefs which caused the sacred springs to have been dedicated to Sulis in the first instance.

Again, at Aquae Arnemetiae (Buxton), in Derbyshire, a native goddess is commemorated at the sacred springs in Roman times.

The basic Celtic goddesses, then, throughout the entire pagan Celtic world, would seem to have been mother-goddesses with all their sexual and maternal implications. Goddesses of war, too, sometimes wielding weapons, sometimes using the powers of their magic to bring about success for the side which they supported. The great Mórrígan is not slow to show her outrage and anger to the hero Cú Chulainn when he ignores her sexual advances. In a mood of grim revenge she comes to him when he is hard-pressed in single combat:

> So the Mórrígan came there in the guise of a white, red-eared heifer accompanied by fifty heifers, each pair linked together with a chain of white bronze. The womenfolk put Cú Chulainn under taboo and prohibitions not to let the Mórrígan go from him without checking

and destroying her. Cú Chulainn made a cast at the Mórrígan and shattered one of her eyes. Then the Mórrígan appeared in the form of a slippery, black eel swimming downstream, and went into the pool and coiled herself around Cú Chulainn's legs. While Cú Chulainn was disentangling himself from her, Lóch dealt him a wound crosswise, through his chest. Then the Mórrígan came in the guise of a shaggy russet-coloured she-wolf. While Cú Chulainn was warding her off, Lóch wounded him. Thereupon Cú Chulainn was filled with rage and wounded Lóch with the *ga bulga* and pierced his heart in his breast. (*C. O'Rahilly, 194*)

The Celtic goddesses, then, controlled the land and the seasons; they were sexually potent and maternally inclined. Many of them have clearly been taken over into folk-tradition where, like the Irish Cailleach Bheara, or the Gaelic Cailleach Beinne Bric, or the sinister, sea-going Muilidheartach, they perform feats and influence spheres which are closely similar to those suggested by the iconography and the textual traditions of the older, pagan world.

BIRDS

Birds, more perhaps even than animals, would seem to have played a very vital and basic role in pagan Celtic religious imagery. The feeling for birds is obviously an ancient one, and clear patterns of attitude to the various species can be determined (*51*). The consistency of the character of certain birds throughout the ages, and surviving down into the oral tradition today, is truly remarkable. Others had a limited period of popularity, but birds in general as well as in particular, appealed strongly to the Celtic

51 Owl, from broken brooch found at Weiskirchen, Lorraine, France
52 Cormorants, on a torc from Breuvery, Marne, France

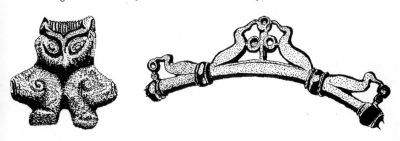

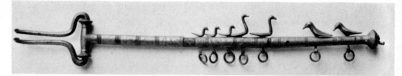

53 Flesh-fork or horse-goad, Dunaverney, Co. Antrim, Ireland

temperament. They were used in various ways. The Druids allegedly drew omens from bird-flight and from bird-calls. There are several charming examples of the meaning of various bird-calls in the textual material. As early as the Urnfield period, in a proto-Celtic context, certain birds figure regularly in what would seem to be clear cult contexts. Water-birds of every kind are associated with the cult of the sun in its healing aspect. Idols are portrayed as sitting in chariots pulled along by birds. The sun itself is represented as being drawn by a cormorant (*52*), a duck or a goose, birds which continued to be represented in the later artistic tradition. Many kinds of duck can be detected, and the accuracy of ornithological observation in the iconographic repertoire of pagan Europe is remarkable. One of the most elegant examples of the use of birds on a functional object which was, however, perhaps reserved for ritual purposes only, is the flesh-fork or horse-goad from Dunaverney, Ireland (*53*). Here, ravens and swans with cygnets are represented, in the round, and the fact that they are all movable suggests that they may have been connected with augury, and the object may thus have belonged to a king or a priest.

Some of the larger, more dramatic birds play a role in the entire tradition. These include the swan, the crane or heron, the raven, ducks of various kinds, and the eagle, which does, however, figure to a much lesser extent than one would have expected. The Celtic Jupiter has the wheel rather than the eagle as his attribute. The swan is consistently regarded as the epitome of purity, beauty, and potential good luck; its sexual associations are obvious. It is frequently the form taken on by lovers of both sexes when they set out on

54 Pommel (?) from Lisnacrogher, Co. Antrim, Ireland, with raven ornament

amorous expeditions. The crane is utterly sinister; it was taboo to eat its flesh in the ancient Celtic world. It was the form adopted when required by hostile goddesses, or by ill-natured and sexually promiscuous women. Always disliked, the abhorrence for this bird continued right down into modern Gaelic tradition. The raven was at once deceitful and dangerous, a bird to be watched carefully and to be propitiated with the correct ritual (*54*). It was the form of the Irish war-goddesses, when they were not in human shape; it was the servant and the messenger of certain of the gods. The Otherworld birds of the pagan Celtic elysium were sweet-singing, pain-killing, conveyors of all delight. They are often portrayed in the iconography and in the texts as belonging to some radiant goddess, a goddess of sexual powers, a being to be wooed and won by gods and heroes alike. Birdlore and bird superstitions abound still in the folk-repertoire of the modern Celtic world, and testify to the deeply fundamental nature of bird symbolism in the religious traditions of the pagan world.

ANIMALS IN CELTIC MYTHOLOGY

Finally, we must briefly consider the role of animals in pagan Celtic mythology. Second only to birds, animals played a very marked and distinctive role in the traditions. The boar would seem to have been the animal *par excellence* in early Celtic society. Evidence for the veneration of this animal is copious from the La Tène period onwards; the evidence from the Hallstatt graves, where pig-bones occur, suggests that it had some ritual significance in earlier times also. The iconography of the Romano-Celtic areas shows many examples of pig or boar imagery (*55*); the insular texts

55 Bronze boar from Neuvy-en-Sullias, Loiret, France; bronze boar from Báta, Tolna, Hungary

56 Stone figure from Euffigneix, Haute-Marne, France

57 1, horse fibula, Schwieberdingen, Ludwigsburg, Germany; 2, Doe, Taunus, Germany; 3, Horse, Silchester, Hampshire; 4, Horse, Friesen, Saarland, Germany

likewise contain many references to this beast both as a supernatural creature and as the favoured food of both men and the gods. It was the best animal in the hunt, a food fit for heroes; and its sexual powers, its physical strength, its heroic defence of itself when cornered, and its passion for the fruit of the sacred tree, the oak, all ensured it a foremost place in Celtic mythology. A Gaulish god is actually named Moccus, 'Pig'; another has a great boar on his torso (*56*); and the mysterious north British god, Veteris or Vitiris as he is also called on the inscriptions, has the

58 Bull featured in bronze chariot fitting from Bulbury, Dorset

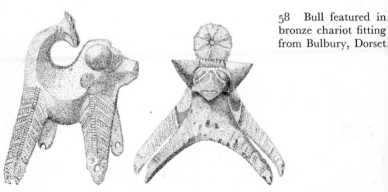

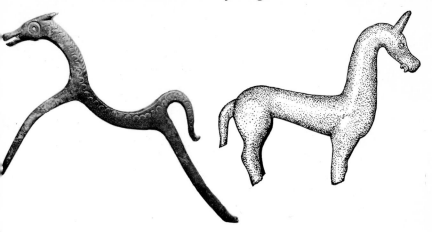

boar and the serpent for decoration on his simple altars.

The stag as an attribute and form of Cernunnos has been noted already (57). The horse was likewise a beast of high cult importance from Urn-field times onwards. The bull (*58*) would seem to have played a some-what subordinate role, but was, nevertheless, still of considerable importance in the native cults. A three-horned bull was favoured by the Belgae in their religious icono-graphy, and some of these, in bronze, reached Britain (*59*). The *Táin* is centred round the huge supernatural bull, the Donn of Cúailnge, which originated as an anthropomorphic deity, subsequently taking on a variety of animal forms and ending up as a powerful bull. The boar and the stag, however, would seem to have had a somewhat greater pre-eminence in the mythologies of the pagan Celts. The ram (*60*), in the form of the mysterious ram-horned serpent, as well as in more

59 Bronze three-horned bull with, originally, three female busts on its back: Maiden Castle, Dorset

171

60 Ram, on gold torc from a hoard found at Frasnes-lez-Buissenal, Hainaut, Belgium; ram on silver torc from Manerbio sul Mella, Brescia, Italy

naturalistic shape, also figures in cult contexts, while the ram-horned god is well attested in the early iconography.

Certain aquatic creatures also played their part in the creation of the supernatural legends. The salmon is the most important of these; it was regarded as a repository of Otherworld wisdom, as the form adopted by certain of the gods, and as the spirit and symbol of the sacred rivers and pools. According to Irish tradition, a salmon used to eat the nuts of a sacred hazel tree as they fell into the pool below, and thereby was enabled to renew its wisdom and supernatural powers. A relief from Gaul figures a human head between two great salmon; this can probably be interpreted as the imparting of magic knowledge to the divine head, just as some of the Gaulish gods, and the Scandinavian Odin got their knowledge of the world and its happenings from two ravens which perched on their shoulders and spoke into their ears.

The dog (*61*) also played its own important part in the mythology of the Celtic peoples. It was, as we know, taboo for the hero, Cú Chulainn, to eat canine flesh; the god worshipped at Lydney, Nodons, was much associated with dogs. In one instance a portrayal of a dog accompanies his name, which suggests that, like the Celtic deities in general, Nodons may have been a shapeshifter, taking on the appearance of his cult animals at will.

THE OTHERWORLD

The Celts believed passionately and joyously in the Otherworld, the home of the gods, the source of all pleasure and satisfaction. They believed in a continuing *material* existence. Their graves were equipped with the articles considered necessary for the journey to the Otherworld and for the feast. A clever, ruthless hero could force his way into the Otherworld in mortal form, by treachery and skill. A goddess could fall in love with a hero and take him with her into her own magical realms. Nowhere do we get the impression that the Otherworld was regarded as a prize for ethical behaviour. Good and bad simply did not enter into the

61 Bronze dog (no provenance)

ideas of life after death, beyond the grave, or while still alive, in the Otherworld with some divine being. It was one's natural heritage, a place as definite and almost as tangible as the mundane world.

The whole of Celtic religion was controlled by magic and affected by the correct or incorrect performance of ritual. The Celtic gods were as crafty and as unpredictable as their own neighbours; if they were properly approached and propitiated according to their individual requirements, with sacrifice and the recitation of charms and incantations, they could be mild and beneficent. If neglected or offended, they could be cruel and relentless. They frequently entered the world of men and played tricks upon those they chanced upon. They were not invincible, nor were they immortal. They were believed to be capable of death like man himself.

CONCLUSION

In this necessarily brief sketch of what is a large and complicated subject, sufficient has been said to make it possible to envisage, in very general terms, something of the basic nature of pagan Celtic religion. Caesar stated that 'The whole Gallic people is exceedingly given to religious superstition', and all the existing evidence at our disposal serves to support his observation. The lives of the pagan Celts—and, to a certain extent, of their Christian successors —were hemmed in and embued with superstitious feelings and petty ritual observances, propitiatory rites, and evil-averting spells and practices. No bird could settle, or fly overhead, without some significance being attached to its movements; the flesh of certain animals could not be eaten on account of religious taboo; buildings may not be constructed without some sacrifice, animal

173

or human, taking place, the remains being buried in the foundations, and so on. In every aspect of their everyday life the Celts felt it necessary to be protected against the gods and the powers of the Otherworld in the manner taught by the Druids in distant antiquity, and perpetuated by each new generation of priests and seers. A bad man was one who did not perform correctly the propitiatory rights, thereby bringing down the wrath of the gods; he was a fool, one lacking in subtlety of reasoning and behaviour.

Barbarous and ill defined though the religion of the pagan Celts may have been, without clear system, without dogma, it impresses by its sincerity, and the tremendous daily part it played in the life of the people. Moreover, it is sufficiently homogeneous over a wide geographical area, and throughout long periods of time, to have its own individual character which makes it essentially an expression of the spiritual life of the people who created it. It deserves, then, a definite place amongst the religions of the ancient world.

7

Celtic Art

By Celtic art we mean, in this context, the art style which originated in the La Tène phase of Celtic society. It is in this highly original and complex series of decorative motifs that the Celts make a real and distinctive contribution to the foundations of European culture. Derived, as it clearly is, from motifs borrowed from a variety of sources, Celtic artists turned these into a composite and remarkably subtle whole by reason of their own peculiar genius in this field. A limited amount of the work must have been carried out with stone as a medium; many more designs would have been drawn on objects of leather, bone and wood. But it is in the metalwork of these artists that the full flowering of the style can be witnessed. There were great regional differences in the basic style, and the art of Britain and Ireland differed considerably from that of the Continent. To many critics, its somewhat more restrained and austere lines make it aesthetically superior to the almost frantic complexity of the later continental work. While it is basically a decorative art, it cannot be separated from the religion and magic which must underlie many of the most typical motifs. In 600 BC a Greek trading station was set up at Massilia (Marseilles), at the mouth of the River Rhône. This opened up the entire Celtic hinterland to Mediterranean influences of various kinds. Amongst other things, the Celts began to import wine from Greece and Etruria. This was sent to them in large vessels called *oinochoai*. These were adorned with Classical designs, stemming from many origins, and having a predisposition for plants and foliage and other naturalistic forms. The Celts enjoyed the contents of these vessels while at the same time the designs clearly made a marked impression on their artists. By combining these Classical patterns with the old indigenous artistic and religious motifs of Bronze Age Europe—the sacred water-birds, the solar

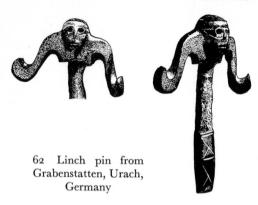

62 Linch pin from Grabenstatten, Urach, Germany

symbols and so on—with Hallstatt geometric forms, and with the splendid animal art of the Persians and Scythians and more Easterly peoples, they evolved this entirely new, original and exciting art style. All these borrowed elements are blended together so subtly that their ultimate individual origin is obscured; naturalism gives way to fantasy, the straightforward motif becomes sheer flowing and complex design. Celtic art is miraculous in its utter intensity and amazing variety. It is possible to study a pattern for hours on end and still come no nearer to understanding its intricacies. Rarely are two areas of any design completely identical, and yet, somehow, there is nothing inharmonious in the whole. In asymmetric patterns one is given the impression of symmetry when it is, in fact, virtually impossible to find two identical pieces of repeated pattern in many of the examples. The designs are fluid, sweeping, and without a clear beginning or end. They simply exist. In their art style, then, we come very close to the essence of the Celtic temperament. It reflects the tortuous and subtle nature of their thought processes; the complexities of their language: it makes manifest the complicated, shifting, oblique nature of their religious attitudes. In short, Celtic art is an impressive summing up of all that is fundamental and distinctive in the spiritual life of the Celts.

This new art style, then, was used to decorate the weapons and the personal ornaments of the aristocracy on whose patronage the artists depended. It was used on cauldrons and on metal wine-flagons, on horse-trappings (62), and, no doubt, decoratively on panels of wood in the houses. It appears on objects of a religious nature, while religious motifs are constantly in evidence in purely functional contexts. Such sacred symbols as the human head (63), the heads of venerated birds and beasts, magical birds, sacred trees and many more such objects, blend into the relentless, flowing pattern, and yet stand out from it in a remarkable way.

Paul Jacobsthal was the first great expert on early Celtic art to

176

63 Examples of Celtic representations of heads

demonstrate the three main sources from which its inspiration was ultimately derived. Today, archaeological researches show that, although Jacobsthal's conclusions were basically correct, the various influences were more complex and diverse than would have seemed to be the case at that time. It seems unlikely that the more exotic borrowings by the early Celtic artists came directly from the Eastern world. These were all to be found in the

177

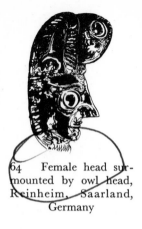

64 Female head surmounted by owl head, Reinheim, Saarland, Germany

Mediterranean regions and it is probable that the Celts took them straight from Italy, together with the more familiar Classical motifs.

Commenting on early Celtic art in general Jacobsthal says: 'The repertory of Early Celtic Art is narrow; the image of man is limited to huge menhir-like statues in stone, in bronze to a few busts or miniature doll-like men and a multitude of heads. There are very few natural animals; most of them are fantastic and highly stylised.' In further demonstrating the essential differences between Classical and Celtic art Jacobsthal says: 'But to the Greeks a spiral is a spiral and a face is a face and it is always clear where the one ends and the other begins, whereas the Celts "see" the faces "into" the spirals or tendrils; ambiguity is a characteristic of Celtic art.'

Early Celtic art has been divided up into styles which correspond with the early, middle and late phases of La Tène culture; these apply solely to Europe. In the British Isles, Celtic art took on such a distinctive quality that it must be considered separately from the development that took place on the Continent. By the time the great votive deposit was made in Lake Neuchâtel, at La Tène, about 100 BC, Celtic art on the Continent had virtually become a spent force. It was left to Britain and Ireland to carry on the tradition and their contribution to its history is noteworthy.

65 Outline of flagon from chariot grave at Waldalgesheim, Hunsrück, Germany

ARTISTIC STYLES

Early Style

On the Continent, then, Celtic art comes into being from the mid fifth century BC and the characteristics of this early period have been defined by the experts on Celtic art. This first phase is known as the 'Early Style'. At this initial stage Celtic art is inevitably experimental and immature, but, even so, it is already a distinct and individual expression and the borrowed elements have been transformed into essentially Celtic motifs. One of the most impressive burials, that of a powerful queen or princess, dating to the early fourth century BC was found at Reinheim near Saarbrucken in 1954. She had been interred in a magnificent grave richly furnished with funerary accessories, this, like the burial at Vix, is suggestive of the power and influence which women could wield in Celtic society. The burial chamber itself was constructed of oak; no vehicle would appear to have been present in the grave. The ornaments placed there were of outstanding richness and beauty. One of the finest pieces is a torc of twisted gold. The terminals are elaborately decorated with female heads surmounted by owl-heads (*64*); the bodies fade away into the decorative foliage. This is possibly a goddess having the owl as her especial attribute, perhaps a Celtic forerunner of the type of the Classical Minerva. A penannular bracelet found in the grave is decorated in a similar fashion. There were also a closed ring bracelet and gold rings in an openwork design, and other objects of gold. One of the finest pieces in the grave was the famous flagon. This is made from bronze; it is spouted, and resembles the flagon from the Celtic grave at Waldalgesheim (*65*). This is interesting because most of the Waldalgesheim grave-goods belong to a slightly later phase of Celtic art—the 'Waldalgesheim

66 One of a pair of early La Tène flagons from Basse-Yutz, Lorraine, France

Style' as it is called—but this flagon is earlier and belongs to the phase considered here (*66*). Elegant in outline, it stands on a pedestal foot; a fantastic animal is figured on the lid. The upper part of the handle is decorated with human heads superimposed on ram-heads.

An earlier grave, dating to about the sixth century BC, and again that of a powerful queen or princess, was found at Vix (Chatillon-sur-Seine). Its proximity to the great hill-fort on Mont Lassois, and the presence near by of another important burial, imply that this was one of the centres of Celtic power and influence. The tumulus contained a plank-built burial chamber in which were a wagon with bronze fittings. One of the finest objects in the grave was a diadem or, more probably, neck-ring of gold, decorated with winged horses. This is an import of Southern origin. The grave-goods also included brooches, bronze bowls, a bronze flagon and a vast *krater* of bronze, from Greece.

Waldalgesheim Style

From this early, experimental style we move on to the second phase of Celtic art, that known as the 'Waldalgesheim Style' (*c.* 325–250 BC). This shows that a new tendency had developed within the earlier style; symmetry was put aside, and the patterns developed a free-flowing quality. The motifs now drifted even further away from their Mediterranean and Eastern prototypes. The style is named after the princely burial found at Waldalgesheim, Kr. Kreuznach. This was the double burial of a man and woman; a chariot with fittings was also placed in the grave. It is one of the last of a series of lavish Rhenish burials. Amongst the rich grave-goods was the flagon, already mentioned, belonging to the earlier style. The body of the flagon is decorated with lightly engraved patterns. A ram's head appears at the upper end of the handle; the lower end is decorated with a bearded and moustached male face having the leaf-crown motif—which Jacobsthal considered to be a sign of divinity—well in evidence above the brow. An animal resembling a horse stands on the reconstructed lid (*67*). The other metal objects in the grave show the new style which was developing out of the Early Style.

The gold objects include a torc with beautiful and elaborate ornamentation of spirals and loops in relief on the terminals and the adjacent parts of the ring. There is also a twisted closed bracelet with beaded decoration between the twists; and there are two magnificent penannular bracelets richly ornamented on the terminals and on the back part of the hoops as well. Human heads are worked into the spiral design (*68*), and the spirals emerging from the brow and continuing up the side of the head look as though they are intended to represent horns. We have seen that the ram figures frequently in La Tène art; and the Celts greatly favoured a horned god, whether antler-bearing or bull- or ram-horned.

67 Horse-like animal originally on the lid of the Waldalgesheim flagon

Two horn-caps or ornamental finials for the chariot-yoke were also found in this grave; they are only slightly decorated. A superb pair of bronze plaques, decorated in the new flowing style, was also recovered. Each is adorned with a head, with typical emphatic eyes, clearly demarcated eyebrows sweeping out towards the side of the face, and a modified leaf-crown. The slim hands are raised in the religious posture, the so-called 'orans' attitude, which the Druids used in prayer. A torc is worn round the neck.

68 Faces worked into the design of a penannular bracelet, Waldalgesheim

This was a style that spread widely throughout the Celtic world. It does in fact appear on one or two scabbards in the great ritual deposit at La Tène itself.

The Plastic Style

This development of La Tène art is dated to somewhere about 275 BC. It is contemporary with the so-called 'Sword Style'. The Plastic Style was much used on objects of bronze made for personal adornment and for chariot-fittings. The great votive cauldron found at Brå, in Jutland, is a fine example of this more robust and inflexible style. As Sandars says, it is balanced between nature and solid geometry. This cauldron illustrates the fact that one style did not stop abruptly and another immediately take over. The cauldron, a ritual vessel with a capacity of 28 gallons, had been deliberately broken up. It provides several excellent examples of the Waldalgesheim Style while being in the main a representative of the newer Plastic Style. The width across the mouth is three feet. The body is made of thin sheet bronze, and the rim is of solid bronze over an iron hoop. There are owls' heads cast in one piece with the attachments holding the three handles; and each handle was flanked by a pair of solid cast bronze bulls' heads. The cauldron was manufactured in the third century B C, probably in Bohemia or Moravia.

Also in this style is a bronze object from France on which a variant of the sacred triple-head motif of the Celts is represented. Into the design of a running spiral three human heads, or more properly superhuman heads, have been fitted. The strange distorted features; the huge eye on one side of the head and the small eye on the other; the streaked-back hair on one side of the head only, and the beard on only one side of the face, together with the mole or wart, are all suggestive, as Sandars says, of such a hero as Cú Chulainn when his distortions were on him:

> Then his face became a red hollow. He sucked one of his eyes into his head so that a wild crane could hardly have reached it to pluck it out from the back of his skull on to the middle of his cheek. The other eye sprang out on to his cheek. His mouth was twisted back fearsomely. (*C. O'Rahilly, 201*)

The Plastic Style was especially applied to bronze objects of personal use. It is a robust style, and less flowing in movement than the earlier styles. The gold torcs of this period are particularly impressive. Three elaborate example's were found with three others at Fenouillet, Haute Garonne (*69*). Some of the human masks used in the Plastic Style have an almost negroid look (*70*). A strong centre of workmanship in the Plastic Style seems to have existed in the territory of the Boii (Bohemia), of which the Brå cauldron is perhaps the finest example.

Finally, in this brief glance at the phases of Celtic art on the

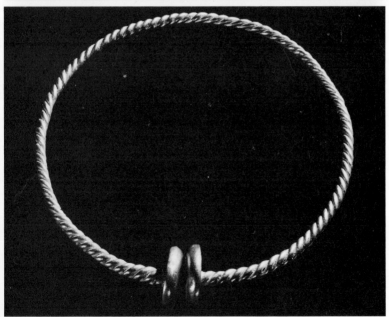

69 Fenouillet torcs, Haute-Garonne, France

70 Human masks with an almost negroid look about them, from Marson, Marne, France

Continent, we come to the last phase, the Sword Style, which was in fact contemporary with the Plastic Style.

The Sword Style

This style, dated to somewhere about 275 BC, is a more original style than the Plastic Style, taking the form of lightly engraved linear designs on metalwork, such as bronze sword-scabbards and iron sword-scabbards, some of which have been found in Hungary and in Switzerland. The style owed a great deal to the example of Waldalgesheim, and favoured the asymmetric designs.

These, then, are the several styles into which it has been found convenient to divide continental Celtic art.

THE BRITISH ISLES

Britain

On contact with Britain the art of the continental parent peoples became subtly changed, as indeed did so much of Celtic culture. Just as we must expect differences in the social details, in the size of the houses, in the degree of domestic sophistication and so on, so must we look for changes and modifications in the art styles.

There are some imported examples of the Early Style in Britain but the whole question of the dating of the native pieces is under consideration. The Celtic artists and skilled craftsmen depended upon princely patronage for their employment. Celtic nobles from the Continent would in the first place, perhaps, bring their artists with them. But even so, right from the start, the differences in style are clear. The predilection for hatching characteristic of British work may perhaps be accounted for by the fact that it was much favoured by the insular goldsmiths catering for the nobility of the Bronze Age. Fox, in his great study of insular Celtic art, discusses 16 objects which he believes to have been imports and to have set the fashion and given rise to a taste for Celtic art before the true insular style got under way. The hanging-bowl from Cerrig-y-Drudion, in Denbighshire (*71*), for example, which was found in a stone cist, is patterned with incised palmette and scroll designs. It is related to the continental late Early Style, and as far as its decoration is concerned its immediate prototypes would seem to lie in north-east Gaul. As the decoration on the base and the projecting rim can only be seen from below it is presumed that the bowl was suspended on four chains at a sufficiently high position to make these fully visible.

The second of these objects discussed by Fox is the splendid scabbard-plate from Wisbech, in Cambridgeshire (*72*). The decoration is similar to that on the Cerrig-y-Drudion bowl, but less complex. As Fox points out, the pattern is again meant to be seen from a specific angle, in this case by the wearer looking down at his thigh, for only in this way is the design of palmettes and scrolls seen in the perspective the artist must have intended. Another example of this designing for viewing from a particular angle is a magnificent head, carved from oak heart-wood, which

71 Underside of rim (restored) of hanging bowl from Cerrig-y-Drudion, Denbighshire

72 Bronze plating of scabbard for short sword, Wisbech, Cambridgeshire

has recently come to light in County Tipperary, Ireland, and which is at present being studied by Celtic Art experts. All the complex and intricate design with which it is ornamented is seen to its best advantage when the head is placed well above the viewer, suspended or on a support. The hatched triangles on the border of the Wisbech scabbard are components of design which are well known in continental decoration. Fox dates this scabbard to the mid third century BC.

A further example of an import from Europe into the British Isles is the remarkable bronze horn-cap from the Thames at Brentford, in Middlesex. This, unlike the two objects already mentioned, is in the Waldalgesheim Style but nevertheless is probably a late piece. True work in this style is rarely found in British-made objects. It has indeed been suggested that this piece was not an import at all, but an insular artefact; but the matter is in question. As we have seen, two horn-caps were found in the Waldalgesheim grave. Fox likens the tendrils on the Brentford horn-cap to duck-heads—and indeed we do find birds, like human heads and animals, regularly worked into fantastic non-natural forms in Celtic art.

There seems to be some slight evidence for the use of red enamel on this piece. The enamel would have filled the background, and the contrast between the brilliant colour and the bright bronze would have been very striking. Enamel was used at an early stage on the Continent; and this horn-cap must date to about the early third century BC.

The palmette forms are much to the fore in this early group of imports. In addition to the objects mentioned, there is a series of daggers with decorated sheaths which must also be considered as having been brought into Britain from the Continent. On those that are decorated the decoration is elaborate, often in the form of bands of geometric design. Fox points out the interesting distribution of these objects. Eleven were found in the Thames above London, between Chelsea and Richmond, and Fox suggests that this may indicate the presence of a trading centre in this area or that there was a centre of invaders in this area that has not yet been identified. The whole group dates to somewhere about the middle of the third century BC.

Having glanced at this group of objects which were seemingly imported into Britain before the full La Tène settlements had taken place there, it is now time to consider Celtic art as it evolved

in Britain. The true beginnings
of the insular art would seem to
be traceable to the Marnian
settlements established in Yorkshire somewhere round about
the middle of the third century
BC from the Marne region of
France. The tribe, the Parisii,
were certainly a component
element in this movement,
though other tribes were probably involved as well. This
early phase of insular art styles
represents the adaptation by
artists working in this country
of the Waldalgesheim, Plastic
and Sword styles.

The evolution of Celtic art in
the British Isles was to span a
period of some 300 years. From
about 75 to 25 BC the full La

73 Back of bronze mirror, Birdlip,
Gloucestershire. There are enamel
inlays on the handle

Tène style became modified, due to Belgic influence. Nevertheless,
some of the finest pieces of Celtic art, in the form of the remarkable
decorated bronze mirrors, are to be found at the very end of the
insular tradition (*73*).

Iron, together with bronze, was used in the manufacture of
these decorated articles. Some of the insular bronzes were
decorated in a linear style, suggestive of an individual school of
craftsmen. This involved a rocked-tracer technique, and basketry
hatching, which reached its full
development in the decoration of
the bronze mirrors. One of the
earliest examples of this style is the
fragment of a shield-mount found at
Tal y Llyn, in Merioneth. It is also
seen on the shield-boss from Llyn
Cerrig Bach, in Anglesey (*74*). Four
roundels on this boss, arranged on
either side of a central rib, contain
triskele motifs. This, like most of
the other objects from Llyn Cerrig

74 Roundel on shield-boss,
Llyn Cerrig Bach, Anglesey

75 Shield from the river Thames at Battersea, London

Bach, must be regarded as an import into Anglesey from elsewhere.

Asymmetric patterns were greatly favoured in Britain, and non-Classical patterns are much more in evidence here than on the Continent. There is a very interesting concentration on zoomorphic and ornithomorphic subjects in Britain. The magnificent Battersea shield, for example, originally gilded, and having red glass insets, is decorated with the so-called 'fold-over' symmetry (75). Though probably dating to the first century AD it has direct links with the earliest examples of insular Celtic art. There is very little in this piece that has not already its place in the repertoire of Celtic art. Animal-like faces have eyes inset with red glass. The design of the central boss is reminiscent of the owl-head with huge staring eyes, again with glass insets. Likewise, in the case of the Torrs (Kirkcudbright) pony-cap, the bird or animal element in the basic design is noteworthy. It contains suggested bird-heads and the stylised human masks which are a typical motif in Celtic art. The date assigned to this unique piece is the second half of the third century BC. This provides another example of the so-called 'fold-over' symmetry, a much earlier example than that which decorates the Battersea shield. The tendril themes are here well developed.

Many of the early features we see here are to disappear with the evolution of insular Celtic art. Fox demonstrates in this case again that the object was designed by the artist to be seen in use, and the pattern would in fact be observed to the best advantage by the chariot warrior standing in the chariot and looking down on to the cap. The foreshortening of the design as seen from this aspect would put it into the proper perspective. The influence of the Waldalgesheim Style is again obvious here.

A pair of drinking-horn mounts was also found in Torrs Moss, and it is likely that these were created in the same 'school' as the pony-cap. The mounts, of thin bronze, terminate in duck-heads— a popular motif in insular Celtic art, as we have seen. The eyes were inset with coral or red glass; the ornament is incised and complex. Fox believes that these objects were actually made in north-eastern England rather than in Galloway, where they were found.

This pony-cap was no doubt used for ceremonial purposes, like so much else that has been recovered from bogs and lakes and rivers—fine bronze shields, for example, must have been made primarily for these purposes because they are too frail for serious use.

Two main schools of Celtic art in Britain then can thus be distinguished, one favouring the linear style, the other what may be called the 'Shield Style'. No actual Celtic workshops have been discovered here or on the Continent, but we know that such *ateliers* must have existed. The artists used compasses but they also used freehand designs which were themselves based on compass technique.

In Britain, the Celtic art style flared up overnight, as it were, in contrast to the slow development on the Continent. As Sandars appositely says, 'at all events it is the overriding consistency and harmony of the insular tradition that strikes the observer'.

Another difference between the creation of Celtic art in this country and on the Continent is the fact that the continental Celts had their scabbards ornamented by the blacksmith, whereas in Britain the bronzesmith did this work. Some of the finest examples of insular Celtic art are found on sword-scabbards; most of these have been found in northern Ireland; the only comparable piece from Britain is from Bugthorpe, in the East Riding of York- shire. Here, an incised shaded pattern is used, resulting in one of the loveliest pieces of insular Celtic art. It is a splendid example of the northern school, especially the chape. This scabbard is closely related to the comparable contemporary objects found in northern Ireland, dating to the first century B C.

Fox points out that bronze collars would seem to have replaced gold torcs by the first century B C. Some of these are very grand and intricate, like the Stichill collar from the banks of the Tweed, in Roxburghshire, with its hinged back—and the impressive collar found in Lochar Moss, in Dumfriesshire (*c.* first century AD), presumptively a votive site. The upper part of the collar is formed of beads, and the front is decorated with a scroll pattern. An openwork strip has been riveted on to the main structure.

There was thus a flourishing school of northern British Celtic art, which was at its height during the years immediately before and after the birth of Christ.

The evidence of Celtic art, religion and settlement in the Dumfriesshire area of Scotland is a remarkable phenomenon; for some reason or another there would seem to have been a flourishing and vital Celtic community here.

Ireland

Ireland is extremely interesting from the viewpoint of Celtic studies in general, for not only is it the sole Celtic country which escaped the direct impact of Rome, but it comments on its own society and its individual peculiarities from within the tradition and in its own archaic language. Not only does Ireland have a limited but striking repertoire of La Tène art objects, but this art style does in fact continue with an unbroken tradition—unlike that of the regions subjected to Roman rule—and continues to flourish, with obvious modifications, well into the medieval period as the magnificent art of Irish Christianity. Stones, metalwork and manuscripts almost groan under the weight of the lavish and magnificent ramifications of the Christian artists. They work as passionately to glorify God with their art as their pagan predecessors had sought to express the feelings of a pagan society towards the deities of the ancient Celtic world. The magic, the hidden meaning, these endure—but now they hint, in the main, at a Christian concept. Sometimes the pagan element is present, to express anti-Christian forces. Sometimes one suspects that the artist is slipping a latent pagan symbol in for his own purposes— seeming to reveal a perfectly understandable unwillingness to commit himself entirely, and thereby to alienate forever the forces by which his and his people's forebears were ruled.

The sudden blossoming of La Tène art in northern Ireland may be accounted for by the coming of bands of Celtic invaders to the country, possibly in the second century BC. These must have entered the country through Britain. An earlier wave of immigrants had reached the west of the country some time in the third or second centuries B C, coming direct from the Continent. This immigration accounts for the presence in Ireland of two groups of La Tène peoples and would, as we have seen, account for the fact that the *Táin Bó Cúalnge*, the earliest Irish epic tale, is concerned with the traditional rivalry between the inhabitants of Connacht in the west and those of Ulster in the north-east.

The finest of the La Tène scabbards from the British Isles do in fact come from northern Ireland. The beautiful scabbards from Lisnacrogher illustrate clearly the subtle skill of the artists. Lisnacrogher is itself an extremely interesting site. In County Antrim, it consisted of a low mound, allegedly a crannóg, in a bog, in which the hoard of objects was originally found. It is believed to have been a votive site, one of those noted throughout Europe in bogs, marshes, ponds, lakes, springs or rivers. In 1882 the site was irresponsibly destroyed and the alleged crannóg was robbed by a collector. This was a tragedy for Irish archaeology. Not only has much invaluable material been lost, but a site which could have helped to throw some light on pagan Celtic practice in Ireland has been completely lost to posterity. Three bronze scabbards were found there. An interesting piece from the same site is the sword-pommel (*54*), so called, which is decorated by a pair of small ravens in the round and with a band of red enamel which has curving lines of bronze wandering through it. The presence of this object, its cult implications suggested by the ravens, helps to strengthen the supposition that this was in fact a votive site. The surviving scabbard has obvious affinities with the slightly later scabbard from Bugthorpe (p. 189) which has already been mentioned. Although, however, the British scabbard has many features in common with the La Tène work of northern Ireland of the second to first century B C, as Fox points out, the Lisnacrogher piece has retained Marnian motifs which the other has discarded. Other closely related scabbards come from the River Bann at Toome and Coleraine. These finds suggest that the origin of this style in Ireland may have been somewhere about 175 B C. Dillon is of the opinion that these objects could have been the product of a single workshop; nothing comparable is known from any other part of Ireland, and they suggest a firm link with the art of the Continent.

Other splendid objects in the La Tène style have been found in Ireland. These include two fine collars, one from Clonmacnoise,

76 Bronze and enamel disc, Ballinasloe, Galway, Ireland

County Offaly, and the other from Broighter, County Derry (p. 215). The Clonmacnoise collar would seem to have been manufactured in Ireland, but it owes much to continental models. The Broighter collar, on the other hand, has affinities with British art, and may be compared with the example from Snettisham. Various other objects suggest a flourishing and individual school of Celtic art in Ireland, which was to lay the foundation for all the later flowering of medieval Irish creative genius.

The early centuries of the Christian era saw the importation of many objects from the Roman-occupied areas. The vogue for things which were originally Roman in design but with the addition of Celtic patterns, continued well into the sixth and seventh centuries. Many bronze pins and penannular brooches were imported from Britain. These penannular brooches stemmed from Roman prototypes. From about the turn of the Christian era these were decorated with enamel. The art of enamelling was known in Ireland and a high degree of skill was shown. The Lisnacrogher sword-pommel has been mentioned already. Another beautiful object was found in Galway in 1959. Dating to round about the early first century AD, it is shaped like a disc, perhaps for mounting on wood or leather, and therefore possibly a decoration for a belt. The design is in relief and openwork (76). It had an infill of red glass which could be seen through the openwork pattern. Its decorative technique can be compared with that on the Battersea shield, for example, with the Hod Hill boss, and with other examples from Britain and the Continent. The technique applied to the making of this Galway disc was, as Henry points out, applied many years later to the creation of the famous Ardagh chalice; but this takes us beyond the range of our inquiry.

Brooches, belt-buckles, and hanging-bowls, derived from Roman models, were used in Ireland, then, and the passion for the technique of *millefiori** and the manufacture of the coloured glass sticks which it involved, all stemmed from this indirect

---

* A decorative glass made by fusing together a number of these coloured sticks of glass of different sizes and then cutting the resultant whole into sections for use as inlay.

contact with the Classical world. The penannular brooch became very popular in Ireland, and by the end of the Roman Empire enamelled penannular brooches were being manufactured, having for their decoration curvilinear designs, and discs of red enamel and millefiori glass; thus the Roman-derived objects were by no means all imports into Ireland. In Ireland, compasses were still in use, whereas in Britain they had gradually died out, due to Classical influence. Bone slips served as pattern books. As Henry points out, it was during this period that all the preparations were being made for the great art of the later, Christian period: 'A remarkable continuity is one of the most striking aspects of Irish art'; and again: 'Only if we realise that a long pagan tradition supplied the first elements and the essential decorative principles of the art, which flourished in the monasteries after the fifth century, will we see the reason for this persistence of outlook.'

The magnificent Celtic art of Ireland in the Christian era draws upon and uses, and benefits directly from this great toreutic tradition of the pagan Celtic world.

So far we have only considered *metalwork* in pre-Christian Ireland. Stone sculpture did, however, exist, and the small amount that has come to light so far is suggestive of much more yet to be recovered or recognised for what it is; it also reminds us that a great deal more must have fallen under the evangelising blows of the Christian Fathers who, like St Patrick when he smashed up the stone idol, Cromm Cruaich, 'plied upon Cromm a sledge, from top to toe'. One cannot help feeling that a lot of other 'strengthless goblins' must have met their fate in a similar fashion. Pagan iconography would, then, be likely to have been destroyed outright, or sanctified and reworked for the good of Christianity. Many stones which are suggestive of an earlier origin in Ireland are decorated with Christian symbols, the offending pagan features having been obliterated or adapted to the Christian formulae. The continuity of the tradition of placing stone heads in prominent positions in churches, in the walls of houses, on farm walls and so on—which went on to an almost bewildering degree in Ireland—would seem to testify to the original strength in Ireland of this pagan belief in the powers of the human head, as does the recovery of certain heads of Iron Age date. These, and the few pieces of monumental sculpture which have been recovered in Ireland to date, together with the textual references to stone idols, point to a stronger tradition of pre-Christian monumental sculpture than the surviving material would suggest. A glance at what does in fact now exist brings us on to the whole question of the use of stone in pre-Roman art.

One of the most exciting and fascinating decorated objects from pagan Ireland is the Turoe stone. It stood, at one time, out-side the rath of Feermore, in the township of Turoe, in Galway. The stone is a granite boulder which has been trimmed into a dome-like shape and covered with decorative motifs. There would seem to be no doubt that the stone is intentionally phalloid in shape and general appearance, and its obvious cult associations would strengthen this conclusion. It is almost four feet high and the patterns which cover it are essentially asymmetric and strongly curvilinear; the basis of the design is to be found in foliage and the disc motif. In general treatment it can be compared with the stone pillar from Pfalzfeld. Its date is problematic and at the present time there are widely divergent views about this question. The decorative motifs would, however, seem to indicate a date round about the third century BC and until more evidence comes to light, this is as far as we can reasonably go. A small object which, in shape, is reminiscent of a miniature Turoe stone, comes from Barnwood, Gloucestershire, and is at present in the Museum at Cheltenham (77). Fox includes it in his 'magical' objects category and this would seem to be a reasonable conclusion to reach, for it can have had little of functional significance. It is decorated with triskeles suggesting a mythological association—the triskele (78) was a solar symbol and one of the stylised representations of the symbol of the cross in the Bronze Age—and one is reminded here of the triskeles which adorn the Llyn Cerrig shield-boss and other objects. The triskeles are incised on this enig-matic object which is 3·7 inches in height, little bigger than a good-sized glass paper-weight in fact. The technique used in its

77 Limestone cone, Barnwood, Gloucestershire—9·4 cm high

decoration suggests a date for its manufacture in the mid first century A D. It is of local manufacture and must, therefore, be the product of a Dobunnic workshop. As we have seen, the Celts worshipped certain stones and believed them to be under the direct influence of certain deities and spirits. It is clear that the Turoe stone was used as a cult object which may have been connected with the fertility rites which formed an essential part of the inauguration of the Irish kings.

78 Triskele decoration on a *phalera* from Écury-sur-Coole, Marne, France

Other stones, decorated in the La Tène manner, are known from Ireland and serve to suggest the vitality of the Celtic artists in this medium, as well as in metalwork. One of these, now fragmentary, from Killycluggin in County Cavan, would appear to be of especial significance (79). It was found shattered, outside a circle of stones and we are reminded strongly of the reference to the breaking up of Cromm Cruaich, the idol which stood in the centre of other stones, in the same county. The figure was decorated with fine spirals, and bears clear affinities to the Turoe stone. This was, again, clearly a cult stone, and the region an important religious site in pagan times. As at Tara, in County Meath, and elsewhere, the site has direct connections back as far as the Neolithic Age at least. As Henry says of such sites: 'They introduce us to a much more remote past in the occupation of Tara; the mound covered a megalithic tomb in whose tumulus 40 or so burials of the Middle Bronze Age had been inserted. These discoveries give to Tara the background of a prehistoric necropolis and sanctuary later adapted by the Celts to new needs and turned into a royal residence still keeping a religious aura.'

All the evidence suggests that in Ireland, as elsewhere no doubt in the pagan Celtic world, ancient sacred sites were used by the innovating Celts for their own religious purposes.

79 Remains of pattern carved upon a stone at Killycluggin, Co. Cavan, Ireland

Another stone, at Castlestrange, County Roscommon, has its surface decorated with an incised, curvilinear design, and again resembles the Turoe stone. It is a granite boulder some two feet high, and is in fact an early Celtic stele of a type known from Brittany and elsewhere.

These Irish examples of stone sculpture are closely paralleled by the iconography of pagan Celtic Europe. One of the most impressive pieces was found at Pfalzfeld, in the Hünsruck, and is now in Bonn Museum. A Rhenish work, it consists of a pillar, clearly phalloid in shape, with the glans placed downwards into the earth. It is elaborately decorated. The top once supported a head, or heads. It is believed to have stood on a barrow. It is likely that the Irish stones originally stood in similar positions, marking perhaps the grave of some ancestor round which religious rites were performed. Each of the four sides of the Pfalzfeld pillar is decorated with a pear-shaped human face, adorned with great swelling horns (or a leaf-crown) and stylised foliage.

A sandstone block from Waldenbuch (Württemberg), of which only the lower part remains, is decorated in relief in the Waldalgesheim Style. A naturalistic arm stretches across the body, comparable to the arm carved above the waist-belt of the remarkable janus stone from Holzgerlingen (*80*), now in Stuttgart Museum. This is a sandstone double statue, the stern features and great horns imparting a grim dignity to the work. The arm, the horns, and the eyebrows depicted in a straight line, would link it with the more dramatic and demoniac figure from Tanderagee, near Armagh (*81*). Coming from the precincts of what must have been a powerful pagan sanctuary—Armagh Hill—this figure has vestigial horns, moustaches, a great mouth, and a general air of frenzied wildness. It has been described as wearing a horned helmet, but this is in fact an illusion created by the long, straight eyebrow line which terminates at the sides of the head and does not continue round the back, as would a helmet. The horns thus grow from the head itself, as do those on continental examples. This figure, too, may have been displayed on some burial mound, or housed in a simple shrine which the Christian establishment was intended to subject and supersede.

Another stone fragment in this early tradition, from Echterdingen, now also in Stuttgart Museum, shows similar decoration.

Ireland has several examples of figure-carving of a monumental nature which would seem to evidence affinities with the northern

80 Janiform stone figure from Holzgerlingen, Böblingen, Germany

⚔ 81 Stone bust from Tanderagee, Armagh, Ireland

82 Stone statue of a warrior found beside a late Hallstatt tumulus at Hirschlanden, Stuttgart, Germany

European examples rather than with the Mediterranean-influenced sculptures of Provence and the valley of the River Rhône. Chronologically, the first monumental stone figure that we know of (many such must have been fashioned in wood throughout the Celtic period) was discovered in 1962. It is remarkable both in its early date and in its great size. Of obvious Classical derivation, it was found when a Hallstatt tumulus near Hirschlanden was in the process of excavation. It consists of the figure of a warrior (*82*) with one arm crossed over the torso and the thumb raised. The excavators suggested that originally it crowned the tumulus, but they found it cast down just outside it, in fragments.

Many more such figures must have existed, but those which were readily visible would have been systematically destroyed in the Middle Ages. This takes us back to Ireland. The horned figure from Tanderagee has already been mentioned; it may be compared with the stone figure found at Blackness Castle, in West Lothian, Scotland (*83*). In all its crude and stark simplicity this figure has much in common with the Irish figures in question here, and must be regarded as yet another cult figure from the British Isles dating to somewhere in the first centuries before or after Christ. Another figure from Armagh is also likely to be early in date. This is the radiate, naked figure, which is apparently the portrayal of some native deity (*84*). It compares well with some of the Romano-British sculptures from north-west England, especially those from the Maryport area of Cumberland, and it may have been that it was from this area that its ultimate inspiration sprang. In Ireland, all the figure sculptures and the decorated stones are found in the north and west.

Two figures found on islands in Lough Erne, Fermanagh, again show affinities with the northern European material. One is janiform, all the emphasis being given to the head with its enormous eyes outlined with a double line, its straight nose and small mouth. The head is basically pear-shaped, and the arms are crossed over the belt. A general air of archaism prevails. The second stone is single, with similar ancient features.

In this same category of crude, vigorous figure sculptures of a north European type we may perhaps include the so-called

83 Bust from Blackness, West Lothian

84 Radiate bust from Armagh, Ireland

85 Stone figure, La Gran'mère, St Martin Guernsey

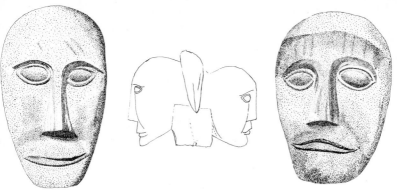

86 Pair of heads from Roquepertuse, Bouches-du-Rhône, France

'Gran'mere' from St Martin's parish, Guernsey (*85*). Bearing more resemblance to the Gaulish mother-goddesses than to any other category of images, she stands outside the churchyard where she was banished from within the Christian precincts. People still make offerings to her, and believe yet that she is capable of making certain movements and responses in the correct circumstances.

From Provence comes a group of early figure carvings of a much more sophisticated and Classically influenced type. A double head, for example, originally painted, and having a great raptor's beak separating the heads at the top (*86*) was found together with five figures, more than life-size, inside the sanctuary at Roquepertuse. The presence of human skulls in niches specially provided for them; a frieze of horses; and the great raptor-like goose that stood above the portico (*87*) complete the Celtic picture. These figures may date to as early as the fourth century BC.

87 Stone goose, reconstructed, from Roquepertuse

Another piece of Celtic figure-carving comes from Euffigneix (Haute-Marne). This figure has the appearance of having been fashioned from the trunk of a tree, and no doubt its immediate antecedents were of wood. A boar in La Tène style is carved on the front (*56*). Here we must have the portrayal of some god whose special cult attribute the boar was.

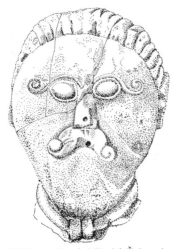

88 Stone head, Mšecké-Žehrovice, Bohemia

89 Limestone head dug up in GLEVVM, Gloucester

As we have seen, the boar was perhaps the most important and sacred of all animals in the Celtic world.

Stone heads are difficult to date, on the whole. Those which come from Roman contexts, which are very numerous, may include some which in fact ante-date the Roman occupation nevertheless. The whole question of dating these heads requires reconsideration. As heads have been considered from the point of view of cult in the last chapter, only one or two of the apparently early ones will be mentioned now. One of the most famous and impressive comes from Mšecke-Žehrovice, Bohemia (*88*). Of rag-stone, it was found in a most interesting context in a site that was both an iron-foundry and a sanctuary. It dates to the second century BC or somewhat earlier. The treatment of the ears is reminiscent of those on the magnificent head from Gloucester (*89*). It also has a 'cigarette hole' on the side of its mouth, a mysterious feature which occurs on Celtic heads over a wide area of Europe including the British Isles.

Strange, Oriental-looking heads are grasped by a fearsome monster in the famous sculpture from Noves. From Ireland comes the three-faced head from Corleck, County Cavan, the strange, austere features of which are typical of early Celtic cult heads (*46*). This tricephalos has no ears. There is a hole in the bottom of the stone for the insertion of a dowel, and presumably the head was originally mounted on top of a pillar in some shrine or sacred enclosure. Corleck itself would seem to have been a cult centre of first importance. When the three-faced head was found, two janiform heads were alleged to have been unearthed with it, but these have apparently been lost. Other heads from the site are, however, being brought to light, and the janiform examples may yet be recoverable.

A head from Cortynan, also in the northern part of Ireland, is another stone which would seem to justify early dating.

A stone head recently recovered from a garden wall in Hampshire has markedly Celtic features, and in some respects resembles the figure from Tanderagee—smallish, round and emphatic eyes; the brow carved in a single arching line; horns—in this case ram's horns—moustaches sweeping up the cheeks; the great mouth—which, although damaged, must always have been generous in size—all these features point to a Celtic origin, and compare with those of the Tanderagee figure. Animal sculpture in stone is also known from the Continent, and from Armagh in northern Ireland (_90_).

These are some examples which help to demonstrate that, apart from decorating metal surfaces with Celtic patterns, and apart from carving heads and figures from wood—and no doubt also decorating these with carv-ed patterns (reminiscent of tattooing) as they prob-  90 Stone figure of a bear, Armagh, Ireland

ably did the woodwork in their houses, their clothes and their leatherwork— the Celts did produce naturalistic figure sculp-tures and heads in stone. The present corpus of sur-viving examples leads us to suppose the former exis-tence of a much richer repertoire in this medium than has been suspected hitherto. The religious zeal of the Middle Ages has no doubt accounted for many of them. Others must await discovery either in the ground or in churches or in private collections, where their real nature has not been appreciated, or in the basements of museums.

BRONZE FIGURINES AND CAULDRONS

Over and above the objects already discussed, the Celts produced some splendid bronzes some of which are worthy of such a modern sculptor as Henry Moore. They would almost seem rather to have their immediate inspiration in the modern world than in ancient Mediterranean or barbarian milieus.

Coming from a site having clear religious associations—on the River Loire, opposite the great Celtic sanctuary at Fleury-Floriac—the remarkable collection of bronzes from Neuvy-en-Sullias, together with vast treasure, which was in all likelihood buried by Celtic priests to protect it from the Romans, indicate a centre of cult here of some magnitude (*91*). One cast-bronze piece representing a woman dancing conveys a marvellous impression of rhythm and movement (*34*). Another bronze portrays a nude man dancing; his features and the style of his hair are typically Celtic (*35*). Again, there is a sense of delicate yet powerful movement and vitality. Among the other figures from this site is one of a man who must have been playing a harp or cymbals—the instrument is missing now. He wears tight, checked trousers (*bracae*) and a checked jerkin top, thus providing an interesting example of at least one type of Celtic dress. His hair, again, is done in a Celtic style (*10*). A splendid boar, measuring over four feet in length and more than two in height, was found here; it was apparently a standard (*55*). A fine bronze stag is also present in this unique collection. The workmanship is all of high quality, showing once more that the Celts were capable of working more or less naturalistically as well as fantastically.

The Celts used cauldrons as domestic

91 Bronze figure of a 'jongleur', Neuvy-en-Sullias, Loiret, France

vessels, but they also made them for ritual purposes. Three of these ritual vessels have been found in Denmark. They appear to have been used as votive offerings to some deity or other. Their presence in Denmark at all is a matter for speculation, but it is in keeping with the entire problem

92 Part of a bronze cauldron, Rynkeby, Jutland, Denmark

of the nature of Celtic influence in Denmark. There is evidence that this was, in fact, considerable, but how it came about we do not yet quite know. It may be that the Cimbri (a northern tribe of Teutonic origin: Strabo mentions the 'wealth of the Cimbri') were responsible, but at present no clear picture can be obtained even though it is clear that Celtic artists must have been at work in this region. One of these cauldrons was found at Rynkeby, on the island of Funen. Made of bronze, and dating probably to the first century B C, which seems to be a fairly general date for these vessels, it is decorated with a human face with stylised hair, large compelling eyes which must originally have been inlaid with some substance, and a small precise mouth (*92*). The neck is adorned with a massive torc with weighty terminals. The head is flanked by delicately worked ox protomes. It also had at one time inner plates fixed round the upper part of the inside. The only one that still exists is decorated with two animals which face each other—a boar, and what is taken to be a lion. The diameter of this cauldron is two feet four inches. It has clear affinities with two buckets imported into England from the Continent and, again, dating to the first century B C. These are the 'Marlborough vat' and the Aylesford bucket, both stave-built wooden vessels bound with decorated hoops and mounts.

The same date is given to another vessel, a great ritual cauldron, the finest of all those yet known, which is an extremely important document for pre-Roman cults. It was found in 1891 in Denmark, at a place named Gundestrup, in Jutland, and is thus known as the 'Gundestrup cauldron'. The vessel, which is made of silver, had been deliberately dismantled and laid on the ground as a votive offering. Both the inside and the outside of the vessel were faced with decorative plates, consisting of busts of deities on the outside of the vessel and cult scenes on the inside. The base of the cauldron on the inside likewise depicts a cult scene and this, together with the divine busts, was originally covered with very thin gold-foil. The eyes of the figures were inset with red and blue glass. Each plate, then, represents either some cult scene, or bears the representation of some distinctive god or goddess together with his or her attendants, cult beasts and birds and symbols, or having some mythological scene in progress in the background. The influence of the Eastern Celtic world is obvious, and a site somewhere near Bratislava has been suggested as its place of manufacture. The silver-working techniques are clearly of Eastern origin, while the scenes and cult figures can be closely paralleled in Celtic iconography and in the insular literatures alike. The basal scene, which represents the slaying of a vast bull, has been claimed to be of Mithraic origin, but this must remain in question. The Irish epic, the *Táin*, has a great, supernatural bull as one of its main characters, and although it does not concern a bull-hunt proper, there is no reason to suppose that some legend of the pursuit and slaying of a great divine bull was not in oral circulation amongst some of the Celts at least on the Continent; but, until some more definite evidence comes to light, this must remain purely speculative. The bull would originally have had horns of some other material; these are now missing. Another important cauldron, which we have already mentioned in connection with the Plastic Style of Celtic art comes from Brå, near Horsens in Jutland. It is earlier than the other cauldrons discussed here, and may date to the late third or early second century B C. Of bronze, it had been broken into pieces and placed in a pit in the ground, and, again, it would seem to represent a votive offering made to some deity. Like the Gundestrup cauldron, its place of origin would seem to have been in the more easterly Celtic world, and the Bohemian-Moravian region is a possible place of manufacture. How these great Celtic cauldrons reached Denmark is not known to us, nor has the general nature and extent of Celtic influence in that country as yet been determined.

CELTIC COINAGE

Another medium for the artistic and mythological expression of the pagan Celtic world is to be found in their coinage. The coins provide a fascinating sphere for study. They cast light on political and economic affairs; they suggest the movements of individual tribes; their motifs help to contribute to our knowledge of Celtic mythology.

There was an early coinage in silver amongst the Celts of Transylvania. As Powell points out, some of the designs struck on silver 'seem to provide illustrations for the Celtic mythology that was preserved in Ireland'. The coins, then, are potentially a repository for mythological tradition, as well as being a stimulating and challenging medium for the display of the Celtic artists' peculiar skills. The coin art came into being at a time when, leaving the British Isles aside, Celtic art had virtually burnt itself out; that is, from the late third century B C, until the time of the Roman Conquest.

One source of inspiration for the native coinage stemmed from the gold staters of Alexander III; these were of more importance in the easterly parts of the Celtic world. Another, and less influential source, was that of the gold staters of Philip II of Macedon. These appear to have reached the West via the Danube, and eventually arrived in Britain through Belgic influence. A further source which stimulated the Celtic coin artists to work in silver this time, was that from Massilia, and the coinage of the western Greeks. But, as Derek Allen points out, the adoption of a certain type of coin must always to some extent have depended upon the individual preference of any one tribe for one motif rather than another; mythological preferences are also likely to have been involved. The Celtic artists took the basic Classical repertoire and changed it as they had changed the Classical and other motifs in the very beginnings of the La Tène style. The formal naturalism of the Classical coins became debased, or elevated according to opinion, into typical Celtic fantasy. Severed heads, the legs of horses which have become detached from their bodies, chariot-wheels trundling along on their own, a great series of cult animals and birds, sun symbols, magical signs and every kind of mythological extravagance are to be found. Later on, and under the influence of the Roman coinage, the coins started to be inscribed, mainly with the abbreviated names of tribes, or individual chieftains and titles. They are thus able to throw some considerable light on changes that were taking place in Celtic society, and on the politics of the time, by reason of their pattern of distribution. In Ireland, as in Scotland, and in other northerly parts of Britain, no native coinage existed.

A move towards naturalism is found in the coinage of the later period, and this is especially seen in coins from the Belgic areas of Britain; it would seem to have stemmed from the influence of the easterly Celtic craftsmen who favoured this style.

Europe, then, in the main, used gold for its currency in the west and silver in the east. This currency would tend to be reserved for foreign trade, and the tribes requiring coinage would be those which traded regularly with peoples outwith the Celtic world. Exchange of goods in kind—barter—would tend to have been the mode of transaction amongst the people themselves. The cow was the unit of value in Ireland, and something similar no doubt served this purpose in Gaul. A slave woman, for example, was equal in value to three cows. Foreigners, however, would not be willing to transport bulky objects across Europe in return for their wares and would require their payment in more convenient monetary form.

The Belgic tribes brought the art of coinage into Britain at the end of the second century BC and mints were subsequently set up at the great tribal capitals, such as Silchester and Colchester. Currency bars of a standard weight were favoured in the west of England. In Britain, again, the coinage and its distribution throws considerable light on the political and economic scene. Inscribed coins dating to the last half-century before the Roman Conquest recording the names of tribes and chieftains in south Britain are also of invaluable assistance in our understanding of the insular Celtic set-up at this time. The early south British coinage shows variety and inventiveness; that of the more northerly tribes is less fluid and less original. The coins of Armorica, however, are perhaps the most noteworthy in this respect. They contain much that is of interest to mythologists, and in the fantastic human heads with their seemingly tattooed faces, wild hair bearing sacred symbols, and their frantic, distorted features, we would seem to come closer to the descriptions of the distorted, semi-divine hero of Irish legend than do we in any other area of the representative repertoire of the Celtic world.

CELTIC MIRRORS

The magnificent bronze mirrors, made in Britain from the late first century BC on, are another medium for some of the finest and most intricate examples of Celtic artistry (*93*). They were status symbols, indicating social wealth and power, and they reached their climax round about AD 30. Their ultimate inspiration lay in Greece and Etruria, and this was followed by Roman example at a later date; but, as they stand, they are, like all other aspects of Celtic art, unique in their complete individuality. Sandars says of the skill of the craftsmen: 'Steadiness and control had been learned long ago in the Bronze Age goldsmith's shop.' A rocked tracer was used to achieve the basketry effect which was much favoured by the mirror artists. Some of the finest examples, such as those from Desborough and Birdlip (73), show a marvellous precision of workmanship that, like the later Celtic illuminated manuscripts, is almost impossible to comprehend. The mirrors are confined to southern Britain and they are all of bronze. The Mayer mirror, one of the loveliest of the series is believed to have been recovered from the River Thames. The mirror designs are based on the circle, three circles being linked together, and combined with the Classical lyre-palmette motif. Sometimes only parts of the mirrors are hatched with basketry-work; sometimes this is used to form the entire background. The handles are in themselves works of art. They likewise are mostly wrought in bronze and show a variety of elegant shapes. The earlier mirrors have more simple handles; later the possibilities for further artistic expertise in this sphere became recognised and they became more complex and varied. The splendid example of a Celtic mirror, found at Colchester in Essex, was found in association with a cremation burial, which included late Belgic pottery.

93 Back of bronze mirror, Desborough, Northamptonshire

The distribution of these British mirrors is, as Fox points out, singular. He would attribute their concentration in or near ports in south-eastern and south-west Britain to the fact that the most progressive and fashionable ladies of the time are likely to have lived in areas which were most open to Roman influence; since mirrors with decorated plates are unknown in Gaul, these cannot be regarded as having been imports. The subtle art of these decorated bronze mirrors, together with that of the coinage, represents two aspects of the art of the Belgae in Britain from about 100 BC until the time of the Claudian Conquest in AD 43. More progressive and sophisticated than the insular Celts, the incoming, innovating Belgic tribes thought in terms of *oppida* (cities), cremation burial, and higher standards of technology. Apart from anything else, they introduced the use of the wheeled plough into southern Britain which had, of course, revolutionary effects on the agriculture of the region.

IRONWORK, POTTERY AND ENAMEL

Perfunctory though this glance at Celtic art and its achievement must be here, it would not be in any way complete without some mention of the fire-dogs and the pottery which are a distinctive feature of the cremation burials. The graves were furnished for the feast of a nobleman and his companion, which meant that they

94 Iron fire-dog: Lords Bridge, Cambridgeshire

95 Amphora stand, Welwyn, Hertfordshire, with five amphorae warming in it

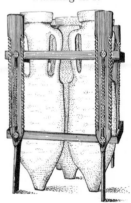

were equipped for two people, not one. The equipment for the
funerary festivities and the gaiety beyond the grave included iron
fire-dogs. These, which are essentially Celtic in form, are simple
andirons (*94*), used to support logs across the hearth. Another
article of this nature is a square frame, intended to take wine-jars
(*95*). It has been surmised that since only one andiron was used in
a single fire, the presence of two of these in Belgic graves is suggestive of two fires, one for the chief and one for his feasting
companion. The Celtic tradition of single combat between two
warriors is forgotten; here we have the chieftain merry-making
with his friend and, no doubt as the Welwyn Garden City grave
indicates, board games would be included in the funerary paraphernalia to while away the time until the Otherworld could be
reached, and the great feast of the gods partaken of. The terminals
of the fire-dogs consist of representations of ox-heads, and some of
these are extremely elegant. The remains of gaming counters and
of musical instruments suggests that the unearthly entertainment
was expected to follow a mundane pattern and would satisfy the
spiritual being as it had pleased the living man.

Belgic pottery is another feature of late Celtic art which is well
represented in these Belgic graves. There were two types of wheel-
made pottery. One, the *tazza*, or footed bowl (*96*), stems from a
metalwork prototype; the other is the elegant pedestal urn, in
which the cremated remains of the dead were frequently placed.
Black and grey were the favourite colours for these Belgic vessels.
Other types of pottery were in existence, and all serve to testify
to the skill and refinement of the Belgic craftsmen.

The elaborate use of enamel presents yet another aspect of the
individuality of Belgic art. Many objects were decorated with this
substance, including terrets, horse-bits and other parts of the
harness. In pre-Roman times the tendency in enamelling had been
to use a single colour, namely red. Spots of blue or yellow added
at this stage were never very satisfactory. The art of enamelling
was much practiced in the eastern counties of Britain, in the
independent Belgic areas. Sometimes blue glass was combined
with the enamel—glass had been used decoratively by the Celts
from Hallstatt times on. In early Belgic contexts the enamel was
used in the form of small studs, in place, presumably, of the coral
studs that were formerly used in similar contexts. At this stage the
work was essentially simple. Late in the first century BC enamel
came to be used for the decoration of larger surfaces and the

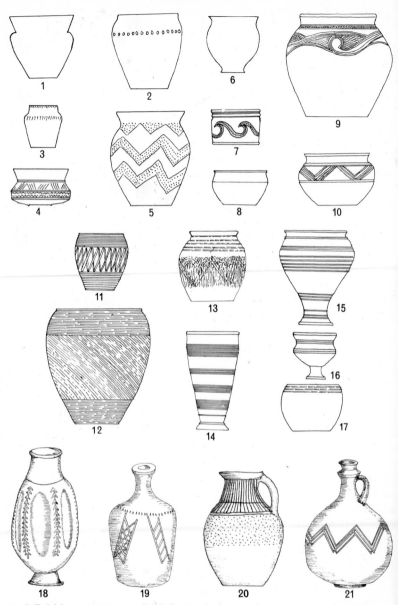

96 British pottery: 1, 2, Park Brow, Sussex; 3, 4, 5, All Cannings Cross, Wiltshire; 6, 7, the Caburn, Sussex; 8, the Trundle, Sussex; 9, 10, Hengistbury Head, Hampshire; 11, Cogdean, Dorset; 12, Rotherley, Wiltshire; 13–17, Swarling, Kent; 18, 19, 20, 21, New Forest pottery, Hampshire

champlevé technique was used (*97*)*; this is only found in Britain and would seem to have originated amongst the Belgic tribes occupying the area between Kent and Suffolk in the immediately pre-Claudian period. Belgic art is used to decorate objects of personal adornment, such as brooches, buckles, heavy armlets, sword-scabbards. In north Britain the art of enamelling continued until the Romans finally swamped the native culture (*98*). Objects such as the remarkable, flamboyant brooch from Aesica (*99*) on Hadrian's Wall in Northumberland, and the extraordinary armlets from Castle Newe in Aberdeenshire, dating to about 100 BC mark the end of independent Celtic art in Britain and herald the advent of Romano-British art—a very different affair.

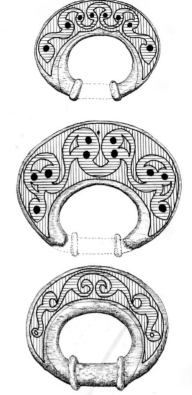

97 Enamelled terrets: 1, Bapchild, Kent; 2, from the Stewartry of Kirkcudbright; 3, Westhall, Suffolk

CONCLUSION

The coming of Rome everywhere in the Celtic world destroyed the structure of the society upon which the native artists depended, and so destroyed the opportunity for the practising of the art itself. The Celtic craftsmen required the patronage of the wealthy aristocracy for their livelihood and their inspiration. A barbaric chieftain must have the appropriate barbaric pomp and personal display. He must be equipped with weapons for parade purposes as well as having sets of purely functional arms. He must have armour, unless he despised the extra protection it would give to

---

* 'Champlevé' is the name given to the technique of filling with enamel voids in the metalwork thereby emphasising the pattern in the colour of the enamel and that of the metal.

98 Dragonesque fibula from Carlisle, Cumberland, enamelled in two shades of blue

him. His chariot and his horses must be suitably adorned with decorative and magical designs; his own and his lady's clothing must be richly embroidered and patterned with gay and mystical signs. The wood in his house must be carved in accordance with his social status and the technique and individual skill of his craftsmen. Once that powerful background is removed, the entire background for creative Celtic art is also removed. With the coming of Rome, Celtic art went underground, as it were, waiting to be revitalised centuries later by the inspired artists of Ireland and Britain working under the aegis of the Christian Church. Only now and again does the native artistic spirit manifest itself, feeble now, but latent. The New Forest potters, for example,

99 Gilt bronze fibula from AESICA, Great Chesters, Northumberland

working in the third and fourth centuries AD, played their humble part in keeping it alive and the simple but essentially native decoration of their wares is an indication that the flame which had been fanned by the Celtic artists in La Tène Europe into a mighty conflagration, was not quite dead. The potters, working in isolation in the Hampshire moorlands and woods, decorated their water-jar with the strange, bird-like goddess with the spiralling body, so reminiscent of the owl-goddess portrayed centuries earlier on the torc from Reinheim (*64*); with the one-eyed, radiate figure with the splayed hands—essentially a Celtic cult figure—and with the strange, armless rider, holding the reins in his mouth and balancing himself upon his awkward, elongated mount (*100*). This isolated group was thus carrying on, in its inevitably limited way, the artistic spirit of its forebears; and protecting its work and ensuring its success by invoking the ancient Celtic deities; and no doubt passing the time by reciting the old cult legends which had formed the entire

100 Pottery jar and cover, Linwood, Hampshire

spiritual background of its more powerful predecessors in the ancient La Tène world.

Now Cú Chulainn possessed many and various gifts: the gift of beauty, the gift of form, the gift of build, the gift of swimming, the gift of horsemanship, the gift of playing *fidchell*, the gift of playing *brandub*, the gift of battle, the gift of fighting, the gift of conflict, the gift of sight, the gift of speech, the gift of counsel, the gift of fowling, the gift of laying waste, the gift of plundering in a strange border.

(*C. O'Rahilly, 152*)

Everything that has a beginning must also have an ending and, like the circular songs of the Hebridean waulking women or the tortuous flowing lines of the Celtic artists, we end here where we began, with the concept of the Celtic 'ideal': the ideal of bodily perfection and strength; the ideal of accomplishment in both physical and intellectual pastimes; the ideal of heroism in battle and skill in raiding; the ideal of perspicacity, wisdom and loquacity. These 'ideals' of appearance and behaviour, together with the concept of the 'fitness of things' do perhaps more than political unity could ever have achieved to bond the Celts together in antiquity and down the ages into a distinctive, homogeneous people, and raise them a little above the common level of Iron Age barbarity. Barbarous and sordid many aspects of their everyday life may have been and undoubtedly were; and their actual behaviour must have fallen far short of the standards so much admired and desired by them. But it is the very fact that they were capable of such ideals and concepts of correct conduct and the 'fitness of things' in the first instance—whether or not they were a true reflection of their everyday dealings—which makes this people remarkable to a degree which their material culture would not necessarily suggest.

In a book which has a prescribed length, it is not possible to cover in any detail a subject which could in fact be almost as long as life itself. I have, therefore, in the foregoing chapters, selected the aspects of the everyday life of the pagan Celts which I, personally, have felt to be the most distinctive features of these people, aspects in which their individuality is more marked and their attitudes less commonplace than those of their contemporaries, in so far as we have knowledge of these. For this reason a considerable part of the book has been devoted to a discussion of their religion and art, two of the most typical aspects of their culture, and to such very distinctive material features as their clothing and personal appearance, their weapons and battle tactics, their learning and their laws. Many topics such as their agricultural methods, their charms and incantations for healing the sick, and their actual medical remedies for illness; their technology, their birth customs and their funerary practices, and a full discussion of their musical instruments, have had to be glossed over. But in these spheres they differed little from other contemporary peoples, and it is in the features of their society upon which we have concentrated that the true essence of their personality can be detected.

As we have seen throughout the book, there is no single comprehensive source, nothing in the nature of reliable history upon which we have been able to draw in order to construct our picture of the everyday life of the pagan Celts. The evidence we use here would not stand up to scrutiny in a court of law. The comments in the summing-up given by the Irish judge in the case of the gold collar from Broighter, in 1903, which was claimed as treasure trove by the Royal Irish Academy, are very apposite here:

> The defendants' suggestion is that the articles were thrown into the sea, which they suggest covered the spot in question, as a votive offering by some Irish sea king or chief to some Irish sea god at some period between 300 BC and AD 100, and for this purpose they ask the court to infer the existence of the sea on the spot in question, the existence of an Irish sea god, the existence of a custom to make votive offerings in Ireland during the period suggested, and the existence of kings or chiefs who would be likely to make such votive offerings. The whole of their evidence (if I may so describe it) on these points is of the vaguest description. (*Praeger, 66*)

I have been able to offer little more evidence of a kind that would satisfy the legal world than could the defendants in the 'Gold Ornaments Case' as it was called. But, evidence of such a nature is neither possible nor necessary in this context. I have started by using a number of indisputable facts and these, together with all that can be inferred from the variety of source materials, both first-class and secondary, at our disposal, have been drawn upon in order to attempt to reconstruct some picture of life in the Celtic Iron Age. This is offered to the reader in the hope that it may help to cast some small ray of light on the lives, with all their human weaknesses, sufferings, joys and aspirations, of these pagan Celtic peoples whose contribution to European culture, while not always discernible, cannot be entirely discounted.

REFERENCES TO SHORTER QUOTATIONS

p.37 Tierney, 248
p.39 Tierney, 249
p.40 Tierney, 250
p.42 C.O'Rahilly, 171, 204
p.43 C.O'Rahilly, 143, 257
Tierney, 270
p.44 Tierney, 268, 251, 252
Dio Cassius, Epitome of Bk
LXII, 3, 4
Hull, 67
p.45 Tierney, 247, 268, 252
p.46 Tierney, 268
p.47 Dio Cassius, loc. cit.
p.48 C.O'Rahilly, 143
p.50 C.O'Rahilly, 171
p.51-2 C.O'Rahilly, 237
p.52 Cross & Slover, 83
p.58 Tierney, 269
p.63 C.O'Rahilly, 209
p.64 Jones, 5
p.65 Tierney, 250
p.68 C.O'Rahilly, 254, 261
Cross & Slover, 157
C.O'Rahilly, 238
p.71 Tierney, 250
p.72 Tierney, 268
p.73 T.F.O'Rahilly, 126
C.O'Rahilly, 170
p.75 C.O'Rahilly, 140-1
Tierney, 250, 272
p.76 Tierney, 268
Bromwich, 31 (Triad)
p.79 Tierney, 249
p.80 (top) Ross (1967), 196, 379

p.81 Jones, 32
Tierney, 260
p.82 Wainwright, 25
p.83, 89 Fox, 145
p.87 Graham, 72
Hull, 63
p.88 Tierney, 268
p.89 Tierney, 252
p.90 C.O'Rahilly, 161
p.94-5 Jones, 145-6
p.98-9 Tierney, 268
p.100 Jones, 117
p.103 Dillon, 75
p.104 Tierney, 248-251
p.108 C.O'Rahilly, 146
p.109 C.O'Rahilly, 190
Tierney, 268, 270
p.111 Binchy, 199, 209-10
p.112 Binchy, 217-18
p.117 Dillon, 44
p.119 Cross & Slover, 203
p.120 Cross & Slover, 493, 29
p.125 Tierney, 267, 272
p.127 C.O'Rahilly, 163
Tierney, 272
p.143 Tierney, 271
Hull, 61
Ross (1967), 263
p.145 Pliny, *Nat Hist*, xxx, 13
p.149 Gwynn, 380
p.155 Livy, X, **26**, 11 (Loeb IV, 459)
C.O'Rahilly, 204
p.178 *Imagery in Early Celtic Art*, 302, 308

BIBLIOGRAPHY

The books listed below consist of those mentioned specifically in the text, and others which may be used for wider reading. Reference to books on more specialised aspects of the subject can be found in the bibliographies of the books named here.

Ashbee, P. 'The Wilsford Shaft' *Antiquity* XXXVII (1963), 116–20

Binchy, D. A. 'The Linguistic and Historical Value of the Irish Law Tracts' *Proceedings of the British Academy* XXIX (1943), 195–227

Bromwich, R. *Trioedd Ynys Prydein* (The Welsh Triads), Cardiff (1961)

Cross, T. P. & Slover, C. H. *Ancient Irish Tales*, London (1936)

Curle, J. *A Roman Frontier Post and its People*, Glasgow (1911)

Dillon, M. 'The Archaism of Irish Tradition' *Proceedings of the British Academy* XXXIII (1947), 245–64

Early Irish Literature, Chicago (1948)

& Chadwick, N. *The Celtic Realms*, London (1965)

Dudley, D. & Webster, G. *The Rebellion of Boudicca*, London (1965)

Faraday, L. W. *The Cattle Raid of Cúalnge*, London (1904)

Feachem, R. W. *The North Britons*, London (1966)

'Medionemeton on the Limes of Antoninus Pius, Scotland' *Collection Latomus* 103 (1969), 210–16

Filip, J. *Celtic Civilisation and its Heritage*, Prague (1960): English translation, London (1962)

Fox, C. *Pattern and Purpose*, Cardiff (1958)

Frere, S. S., (ed), *Problems of the Iron Age in Southern Britain*, London (undated, but 1961)

Giraldus Cambrensis *Topographia Hibernica*, tr. T. Forester, London (1881)

Graham, A. 'Archaeological Gleanings from Dark-Age Records' *Proceedings of the Society of Antiquaries of Scotland* LXXXV (1950–51), 64–91

Grenier, A. 'Sanctuaires celtiques et tombe du héros' *Comptes Rendus d'Academie des Inscriptions et Belles Lettres* 1943, 360–71

Gwynn, E. 'The Metrical Dindshenchas' *Royal Irish Academy Todd Lecture Series*, Vol XI (1924), Dublin

Henry, F. *Irish Art in the Early Christian Period to A.D. 800*, London (1965)

Hull, V. *Longes Mac N-Uislenn*, New York (1949)

Kendrick, T. D. *The Druids*, London (1928)

Jackson, K. H. *A Celtic Miscellany*, London (1951); *Language and History in Early Britain*, Edinburgh (1953); *The International Popular Tale and Early Welsh Tradition*, Cardiff, (1961); *The Oldest Irish Tradition: A Window on the Iron Age*, Cambridge (1964); *The Gododdin*, Edinburgh (1969)

Jones, Gwyn and Thomas *The Mabinogion*, London (1949)

Joyce, P. W. *A Social History of Ireland*, I and II London (1903)

Knott, E. *Togail Bruidne Da Derga*, Dublin (1936)

Lewis, M. J. T. *Temples in Roman Britain*, Cambridge (1966)

Loe, Baron De *Belgique Ancienne*, Vol. II *Les Ages du Metal*, Brussels (1931)

Lubbock, J. *Prehistoric Times*, London (1872)

Macneill, Máire *The Festival of Lughnasa*, Oxford (1962)

Mahr, A. *Prehistoric Grave Material from Carniola*, New York (1934)

Megaw, J. V. S. 'Problems and non-problems in palaeo-organology: a musical miscellany' *Studies in Ancient Europe* 333–58, Leicester (1968)

Nenquin, J. *Salt*, Brugge (1961)

O'Curry, E. *On the Manners and Customs of the Ancient Irish*, Vols I–III, London (1873)

O'Lochlainn, Colm. 'Roadways in Ancient Ireland' *Essays and Studies presented to Professor Eoin Mac Neill* 465–74, Dublin (1940)

O'Rahilly, C. *Táin Bó Cúalnge*, Dublin (1967)

O'Rahilly, T. F. *Early Irish History and Mythology*, Dublin (1946)

Piggott, S. *William Stukeley: An 18th Century Antiquary*, Oxford (1950)
  Ancient Europe, Edinburgh (1965); *The Druids*, London (1968)

Polybius *The Histories*, Loeb Library, London (Reprinted 1960)

Powell, T. G. E. *The Celts*, London (1958)
  Prehistoric Art, London (1966)

Praeger, R. L. *The Way that I Went*, Dublin (1939)

Proceedings of the Second International Congress of Celtic Studies, held in Cardiff 6–13 July, 1963, Cardiff (1966)

Rhys, E. (ed.) *The Journal of a Tour to the Hebrides with Samuel Johnson LL.D. by James Boswell*, London (1941)

Rivet, A. L. F. (ed) *The Iron Age in Northern Britain*, Edinburgh (1966)

Ross, Anne *Pagan Celtic Britain*, London and Columbia (1967)
  'Shafts, pits, wells' – sanctuaries of the Belgic Britons? *Studies in Ancient Europe*, 255–85 Leicester (1968)

Rybova, A. and Soudsky, B. *Libenice*, Prague (1962)

Sanders, N. *Prehistoric Art*, London (1968)

Sjoestedt, Marie-Louise. (tr. M. Dillon), *Gods and Heroes of the Celts* London (1949)

Thurneysen, R. *et al. Studies in Early Irish Law*, Royal Irish Academy, Dublin (1936)

Tierney, J. J. 'The Celtic Ethnography of Posidonius' *Proceedings of the Royal Irish Academy* Vol. 60, Section C, No. 5 (1960) 189–275

Vouga, P. *La Tène*, Leipzig (1923)

Wainwright, F. T. (ed), *The Problems of the Picts*, Edinburgh (1955)

Williams, I. *Pedeir Keinc y Mabinogi*, Cardiff (1930)

INDEX

The numerals in **bold** type refer to the figure number of the illustrations

Index

Index